BRING ME THE HEAD OF
TREVOR BROOKING

2011

Merry Christmas,

love,

Max

KIRK BLOWS is a freelance journalist who has been reporting on West Ham United since the mid 1990s. He is formerly the editor of *Hammers News* and has written or co-authored five previous West Ham-related books: *Terminator: The Authorised Story of Julian Dicks*; *The Essential History of West Ham United*; *Claret & Blue Blood*; *Hammers Heaven & Hell*; and *Fortune's Always Hiding*. He currently contributes a weekly West Ham column to the *East London Advertiser* and *Barking & Dagenham Post*.

BEN SHARRATT is an editor and freelance journalist. He is the co-author of *Claret & Blue Blood*, the story of West Ham United's academy, and has written on football for many magazines and newspapers, including the *London Evening Standard*, *FourFourTwo* and *Match of the Day* magazine. He also worked as assistant editor of *Hammers News* and wrote for the Charlton Athletic matchday programme for ten years.

BRING ME THE HEAD OF TREVOR BROOKING

THREE DECADES OF EAST END SOAP OPERA AT WEST HAM UNITED

KIRK BLOWS
AND BEN SHARRATT

MAINSTREAM
PUBLISHING

EDINBURGH AND LONDON

First published in Great Britain in 2010 by
MAINSTREAM PUBLISHING COMPANY
(EDINBURGH) LTD
7 Albany Street
Edinburgh EH1 3UG

ISBN 9781845966614

All photographs © Steve Bacon

A catalogue record for this book is available
from the British Library

Typeset in Champion and Concorde

Printed in Great Britain by
Clays, St Ives plc

1 3 5 7 9 10 8 6 4 2

Acknowledgements

THE AUTHORS would like to thank: Karen Glaseby, Kaz Lever, Lily Sharratt, Patricia Laker, Karen, Jessica and Lewis Blows, Jo Davies, John and Rachel Laker, David, Jennifer and Helen Laker, Brian and Doris Mattingley, Valerie Blows, Julian Dicks, Harry Redknapp, Rachel Anderson, Steve Bacon, Tony Carr, Greg Demetriou, Rob Pritchard, Laura Burkin, Trevor Davies, Dave Evans, Steve Blowers, David Powter, Tony McDonald, Matt Diner, Ross Davies, Simon Hayes, Jim Lever, Joe Sach, Gerry Levey, John Raven, Brad Ashton, Justin and Yulia Allen, John Matthews, Gary Hawkins, Arthur Renard, Chris Wilkinson, Gary Miller, Dave Pitchford, Gary Martin and Jim Fone.

Contents

Foreword

I HAD ten great years at West Ham and when people ask me what the highlights were during my two spells at the club, one of the best memories was returning to Upton Park in 1994 following my disappointing season at Liverpool. It felt like coming home.

It's been 11 years since I was forced to retire through injury and when I think about what I miss most about football, it's not the money or the banter with my old team-mates. It's playing at Upton Park – and that's because of the supporters. For me, that's what sets West Ham apart from so many other clubs.

I will always remember that incredible show of support during the 1991 FA Cup semi-final against Nottingham Forest at Villa Park. I didn't play because I was sidelined with the first of my two serious knee injuries but to see the fans singing their hearts out with the team 4–0 down was amazing. That says everything about the West Ham support. They have always remained loyal to the club through thick and thin. There are always lots of ups and downs at the club but I don't think the fans would have it any other way. It's all part of the adventure.

West Ham were near the bottom of the table towards the end of the 1987–88 season but that didn't deter me from signing for them. As soon as John Lyall spoke to me my mind was made up, regardless of what money they offered. I had the utmost respect for John, both as a manager and a person. He was one of the most honest people you could ever meet and as a manager he got the best out of his players. When John signed me, he asked, 'What do you know about West Ham?' And I just said, 'Billy Bonds.' Billy was a player I liked because he always gave 110 per cent. He didn't have the best ability in the world but I'd always have had him in my side ahead of anybody else.

You have to work hard for the West Ham supporters and I think that's why I enjoyed such a good relationship with them. Even when you were losing 2–0 or 3–0, you still worked hard. The fans paid their money and, for me, it was about giving them everything I had.

Being made West Ham's captain was a very proud moment for me and it was a real honour, because I was following in the footsteps of people like Bobby Moore, Billy Bonds and Alvin Martin. Billy and Alvin were two of the players I particularly looked up to when I joined the club and when I consider the quality we had – people like Alan Devonshire, Liam Brady and Tony Gale, for example – I can't help but think we should have achieved more.

But I just wanted to play and be part of a team that played football the way it should be – with the ball on the floor. If trophies came along, then that would obviously have been great. As a footballer, you want to be competing for trophies but apart from the FA Cup final in 2006, when they were unlucky to lose to Liverpool, West Ham haven't done enough of that over the last 30 years.

West Ham fans are not stupid; they know their team is never going to win the Premier League but they do like a cup run. I would love to have got to a cup final and played at Wembley but during my time at the club it never materialised. We did win promotion twice but there are no medals for finishing second, as we did in 1991 and 1993. The second promotion season does hold some special memories, though. If I were forced to pick just one game from my West Ham career that represents the highlight, I'd have to say the 2–0 win against Cambridge on the final day when I set up Clive Allen to score in the last minute, which guaranteed we were going up.

I'll also never forget the home match against Tottenham in February 1997 – it's always nice to beat Spurs. And then there's the Manchester United game that same season when we fought back to draw 2–2 after being two goals down. But even though I won no trophies with West Ham, I wouldn't change a thing about my time there. When you think of some of the legendary names to have played for the club, I just feel privileged to have pulled on the claret and blue shirt.

There have been a lot of changes at Upton Park in recent years but I feel confident about the club's future under David Sullivan and David Gold. They're genuine West Ham fans and, therefore, understand the mentality of the supporters. The new owners can only be good for the club. Avram Grant is a proven manager and his Portsmouth side worked their nuts off under him – and that's what we want to see at West Ham. If the current squad can get that work ethic into their game, who knows what they will be able to achieve?

Julian Dicks
June 2010

Introduction

Bring me the Head of Trevor Brooking

SYMBOL: Ag. Atomic number: 47. Otherwise known as 'silver'. The club shop sells it in the form of pendants, necklaces and earrings. It's the colour of choice for many of the luxury vehicles on show in the VIP car park outside the Boleyn Ground, including little David Sullivan's king-size Roller. There's even a district of Newham called Silvertown just a mile or so from the ground.

Talk about adding insult to injury. For the unsettling truth is that in terms of major trophies, silverware has been conspicuous by its absence from Upton Park for more than a generation. Only seven of the 2009–10 squad were even born the last time it was seen around these parts.

In the three decades prior to and including 1980, twenty-seven different clubs won one or more of the big three: the First Division title, the FA Cup or League Cup. Since 1980, that total has dropped by a third as wealth, rather than sporting chance, has come to dominate the sport.

Back when £100,000 was a decent sum to pay for a player, rather than his weekly wage, not many people thought West Ham had much of a chance of beating Arsenal in the FA Cup final. The Hammers' winning goal came from the most unlikely of sources, Trevor Brooking's head: probably the left temple or maybe the crown. It happened so fast that even now, with the power of YouTube, it's hard to tell.

Today, that same majestic head adorns one corner of the Boleyn Ground. Its unmistakeable features – the black wavy hair, wide smiling mouth, tongue characteristically stuck in his left cheek as he floats past another bamboozled defender – are imprinted on the minds of every West Ham supporter who followed the team between 1967 and 1984, and many more since who have heard stories and seen footage of the great man. Sir Trevor Brooking represents West Ham, in every sense.

Much is made of the club's very nature reflecting the 'Just like our dreams, they fade and die' line in the terrace anthem 'I'm Forever Blowing Bubbles', but there really was a time when West Ham were successful. Supporters crave that winning feeling brought to the club by the heads of Brooking, Ronnie Boyce and Geoff Hurst, as well as the feet of Alan Taylor, Alan Sealey and John Sissons. At the same time, there is a certain satisfaction to be had from the knowledge that, silverware or no silverware, life is never dull at Upton Park. Perhaps only Newcastle United and Manchester City can rival the Hammers for the constant stream of on- and off-field controversies, tantalising tales of so near yet so far, cult figures, ownership wrangles, dazzling teams and talents and woefully disappointing individuals and performances.

For the first time, *Bring me the Head of Trevor Brooking* compiles the 60 biggest talking points of the last 30 years at Upton Park – the people, the incidents, the laughter, the tears, the action – with the progression of the chapters reflecting this roller-coaster ride. It's the good, the bad and the ugly of West Ham and serves as a reminder that, much as Hammers fans pine for another moment of magic from a modern-day Trevor Brooking, there is so much else about this club that stirs the soul. Surely that's worth celebrating?

■■■■■■■■■■■■■■■■■■■

Qué Será Será

'Paul Allen is crying his eyes out' – Brian Moore, May 1980

ON 19 JANUARY 1981, in a third-round tie that went to two replays, bogey team Wrexham knocked West Ham United out of the FA Cup. The most beautiful, evocative trophy in sport, crafted by Fattorini & Sons of Bradford, disappeared from the clutches of an East End that had seized it a remarkable three times in sixteen years.

Considering the barren years that followed, it is just as well that West Ham's journey to, and victory in, the 99th FA Cup final the year before packed in enough emotion and romance to last a lifetime. In only the third all-London final, the Second Division Hammers upset the odds by beating Arsenal 1–0. As sensations go it wasn't quite up there with Sunderland beating mighty Leeds United seven years earlier but for dramatic sub-plots it left that game in its wake. West Ham remain the last team from outside the top flight to take home the trophy.

Terry Neill's Gunners were playing in their third FA Cup final on the spin and enjoying yet another season of silverware potential, both domestically and in Europe. In contrast, for John Lyall's West Ham, this was the fifty-eighth game of a campaign in which their promotion aspirations had tailed off with a whimper – just four wins in their last fourteen games.

On the flipside, it was the first time the Hammers had reached the quarter-final stage of both cup competitions. Nottingham Forest, whose brilliant but bumptious manager Brian Clough would play the pantomime baddie to Trevor Brooking's Prince Charming in the build-up to the 10 May date at the Twin Towers, eventually did for West Ham in the League Cup. And but for Phil Parkes' brilliance between the posts, West Bromwich Albion would have done the same in the third round of the more prestigious competition. Ex-Manchester United marksman Stuart Pearson, who was to appear in his fourth FA Cup final in five seasons, helped Parkes save the day before Brooking and Geoff Pike finished the job in the replay.

A Ray Stewart brace sealed a 3–2 victory against locals rivals Orient in round four and, following a 2–0 win over Swansea City in the next round, it was the young Scot who proved the hero again in the quarters.

In front of the South Bank at Upton Park, 'Tonka' kept his cool to smack in an 89th-minute penalty and put Aston Villa to the sword. That strike would make him the Irons' top scorer in the competition but it meant something much more to the defender who had joined the previous year from Dundee United for £430,000. Stewart said his 'greatest-ever penalty' made him feel 'truly accepted by the West Ham supporters. It was as if I became an East Ender for life that afternoon.'

The team celebrated the victory at Frank Lampard's pub, the Britannia, in Stratford. Little could anyone imagine that the mantle of hero would shift onto the wily old full-back's shoulders in the semi-final.

First the Hammers and Everton played out a cat and mouse 1–1 draw at Villa Park, made all the more memorable for a lamentable performance from referee Colin Seel. Everton took the lead from the penalty spot when Alan Devonshire was harshly adjudged to have shoved Andy King. Toffees target man Brian Kidd was then sent off for a touchline tussle with Stewart – who should also have walked having already been booked. Pearson netted the equaliser, then Hammers' teenage prodigy Paul Allen had a goal cruelly disallowed for an offside ruling against Brooking.

The *Daily Express*'s Alan Hoby wrote that he had 'never seen a cup game like it for drama and excitement'. Hoby had to wait just four days to give serious reassessment to that claim but another *Express* reporter did it for him: 'Never has there been such an unforgettable match in West Ham's history than this one that took them back to Wembley.'

Leeds United's Elland Road was the setting for a piece of football theatre that would become enshrined in the top five games in West Ham's history – and the undisputed Number One for many of those who made the long journey north to observe both the 'curious fishy smell emanating from the terraces' and the unerring sense that they were about to witness something special.

Stewart, deputising at centre-back for the tonsillitis-stricken Alvin Martin, and Devonshire would each rate this game as their finest performance for the club. 'It was as near to perfection as I ever got,' said midfield talisman Devonshire. It was he who finally broke the deadlock after the opening 90 minutes had remained nail-bitingly goalless. A purposeful dribble, a refusal to fall after a defender's stab at his ankles, a crisp shot past Martin Hodge, an ecstatic, Bambi-like celebratory run: it was Dev's gifts in microcosm.

Before the crowd could catch its breath, the emotions were dragged kicking and screaming in the other direction. Blues' No. 9 Bob Latchford dived to meet a cross with a superb header, then pounced like a manic baboon onto the railings behind Parkes' goal to emit a primordial rallying cry to the Everton troops.

If that header was exceptional, the next was a miracle. With two minutes remaining, full-back Lampard, following instinct rather than instruction, found himself fifty yards out of position in the Everton penalty area. It was the perfect time to go walkabout. Via a Brooking cross and a David Cross nod, the ball flew off the falling Lampard's forehead and beyond Hodge. No corner-flag choreography before or since has ever matched it for unadulterated joy.

The Hammers had taken three top-flight scalps so far. Thanks to manager Lyall's tactical masterstroke, they were about to take the biggest and the best, but not before Clough churlishly tried to steal some of the limelight by writing in a newspaper, on the day of the final, that Brooking 'floats like a butterfly and stings like one too'. Brooking, whom Clough had failed to sign along with Bobby Moore for Derby County in the early 1970s, answered the criticism in the only way he knew how – with his head!

That England's midfield maestro was able to find himself unmarked deep inside the opposition's penalty box was due, in part, to the confusion wreaked on the Arsenal defence in the first 20 minutes of the cup final. Lyall surprised everyone by pulling Pearson back into the hole and playing a lone striker, David Cross. 'John Lyall told me at quarter to three on the day of the final that I'd be playing up front on my own with "Pancho" Pearson dropping back,' said Cross. 'I think John purposefully kept me in the dark because he didn't want me stewing over it the night before the big game.'

Cross had to sacrifice his chance of glory for the greater good – and Lyall's plan worked a treat. By the time Arsenal's centre-half pairing of David O'Leary and Willie Young had stopped looking over to manager Neill for guidance and sussed who was marking who, Brooking had stooped to conquer.

One of the most famous Wembley goals of all time came in the 13th minute, with Devonshire skinning Pat Rice and Brian Talbot on the left flank and pivoting to send in a tantalising cross with his weaker left foot. Cross met it with a side-foot from the right-hand edge of the six-yard box, it came back out and there was Pearson to drill it home past Pat Jennings. Or at least that's what the watching TV millions at home thought as ITV's Brian Moore exclaimed, 'Cross almost got it in there . . . and Pearson has!'

As 50,000 Hammers fans went berserk, the camera glued itself to Pearson's trademark clenched-fist celebration. An age seemed to elapse before Moore finally identified Brooking as the scorer of a goal that required acute anticipation, a fact seemingly lost on ubiquitous irritant Clough, Moore's co-commentator, who could only offer a weasely, 'That's incredible to see Brooking in the six-yard box. If he hadn't headed it, it would have knocked his head off, Brian.'

Something the cameras had no problem picking out was the breathtaking backdrop provided by the crowd that day. Wembley was not so much a sea as an ocean of flags – and the noise from both sets of fans put *The Last Night of the Proms* to shame. Arsenal skipper Rice's surname seemed to grace at least half the West Ham banners, by way of spray-painted claims that he would be creamed on by Devonshire or eaten by Billy Bonds. The wits weren't far wrong, yet it was Rice's defensive colleague Young who had the fans searching for fruitier adjectives with which to describe an act of pure cynicism late in the game.

It was Young who took Allen's legs from underneath him as the youngest player to win the FA Cup, at 17 years and 256 days, sprinted towards goal with a real chance of doubling West Ham's lead. Widespread condemnation of the so-called 'professional foul' resulted in it later becoming a sending-off offence but Allen was always remarkably diplomatic about a five-second phase of action which defined his career. 'The incident was not a problem for me. I still had to beat Pat Jennings and that's not easy, is it! If Arsenal had earned a replay and gone on to win, I might have felt a bit different.'

When referee George Courtney blew the final whistle, the magnitude of the win and the occasion finally got the better of the youngster who had started the season playing in the South East Counties League with the youth team. While being congratulated by the injured Pat Holland, and with Martin jumping for joy in a huddle with Bonds and Brooking yards away, Allen's tears started to flow. They didn't stop until he'd made it back down the Wembley steps with his winners' medal. Commentator Moore was instantly enchanted. 'Look at the little man! Poor Paul Allen is crying his eyes out . . . and every mother will be weeping with him.'

Allen was superhuman that day, marking future Hammer Liam Brady out of the game. So, too, Devonshire, Stewart, Pike and Bonds. The skipper, who had narrowly avoided a ban from the final due to being red-carded in a league game against Birmingham City, marshalled his team superbly to nullify the threat of Gunners strikers Frank Stapleton and Alan Sunderland. Parkes was barely troubled in West Ham's goal and had a second reason to celebrate, having scooped £40 on the greyhounds at Wembley dog track the night before!

The customary parade the following day, on an open-topped Lacey's single-decker coach to East Ham Town Hall, saw 200,000 pack into Newham for a glimpse of their heroes, among them a rather groggy Stewart. The right-back drank a whole bottle of champagne in the bath after the game and reportedly ended up being violently ill during the West End reception.

A fifteen-year-old Hammers associate schoolboy called Anthony Cottee was one of the hundreds who climbed up lamp posts and on to shop canopies to get a better view. Martin, black eye throbbing proudly in the bright sunshine, obliged by sitting on the edge of the coach roof with his feet dangling over the side, before the players, management and family members crammed onto the town hall balcony to be assailed with 'Bubbles' and 'One team in London'. A dream weekend ended as it had begun: with Lyall's men looking as confident, happy and relaxed as any underdog ever has.

Twenty-five years later, multimillionaire West Ham supporter David Gold, then Birmingham City co-chairman, bought the 1910 version of the FA Cup at Christie's for £430,000. Hammers supporters can only hope that such an obvious passion for the game and willingness to invest in quality will result in Gold helping to bring silver back to an Upton Park now under his aegis.

The Italian Job

'I'm working very hard and my brain is hot' –
Gianfranco Zola, October 2008

IT'S HALF an hour after West Ham have been beaten 2–1 at soon-to-be-relegated Burnley – a side that hadn't won in a dozen league games – and Gianfranco Zola is standing in a Turf Moor courtyard wishing he was some place else. Asked what he liked about Brazilian striker Ilan, who had just scored a late consolation goal on his Hammers debut, the Italian shrugged, 'Er, well, he's only been with us a few days, so it's difficult to judge.'

It was a familiar scenario as West Ham battled against the drop during the 2009–10 campaign, with the manager struggling to explain another defeat while giving the strong impression that he was not in complete control at Upton Park. It was clear he'd had little involvement in the signing of Ilan – one of three strikers recruited in an act of desperation in January 2010 – with it becoming increasingly obvious that he saw the training pitch as his main place of work while everything else was peripheral. It was a philosophy that frequently undermined his aspirations as West Ham's 12th boss and ultimately resulted in his demise.

Zola's trademark smile, although looking rather forced during the more difficult periods of his reign, not to mention his dignified demeanour while under extreme pressure, ensured patience from punters and sympathy from the media when positive results were thin on the ground. Everybody wanted the highly likeable Italian to succeed after taking charge of West Ham in September 2008, not least because he personified all the good things about the game – that football should be played in an attractive style and with a spirit of fairness.

He had established this reputation during a seven-year period with Chelsea in which he scored eighty goals in three hundred and twelve games to become one of the west London club's greatest ever players.

Despite having no club managerial experience, Zola was deemed to have 'ticked all the boxes', according to a Hammers source, as the Boleyn board sought a replacement for Alan Curbishley. His coaching role with the Italy Under-21 side and knowledge of the English game led West Ham chief executive Scott Duxbury and technical director Gianluca Nani to believe they had the ideal man to develop the club's young players and return the first team to its stylish traditions.

'I only know one way to play – attacking football, with the ball on the floor,' said the 42 year old upon his appointment. 'I want to excite people.' Indeed, with defensive coach Steve Clarke leaving his post as assistant boss at Chelsea to provide experienced support, the Hammers appeared to have the perfect partnership. Clarke was Mr Organisation; Zola was Mr Inspiration.

'Mr Zola has expressed his desire for us to play a more creative brand of football,' confirmed skipper Lucas Neill, and it was something the players quickly took on board as they developed a short passing game that was immediately more pleasing to the eye. Sadly, it was initially rather too pretty – pretty ineffective, in fact – as the Hammers lost four successive games during a run of seven outings without a win at one early stage under Zola's control. If the players had been cagey in their approach under Curbishley, they appeared equally cautious under Zola for fear of giving the ball away. 'We knew West Ham would have a lot of possession but all they seemed to do was go square or backwards,' said Bolton boss Gary Megson after his side's 3–1 win at Upton Park in October 2008. It was a similar story up at rain-lashed Hull a fortnight later as Zola's men, one goal down with five minutes to play, continued trying to score the perfect goal instead of taking advantage of the miserable weather conditions and forcing a mistake. 'We played the game the way it should be played,' said the manager defiantly after the 1–0 defeat.

By this time, West Ham had suffered a number of setbacks, with Sheffield United winning their multimillion-pound compensation claim against the club, sponsors XL going bust, key striker Dean Ashton afflicted with ankle problems and Carlton Cole being arrested on suspicion of drink-driving. 'This is a big job and involves many things I wasn't aware of,' confided Zola, who seemed to age several years in a few short months. 'I'm working very hard and my brain is hot.' He also denied suggestions he was 'too nice' to be a successful top-flight manager. 'Being nice doesn't mean I'm stupid,' he insisted.

Much more serious news arrived with the collapse of chairman Björgólfur Guðmundsson's Landsbanki empire, with Zola consequently being told there would be no money to spend when the transfer window opened in January. So much for the bold new 'project' that Zola and Duxbury repeatedly referred to; it looked more like a case of Project Relegation as the Hammers slid down the table following one win in a dozen games. Indeed, 'we need to find solutions' became something of a Zola catchphrase.

Given the financial circumstances, it seemed absurd to invest a large chunk of the £14 million received from the mid-season sale of Craig Bellamy to Manchester City on Ugandan-born German teenager Savio, who never looked anywhere near ready for regular Premier League football. The failure of the Germany Under-20 international to make an impact was disguised by the team's sudden upturn in results during the second half of the 2008–09 campaign – sparked by a shock 4–1 win at Portsmouth on Boxing Day – but the Savio episode was the first example of Zola appearing to go along with a big decision rather than actually making one. Of course, this is what West Ham wanted, with former boss Curbishley having walked out because key managerial decisions over the recruitment and sale of players were taken out of his hands.

Not that the fans were overly concerned about such political matters, with the Hammers going on a brilliant run of six wins in seven games to push themselves into contention for a European place. Zola had taught Cole how to hit the net again with the striker scoring in five successive games and the side was playing the exciting football that the boss had promised. Everybody was suddenly singing the manager's praises, although Curbishley was a little miffed by the suggestion that his successor had invented entertainment. 'Because of the injuries,' he grumbled, during one conversation, 'I played 4–5–1 or 4–3–3 and people saw it as being negative. Zola has played 4–3–3 or 4–4–2 with a centre-forward dropping off and it has been classed as something new – and it isn't.'

Zola claimed he could 'smell' something happening at Upton Park and it wasn't the cooking of greasy hot dogs before games. 'We feel we're building something important here,' he declared. Ultimately, the loss of key players to injury, not least Cole, undermined West Ham's efforts to qualify for the newly formed Europa League but a ninth-place finish in his first season was still very respectable, all things considered.

The decision to hand both Zola and Clarke new four-year contracts a month before the campaign had ended seemed somewhat premature given they had been at the club for just seven months but the prospects for the 2009–10 season looked promising, with the manager insisting, 'Europe will be our target.' The Hammers had succeeded in holding on to key players such as Cole, Matthew Upson, Scott Parker and Robert Green, although Zola was desperately short of strikers following the release of David Di Michele and Diego Tristan, the continued injury woe of Dean Ashton and the failure of Savio. 'I can only choose Carlton Cole . . . and myself,' he joked, although the Italian's dazzling display in Tony Carr's testimonial at the end of the season suggested that such an idea might not have been quite as ridiculous as it sounded.

The striking problem appeared to be largely solved with the capture of Alessandro Diamanti from Livorno, with the Hammers openly admitting that new sponsors SBOBET had advanced cash to fund the reported £5 million deal. The club's website described the Italian as a 'forward' who would 'provide extra firepower' but halfway through the new campaign – one of constant struggle – Zola admitted he was nothing of the sort. 'Diamanti can't play up front,' he said. 'His best quality is setting up balls for others.' With the club hamstrung financially after falling into the hands of Straumur-Burdaras, a debt-ridden Icelandic banking institution, it was beyond belief that they would invest what little funds they did have available to them on yet another playmaker they didn't need – or that Zola, as manager, could happily allow it to happen.

It's in this context that the decision by the club's new owners, David Sullivan and David Gold, to terminate Zola's contract in May 2010 – after the Hammers finished just one place above the relegation zone –

should perhaps be judged. Yes, the Italian was hampered by financial restrictions, speculation about the club's ownership and financial footing, as well as a succession of injury problems to his players. But Gold and Sullivan wanted a fully fledged manager – not just a positive-thinking coach – in charge of their team: one experienced enough to know how to solve big problems when they came along and somebody who accepted final responsibility for the shape of his squad. Zola denied ever suggesting he had no interest in the signing of players – 'It is incorrect to say I didn't want to be involved in transfers,' he insisted after Sullivan had reportedly revealed that to be the case. However, if he was 'involved' in the ones made under the previous hierarchy, even with Nani's influence, then that did not reflect well on him.

Nor did the humiliating 3–1 home defeat by Wolves on 23 March, which prompted Sullivan to write an open letter to fans describing the West Ham performance as 'shambolic', 'pathetic' and 'disorganised'. Zola took the criticism personally and believed his new bosses were undermining him, especially when reports claimed they wanted the entire squad and management to take a pay cut at the end of the season. The Hammers were also linked with potential new signings, such as West Brom's Graham Dorrans, which Zola seemed to know nothing about. 'You don't know the half of it,' he said in the Upton Park corridors after one game as to what was going on behind the scenes.

Despite knowing his days were numbered, Zola refused to throw in the towel – although he admitted that he was considering his future after Stoke's 1–0 win at Upton Park in March made it six defeats in a row for the Hammers. And he achieved what he set out to in making sure West Ham avoided the drop, not that 35 points from 38 games would usually be considered a success.

The fact that Zola would be leaving at the end of the season was one of football's worst-kept secrets but it was still a shock when it was suggested he was sacked for gross misconduct – apparently for publicly questioning Sullivan's claim that all the West Ham players, with the exception of Scott Parker, were potentially on the market. 'I have been surprised so many times this year, so I am not surprised that

I am surprised,' Zola had previously said. And after his dismissal, he fired a parting shot at his former employers. 'I have been the subject of various adverse comments from within the club,' he said. Thankfully, with a bit of help from the League Managers' Association, the dispute was quickly resolved in the form of an agreed settlement figure, with Clarke also leaving the club.

Yet despite Zola tasting victory in just 23 of his 80 games in charge – a mere 28.75 win percentage – West Ham fans will generally remember him in a fond light. Maybe that's no surprise. After all, how can anyone fail to warm to a man who, on the day of his sacking, opens his front gates to greet members of the media with a tray of coffee and duly does the honours? 'One lump or two?' And yes, he could still raise that obligatory smile.

....

United We Stand, United They Fall

'He tried to stop me. He tried to make my brain a little confused' – Paolo Di Canio, January 2001

ONE WAS from Rome; the other lived in Romford. One was dark, lithe and mysterious; the other was blond, rotund and just a little maligned. Paolo Di Canio and Geoff Pike were two West Ham players who could barely be further apart in terms of idolatry among Hammers fans yet the pair are inextricably linked by heroic events separated by almost exactly fifteen years.

The place: Old Trafford. The competition: the FA Cup. The common bond? Each scored a goal against Manchester United that would go down in West Ham folklore.

Away games, especially up north, can be an arduous and dispiriting affair. However, no amount of triple-pack sandwiches, traffic jams, train delays or cramp-inducing coach journeys could take the shine off two particular Sundays spent getting to and from Manchester. On each occasion – 9 March 1986 and 28 January 2001 – the Irons' travelling hordes, plus millions more watching live on TV, were sent delirious by that rarest of pleasures: a cup win over the Red Devils on their own hallowed turf.

In 1986, the 2–0 victory starring Pike was particularly sweet as United were the current cup holders, they had beaten Hammers in the FA Cup in two of the previous three seasons and they had won a Milk Cup encounter earlier in the season. More cynical sections of the Hammers faithful may have often referred to him as 'Stupid Boy' in reference to his namesake *Dad's Army* character but this was the second crucially important goal Pike registered against United, having scored against them in the final game at Upton Park in 1976–77, which the Hammers needed to win to stave off relegation.

Nine seasons later, the occasion was a fifth-round cup replay following a 1–1 draw at Upton Park (itself delayed four times by the Siberian weather), in which Frank McAvennie scored his first FA Cup goal and United's injury-prone 'Captain Marvel' Bryan Robson hobbled off with a dislocated shoulder after tangling with Tony Cottee. Cottee had been the goal hero in the previous two rounds, scoring the only goal of the game against Charlton, then the winner against Ipswich Town after an epic three-game fourth-round tussle. But it was Pike, another pint-sized, home-grown product, who had the fans rubbing their eyes and bouncing for joy at Old Trafford's Scoreboard End.

Only 18 minutes were on the clock when the central midfielder leapt like a pike to put Hammers in front and make amends for what, in contrast to the rising fortunes of most of his team-mates, was proving to be an irksome 1985–86 season. A hernia from the previous campaign, compounded by a torn stomach muscle and the consistent form of Neil Orr, meant Pike was restricted to just a handful of starts as West Ham finished a best-ever third in the First Division.

All those frustrations were forgotten as one of the club's longest-serving players met a Mark Ward corner on the edge of the penalty area and sent a long-range header looping into the United net in front of a dumbstruck Stretford End. As Pike recalled in *Boys of '86*, 'People asked afterwards if it was something we'd practised on the training field but there was no way in a million years that we ever did. Wardie miscued the corner and I just happened to be there.'

With penalty king Ray Stewart coolly dispatching another spot-kick, after Alvin Martin was adjudged to have been shoved in the back by Frank Stapleton, West Ham sealed a victory which manager John Lyall rated as one of his happiest memories of the campaign – especially for Pike's contribution. 'I was delighted for him,' said Lyall. 'He was one of our unsung heroes that season.'

Not being sung about was never a humiliation Paolo Di Canio had to suffer during his celebrated career in claret and blue. Indeed, long after the Italian left the club, his worshippers still revelled in warbling a few verses of 'La Donna è mobile' whenever a burst of moist-eyed nostalgia was required to lift the crowd.

Di Canio took a massive step towards terrace immortality with an ice-cool piece of finishing in the deep midwinter of 2001 during a fourth-round tie at the Theatre of Dreams. In truth, the notoriety of the goal, which earned the Hammers a shock 1–0 win against Sir Alex Ferguson's all-conquering Reds, was as much down to the antics of United goalkeeper Fabien Barthez, whose comical error of judgement made worldwide sporting headlines and bizarrely resulted in this game being merited by *The Independent* as the 'Number One FA Cup Upset of All Time'.

Harry Redknapp's men had made it to Old Trafford via a nervy 3–2 win over Walsall in round three. United had beaten them at home 3–1 in the Premiership four weeks earlier, while a horrific 7–1 Manchester mauling was still fresh in the memory from the previous season. The omens were not good, although residual ill-feeling towards United after they had pulled out of the cup to play in an utterly superfluous FIFA public-relations exercise (otherwise known as the Club World Championship) in Brazil in 1999–2000, meant the goodwill of the neutrals watching on Sky was with the Hammers. Extra spice came with the fact that Ferguson, a huge admirer of Di Canio, was perennially reported as being on the verge of luring the Italian from Upton Park.

Not that any of these factors favoured West Ham for the first three-quarters of the game. As predicted, it was all hands to the pump, with Ryan Giggs, Roy Keane and co. putting an injury-stricken Hammers side under intense pressure. Goalkeeper Shaka Hislop was carrying a leg wound which forced Stuart Pearce to take the goalkicks; on-loan Finn Hannu Tihinen was the only orthodox centre-half, while the Hammers' bench included untried Norwegian defender Ragnvald Soma and veteran Steve Potts who, remarkably, had been a youthful first-team squad member way back at the time of the 1986 Old Trafford win.

No bother, for cometh the 76th minute, cometh the Italian Stallion. The decisive move started with French wing-back Sébastien Schemmel, another 'loanee' who was making only his second West Ham appearance. He skipped up the right flank before playing a ball inside to his compatriot Fredi Kanouté, whose forward pass was perfectly weighted for Di Canio's angled run – and with Denis Irwin crucially playing the striker onside.

It was down to a Spaghetti Western-like battle of wits between two of the Premiership's great eccentrics. Di Canio (Clint Eastwood) advanced forward purposefully, taking a split second to glance at the unraised flag of the linesman. In response, Barthez (Lee Van Cleef) drew on all the acting abilities of his supermodel girlfriend Linda Evangelista in one of her cosmetics adverts by raising his right arm to the heavens to signify that an offside had been flagged. Cunning, but not cunning enough. Too wily to have either his leg pulled or his arm lifted, Di Canio moved on a couple of yards, looked up, then bent the ball round Barthez as the French World Cup-winning goalkeeper ineffectually fell on the floor grasping at air.

Old Trafford fell eerily silent for a split second . . . then 10,000 West Ham supporters erupted in a crescendo of Cockney glee and Di Canio adoration, which lasted until well after the final whistle. Down in the Manchester United changing room, one could only imagine the intensity of the 'hairdryer treatment' Ferguson was giving Barthez – an utterly futile exercise in more ways than one.

The man of the moment was, perhaps, a touch more measured about the incident than Sir Alex. 'He tried to stop me. He tried to make my brain a little bit confused,' Di Canio told the titillated press pack. 'But I have played for 15 years at the top level and have a little bit of experience in these situations. It is better to score and then see whether the goalkeeper is right or wrong. I am very happy. We have given the fans a dream day.'

With the dot.com era in full swing, what became a dream for Irons' supporters immediately became a cyber nightmare for Barthez. Doctored commentaries and video footage of the incident soon appeared all over the Internet, the most common dig being that Barthez was hailing a taxi ahead of his inevitable ejection from Old Trafford, which didn't in fact occur until two and half years later.

A BBC online caption competition summed up the giddy post-match media reaction and included these gems:

'Garçon, two teas and some egg for my face, please!'

'If I pretend to be the ref he might push me over and get sent off!'

'Friends, Mancunians, Southerners . . . lend me your hairs.'

'Hands up if you've got money on West Ham to win the cup?'

Sadly, the last of these captions did not prove prophetic. Just as in 1986, West Ham got knocked out at the quarter-final stage as the first piece of major silverware since 1980 remained elusive. Few would argue, however, that on both occasions the arduous FA Cup journey – especially 'up norf' – wasn't worth it.

Moore Than a Legend

'I had to go, I had to be there' – Sharon Nunn, date unknown

WHILE DISPLAYS of silverware have been notable by their absence at Upton Park in the last three decades, one cannot, never could and doubtless never will be able to say the same thing about displays of emotion.

Untrammelled excitement, trepidation, overflowing joy, un-controllable anger – they come and go on the ever-changing emotional tides that seem to sweep over this football club more than most.

When it comes to outpourings of sadness, there was one event that put any upset caused by relegation, cup exits or the sale of a favourite player completely in the shade: the death of Bobby Moore OBE.

West Ham's greatest-ever player died from bowel cancer at 6.36 a.m., on 24 February 1993. For thousands of Hammers fans and millions of his admirers throughout the world, there was a strange incomprehensibility to his death. Granted, it was widely known that he had been battling cancer for some time but this was *Bobby Moore*. Our Bobby from Barking. Mooro. He of Moore, Hurst and Peters. He of the angelic blond hair and immaculate looks. He of the Swinging Sixties, Jules Rimet, 108 caps, the tackle on Pelé . . .

One minute Bobby Moore was a real, living icon of sport and British culture, the greatest treasure West Ham and England ever unearthed. The next he was gone. Rarely had someone's death felt so unreal. Or, at just 51 years of age, so sad.

The first Hammers game after he died, an away fixture at Sunderland, started as all others did that day with a minute's silence. Both teams should have packed up and left after the minute was up because the ensuing game had all the signs of being played by 22 men – including Ian Bishop wearing Moore's famous No. 6 shirt, which was later 'retired' from the Hammers' squad list as a tribute – for whom chasing a ball around a field suddenly seemed perversely insignificant.

The mourning process has never really ended for West Ham fans, even those too young to have heard Moore on the radio or to have read his newspaper columns in the latter years of his life, never mind seen him play.

Within hours of his death making front-page headlines around the globe, people began making the pilgrimage to the Boleyn Ground. Whether Irons fans or not, they were sucked down Green Street in their thousands, to lay scarves, shirts, flowers and photographs, many attached with heartfelt personal messages of respect for English football's finest.

Soon, the main entrance to Upton Park was completely saturated in mementos left in honour of Moore, making a stroll around the forecourt impossible to do without fighting back the tears. A scroll around the Internet can be just as moving when happening upon one of the Bobby Moore online tributes, which continue to serve the needs of people who simply feel the need to say: 'Thanks, Bobby.'

Take this memory of the day Moore passed away, posted on www.bobbymooreonline.co.uk by Sharon Nunn: 'I was at work when I first heard. My very emotional brother phoned me, he had heard it on the radio. At the time I just remember feeling a sense of disbelief. At home watching the news, I just sat there in stunned silence.

'On the Friday I went to the ground – I had to go, I had to be there. I bought six red roses, had them sprayed in C & B colours, and my favourite West Ham scarf. As I turned into Green Street what I saw was so overwhelming, the memories still move me to tears now. There were hundreds of people and you could not see the gates or railings for flowers, scarves and messages. It was a sea of claret and blue and said everything about the great man and how he was our hero.

'There was a presence and an aura about Bobby that very few people possess. And yet, before his death, I never felt the club gave Bobby the recognition he deserved.

'Rest in peace Bobby Moore. You really were a hero in my eyes.'

Sharon Nunn touches on a nagging irritation often voiced about Moore's post-playing career. There was little about the club to suggest it had once been home to the only West Ham skipper to lift a European trophy, the only England skipper ever to lift the World Cup, a player whom his great friend and adversary Pelé deemed the greatest defender he had ever played against.

A nagging irritation, too, that a man who contributed so much to the pride of a nation should have been reduced, in his last few years, to writing a column for the downmarket *Sunday Sport* newspaper and providing analysis on Capital Gold. As an impassioned Harry Redknapp, his former team-mate, put it in his autobiography: 'One of my most saddening sights was seeing Bobby Moore sitting in the back of the stands at Grimsby, eating fish and chips out of a newspaper and freezing his nuts off, just to earn a couple of bob helping out a radio station. This was the England captain who lifted the World Cup but no one gave a shit.'

On some level, Jonathan Pearce, the commentator for whom Moore acted as sidekick, no doubt agreed with Redknapp's sentiment, although the focus of an article he wrote for the BBC centred instead on his own, tender memories of his colleague's last days: 'On 13 February 1993, he phoned, just as I was leaving for Arsenal against Forest in the cup. "I've got bowel cancer, Pearco. There's nothing they can do. I'm dying, old son." I cried out loud and I weep every time I remember him. He was peerless.'

West Ham, and the FA, have belatedly got their act together since Moore died. At the Boleyn there is a stand named after him and a bronze bust in its foyer. Across town at Wembley is another statue, with Bobby standing atop a plinth decorated with the rest of his heroic compadres from 1966. Back east, the Bobby Moore Cup was launched in 2008 – 50 years after his Hammers debut – with a showpiece game against top European opposition being used to raise money for the Bobby Moore Fund for Imperial Cancer Research, the charity established by his widow Stephanie.

Meanwhile, on the corner of Green Street and Barking Road, another statue, based on a famous photograph taken on the pitch at Wembley in 1966, has Moore being victoriously hoisted aloft by Geoff Hurst, Martin Peters and England left-back Ray Wilson. It was as a home-grown triumvirate with the first two that Moore enjoyed such success in a Hammers shirt. Not as much success as his talents deserved but success all the same: the FA Cup in 1964; the European Cup Winners' Cup in 1965 – the game Moore rated as his finest of all; Footballer of the Year in 1964; and four times Hammer of the Year.

Fittingly, it was Hurst and Peters who placed a floral replica of Moore's No. 6 shirt on the centre spot at the first home game after his death, a 3–1 win over Wolves, in March 1993. Four months later, the entire '66 squad, plus a host of dignitaries and celebrities, attended a memorial service at Westminster Abbey.

After West Indian cricketer Sir Frank Worrell, Moore was only the second sportsman to be honoured in this manner and in March the following year, the club staged a memorial game between West Ham and a Premiership XI attended by all of Moore's team-mates from the mid-'60s glory years.

Contrary to popular belief, Bobby Moore was only human: he made mistakes on and off the field. There was his costly slip-up against Poland during World Cup qualification failure in 1973, and the Blackpool affair, when boss Ron Greenwood dropped him for two weeks for visiting a nightclub on the eve of a 4–0 FA Cup humiliation against the Seasiders in 1971. More controversy, still: the 1970 Bogotá 'bracelet' affair and in the same year a kidnap threat against his first wife Tina and their children.

Finding chinks in Moore's ice-cool persona isn't that hard, it's just that eulogising about him comes so much easier: everything from his God-given sense of timing as a defender to his magnetic presence during a night on the town.

Former colleagues will say that he was not just the best player by a mile but that he also had the best manners (Frank Lampard Snr: 'He knew how to handle himself. He never said too much or anything bad'); was the best trainer *and* the best drinker ('60s teammate Jimmy Lindsay: 'Nobody could drink like Mooro but he'd be in every Sunday morning training on his own with a great big wetsuit on under his kit. He must've sweated out ten gallons of beer'); and was the most fun to be around (Rcdknapp: 'We'd get invitations to all sorts of places because of Mooro').

Even his closest pals and most ardent admirers admit that Bobby had his weaknesses, from his business dealings to his difficulty expressing emotion. In that respect, he was no different from most people.

But in so many others, he was.

....

In Praise of Paolo

'The bloke is a genius' – Harry Redknapp, January 1999

PAOLO DI CANIO is sitting behind the wheel of his rather modest hire car, which is loaded up with dirty washing, when a glint appears in his eye. 'I've always liked Sharon Stone,' he pants. 'She's an incredibly sexy actress – she's beautiful.' The Italian sees beauty in lots of things, whether it's football, cinema, clothes, fine wines or the people he idolises. Indeed, as the title of one of his favourite films suggests, life is beautiful. 'I am very happy now,' he smiles. 'This is where I belong.'

For West Ham fans who yearn for the days when Di Canio belonged to the East End, nostalgic thoughts inevitably turn to the striker's FA Cup fourth-round winner at Manchester United, the sensational scissors-kick goal against Wimbledon, his match-winning double against Arsenal or his stunning strike in the 3–2 victory at Chelsea – each an example of his unique brilliance.

The most pertinent date of all, however, is 26 September 1998, when Di Canio allowed his emotions to get the better of him to the extent that he tempestuously pushed referee Paul Alcock to the ground during Sheffield Wednesday's home game against Arsenal. Since none of the aforementioned magical moments in West Ham's colours would have been possible had he not incurred an 11-game ban and rendered his position at Hillsborough untenable, it should therefore be remembered as an important day in the history of West Ham United. 'I wouldn't have been able to buy Paolo under any other circumstances because Wednesday would not have sold him,' admitted Harry Redknapp after bringing him to Upton Park in January 1999.

It's fitting that Di Canio also lists Stone and Robert De Niro's *Casino* among his top films, because West Ham's £1.75 million investment in the Italian was certainly considered a huge gamble. Di Canio might have described himself as 'sentimental' rather than temperamental but the critics considered some of his behaviour just plain mental. Yet Redknapp refuted claims that he was putting his neck on the line. 'The bloke is a genius,' he insisted. 'He can do things that other people can only dream of and the crowd will love him. It's not a gamble at all.'

Not that Di Canio was the only volatile character at the Boleyn when he arrived, with Ian Wright and Neil Ruddock – neither of whom were strangers to controversy – having celebrated the former's winner against Southampton by re-enacting the infamous push on Alcock in comical fashion. 'Hey, you two, you take da piss or what?' Paolo joked when meeting his new teammates for the first time. But when push came to shove, the striker was desperate to put the events of the past behind him. 'I want people to remember Paolo Di Canio for his footballing skills – the dribbling, passing and goals – not for what happened against Arsenal,' he said while sitting in that hire car, after putting Sharon Stone out of his mind. 'I want to show the people here my qualities and positive attitude for the game.'

It's no understatement to suggest that's the very least he achieved as he captured the hearts of the adoring Upton Park faithful, who regaled him with renditions of 'La Donna è mobile'. After helping West Ham qualify for Europe, he top-scored with 18 goals in his first full season with the club to win the Hammer of the Year award. He grabbed both goals (while wearing his shorts back to front) as West Ham beat Arsenal for the first time in 14 attempts in the early part of that campaign, a period when he also scored twice in a 4–2 home defeat against Manchester United when he was seen beating the pitch with his fists in frustration. His spectacular strike against Wimbledon, displaying the kind of audacity very few players possess as he switched feet in mid-air to volley home with his right boot, won the BBC Goal of the Season award. Di Canio remembers the campaign as 'the best of my life'.

Yet it was also one that confirmed how unpredictable, unstable and erratic he could really be, his bizarre antics in a home game against Bradford living long in the memory of all those present. With the Hammers trailing 4–2, the Italian went ballistic when referee Neale Barry ignored a second strong penalty claim and he strode over to the bench to demand his substitution. He later claimed he had been 'kicked and shoved, grabbed and gouged' without the slightest hint of protection.

After the referee had waved away his protests, now it was the turn of Redknapp who told him to 'get back out there and fight'. Within ten minutes, Di Canio was literally doing just that by wrestling with team-mate Frank Lampard for the right to take a penalty after Barry had finally pointed to the spot. He (inevitably) won the battle, stuck the ball into the net and inspired the Hammers to a thrilling 5–4 victory. 'That game probably summed up my career at West Ham,' he later declared. 'I went through every emotion possible and, at the end, I looked around and realised that I had found my true home in football.'

Di Canio may have been a maverick with majestic talents but he had also displayed nomadic tendencies, having played for seven clubs before joining West Ham – Ternana, Lazio, Juventus, Napoli and AC Milan in his homeland, plus Celtic and Wednesday following his move to Britain. Yet from the day he arrived at Upton Park, the 30 year old insisted he felt a kinship with the club's supporters and the bond between them only intensified over the four-and-half-year period in which he made 141 appearances and scored 52 goals.

The histrionics and hysteria were evidence of his undeniable desire to succeed and if there's one thing Hammers fans want, as well as class from their players, it's commitment. 'People may feel I have an attitude and that I sometimes protest too much because I wave my arms about but that's because I'm Italian and come from another culture,' he said. 'I want to win and to do that you have to have a strong attitude. I give my body for my team-mates.'

The 2000–01 season saw Di Canio make headlines for denying himself a goalscoring opportunity by catching the ball to allow injured Everton goalkeeper Paul Gerrard to receive treatment, for which he won the FIFA Fair Play Award, as well as helping the Hammers to stage a rare FA Cup shock at Manchester United. He was predictably sorry to see Redknapp sacked towards the end of that campaign – 'He understood me,' he said – and was less than impressed with his successor Glenn Roeder, whose appointment he questioned and with whom he eventually had a huge bust-up after one substitution too many. His final season was illuminated by goals against Chelsea as the Hammers completed an unlikely double despite heading for relegation in 2003 but it also coincided with the expiry of his contract. 'My four years at West Ham was an experience I will hold in my heart for ever,' he said.

And so it was no surprise that Di Canio put his name forward when the Hammers were searching for a successor to manager Alan Curbishley, following his resignation in September 2008. 'My dream would be to manage West Ham,' he said. 'The fans are fantastic there and the atmosphere at Upton Park was always so special.' His agent

Phil Spencer said: 'Paolo wouldn't be putting himself up for the job if he didn't think he was capable of doing it.'

Despite their tremendous worship of Di Canio as a player, Hammers supporters would surely be divided as to whether he would make a successful manager, although there's little doubt that he would capture people's imaginations. His lack of experience seemed to be the most obvious concern, although that didn't stop fellow Italian Gianfranco Zola from being appointed West Ham boss instead, and he continues to dream. 'For me, the shirt still feels like a second skin,' he says. 'Nobody can doubt my passion. And the club needs to have somebody who can light up the hearts and minds of the fans.'

As the reception given to Di Canio when he appeared for academy director Tony Carr's testimonial game in May 2010 would suggest, few people – if any – did that better.

■■■■■■■■■■■■■■■■■■

Life Beyond the Vitriolic Old Slaphead

'Come on you Irons!' – Stinky Turner, May 1980

IT WASN'T every football fan who could look forward to their favourite team being name-checked each week in a television sitcom watched by millions.

In the 1970s, Britain was served by only three TV channels – and one of these was little more than an advert for the Open University. So West Ham supporters had much to be grateful for in the shape of that vitriolic, slapheaded old scrote Alf Garnett, an exaggerated Cockney stereotype whose bigoted frustrations with modern society, especially the influx to Britain of people he regarded as having an unfortunate similarity to Clyde Best, were softened only by his affection for 'West Haaaam!'

Seeing a claret and blue scarf round Garnett's scrawny neck or hearing him harp on about West Ham winning the World Cup was like cultural gold dust for watching Irons fans. If there was a nagging irritation (other than his racist yapping) it was that *Till Death Us Do Part* had such a grey, cardigan and slippers feel to it. Worse, in real life, actor Warren Mitchell, who played Garnett, was a Spurs fan!

The only other TV and media reference points around did little to suggest youthful vigour had any part to play in Upton Park's cultural sphere. Radio 1 DJ Noel Edmonds and gypsy crooner David Essex were both unfashionably in their 30s, while 'funnymen' Kenny Lynch and Reg Varney were veritable antiques. Manager John Lyall didn't help matters with his 1950s DA hairstyle and first-teamers like Frank Lampard, David Cross and Billy Bonds actually went out of their way to make themselves look older by sporting the scraggy-bearded Catweazle look.

Finally, in 1980, seventeen-year-old Paul Allen and four herberts from Custom House made sure the kids were all right. The former did it with his tears, flushed cheeks and squeaky voice at Wembley. The latter went one step better: they did it on *Top of the Pops*.

Protagonists of 'Oi!' punk, an acquired musical taste popular among insolent boys at the back of the classroom, the Cockney Rejects celebrated West Ham's ascent to the FA Cup final by releasing a jerky, hectic version of 'I'm Forever Blowing Bubbles'. Three minutes of pure pogo-inducing Irons bravado, the record came in a sleeve sporting the Hammers' iconic V-design Admiral home shirt of the time, which vocalist Stinky Turner wore on *TOTP* as he executed a masterclass in how not to lip-synch.

'Bubbles', with its territorial terrace stomper B-side 'West Side Boys', spent five weeks in the charts, climbing to a high of No. 35. *TOTP* presenter Mike Read didn't look too enamoured of introducing a bunch of lippy East End bovver boys in football tops onto his show and, against the odds, around the same time an even noisier bunch of ne'er-do-wells from Leytonstone also appeared on the programme similarly clad in West Ham regalia.

With the minor chart success 'Running Free', Iron Maiden confirmed both their arrival in the foothills of heavy metal and that Garnett didn't have it all his own way where West Ham fandom was concerned.

For young Hammers fans, sitting transfixed on the living room floor watching *TOTP*, with their parents tut-tutting behind them on the sofa, it was all too good to be true.

The rise and rise of Iron Maiden – led by bass player Steve Harris, a Hammers nut and once on the club's books as a junior – coincided with that of an intense young Cockney actor with a menacing glower and an equally fierce devotion to all things claret and blue.

Thanks to a sockful of snooker balls and a sack full of talent, Ray Winstone shot to cult stardom in the controversial borstal flick *Scum*. Over the course of the next 30-odd years he would appear in some of British cinema's biggest successes (*Sexy Beast, Nil By Mouth*) and play alongside the likes of Jack Nicholson in *The Departed* and Harrison Ford in *Indiana Jones and the Kingdom of the Crystal Skull*. Yet when interviewed, Winstone always seems as keen to talk about his football team as he is about screen presence or box-office takings.

With the Hammers looking doomed to relegation in the spring of 2010, Winstone diverted attention away from his 'Outstanding Contribution to British Film' gong at the Empire Film Awards by expressing his West Ham woes on the red carpet, doing so in typically forthright fashion. 'I can't see us staying up now. They're trying their hearts out but when your confidence goes in any profession, you're knackered. Someone said they were putting the clocks back this morning. I said, "I'm putting mine back to 1860 so there'd be no West Ham and there'd be no pain." That's how you feel.'

Winstone's thousand-yard stare is unlikely ever to feature in *EastEnders* but since 1985 the BBC soap has been another fertile hunting ground for Hammers touching points. Nick Berry (as Wicksy) was the first of several characters over the years to find time to espouse his love of West Ham amid all the mayhem and misery of life in Albert Square. Like Perry Fenwick and Leslie Grantham, the soap's ultimate baddie Dirty Den, Berry is a West Ham fan in real life.

On the literary front, the standard that Nick Hornby set in describing the travails of following Arsenal in *Fever Pitch* was always going to be a hard one to match for writers associated with other teams. Not even someone with an imagination as vivid as Hornby's, however, could have predicted that West Ham would be served on this front by the outlandish witterings of a Grays-born comedian/ actor/author/dandy, whose fascination with sex is matched only by his lust for the Irons.

Through his brilliantly abstract *Guardian* column and books like *Articles of Faith*, Russell Brand has achieved the impossible by turning the minds of the chattering classes away from the pretensions of Old Trafford and the Emirates and towards little old Upton Park. Even more incongruous, in 2009 he managed to get his American pop star girlfriend Katy Perry to perform in claret and blue lingerie, prompting the club to sell a limited-edition range of underwear through its merchandising operations. G'awd bless the incorrigible ol' rapscallion!

Some might say it is apt that comedy and West Ham United seem so intertwined. As well as Brand, *Never Mind The Buzzcocks*' Phill Jupitus and James Cordon of *Gavin and Stacey* both show a welcome keenness to fly the West Ham flag. Funnier still, US President Barack Obama is rumoured to be a fan. What Chairman Alf would make of any of these figures doesn't bear thinking about, let alone printing, but even he would have to grudgingly concede that from rock music to film, sit-coms to superpowers, 'West Haaaam!' are better represented than most.

....

We're (Nearly) Gonna Win the League

'West Ham are the best team in the land' –
Joe Melling, Daily Express, December 1985

'WEST HAM deserved the league championship that season because we played the best football over 42 games, entertaining crowds up and down the country with our own brand of exciting, attacking football.' So said Tony Cottee when reflecting on the magical 1985–86 campaign that saw the Hammers secure not only a best-ever finish of third but also hassle eventual champions Liverpool to the final weekend for the title. John Lyall's men won twenty-six of their league games – as many as the Reds and second-placed Everton – while the eighty-four points they amassed would have been enough to see them crowned champions in two of the previous three seasons. As Patrick Collins wrote in the *Daily Mail*, 'West Ham have proved that attractive football can also be effective football. They have grown into the most appealing side in England.'

West Ham challenging for the league title was not the only unbelievable aspect of that unique campaign. For a side that had finished sixteenth in 1985 – just two points above relegated Norwich – and seen Hammer of the Year Paul Allen defect to rivals Tottenham, they were unlikely to be transformed by the arrivals of an attacking midfielder from St Mirren and a winger from Oldham. Nobody had heard of Frank McAvennie or Mark Ward. It's also astonishing that between 19 January and 14 March they would play just a single league game – as a result of inclement weather – and therefore see the final eleven fixtures compressed into a crazily intense five-week period that put the Hammers at a considerable disadvantage compared to their Merseyside foes.

In essence, the whole season was one of upsetting the odds, taking people by surprise and overcoming obstacles, before finally making a little bit of history that has since been commemorated in the form of books, reunion dinners, golf days and a whole host of tribute functions. *Boys of '86: The Movie* anyone? Why not, for as midfielder Alan Dickens once said, 'It seems strange to be celebrating finishing third but, in a way, it's not really about our final position in the table, it's more about the characters in that team and the special spirit we had.'

The effervescent McAvennie and Ward, who had arrived for fees of £340,000 and £220,000 respectively, definitely introduced more personality to the dressing-room, although early results suggested another season of struggle was on the cards. McAvennie was making his mark after being pushed up front following Paul Goddard's injury in the opening-day defeat at Birmingham but one win from the first seven league games left the Hammers down in 17th place and looking highly unlikely to cause the big boys any sleepless nights.

'People don't realise how poor we were at the beginning of that season,' recalled Neil Orr, who came into the side as a replacement for the injured Geoff Pike. 'That start really cost us and was really annoying. But once we got some momentum going we were unstoppable.'

The real fun began with a run of 18 unbeaten league games in the autumn to equal the club's record at that time. In October, they shifted into a whole new gear completely, racking up nine successive victories that thrust them up from eleventh to third place in less than two months. Cottee and McAvennie were banging in the goals as they gleefully exploited the chances created for them by Alan Devonshire, who was enjoying a great season after recovering from a serious knee injury, fellow midfielder Dickens and, in particular, Ward on the right. 'Nobody had really heard of Wardie,' said Orr. 'But his work rate was incredible; he had great pace and could put a great ball across.'

By Christmas, the Hammers had collected 45 points from 22 games, compelling Joe Melling to write in the *Daily Express*, 'On current form, West Ham are the best team in the land.' However, like most observers, he predicted that their bubble would soon burst. 'The feeling remains that their title challenge will fade.'

That appeared to be the case when West Ham lost three games out of four – at Liverpool, Arsenal and Aston Villa – and also had defenders Alvin Martin and Ray Stewart sent off. Those defeats, which dumped the Hammers back down to seventh, had been spread over a two-month period with the appalling weather playing havoc with the schedule and destroying the team's momentum. At one stage, they had four games in hand over leaders Everton.

However, a sensational 4–0 thrashing of Chelsea (not out of the title hunt themselves) at Stamford Bridge at Easter confirmed that West Ham were back on the march. Two-goal Cottee later described that result as 'our most complete performance of the season', adding, 'That was the result that made people sit up and take notice. Not only that but our players suddenly started to believe that perhaps we could challenge for the title.'

It's one of a number of outstanding highlights during a wonderful run-in that saw the Hammers win 11 out of 13 games while the championship was still a possibility. Another was the 8–1 thumping of

Newcastle that is famously remembered for Martin writing his name into the record books by scoring against three different goalkeepers to claim the only hat-trick of his career. With Martin Thomas and emergency stand-in Chris Hedworth both beaten by the defender before being forced off injured, England attacker Peter Beardsley found himself between the sticks when the Hammers won a late penalty with the score at 7–1. 'Ray Stewart picked the ball up because, as ever, he wanted to take it,' remembered Martin. 'It wasn't until the crowd started chanting my name that it became embarrassing for me not to take it. Sending Beardsley the wrong way from the spot – it was the pick of the three! But John Lyall wasn't amused that I'd taken the penalty and made the point that the title could have been decided on goal difference.'

Incredibly, West Ham were forced to follow up that result with a run of four games in a week – the first three thankfully at home. Coventry were beaten 1–0 on the Saturday, as were Manchester City on the Monday, before struggling Ipswich arrived at Upton Park two days later for a tension-filled tussle that was won by Stewart's late penalty, after a brilliant curler from Dickens had wiped out Kevin Wilson's shock opener.

That victory lifted the Hammers to within four points of leaders Liverpool with a game in hand and, with just trips to West Brom and Everton remaining, the players saluted the Boleyn faithful from the directors' box where they were met with chants of 'we're gonna win the league'.

For that to happen, West Ham needed to win at the Hawthorns and hope Liverpool were denied all three points in their final game at Chelsea that same afternoon. The Hammers battled their way to a 3–2 victory and, with mixed messages coming off the terraces about the events at Stamford Bridge, returned to their dressing-room with the belief that their title dreams were still alive. Suddenly an official appeared and announced, 'Sorry, lads, Liverpool have won.' Player-boss Kenny Dalglish had scored in a 1–0 win as the Reds wrapped up their league campaign with their 11th triumph in 12 outings. To say the least, the news was hard to stomach. McAvennie recalled, 'We crashed from victorious delirium down to bleak depression in a second. You could have heard a pin drop in that dressing-room.'

Typically, manager Lyall was able to put his immense disappointment to one side, insisting his players be proud of what they had achieved. Not surprisingly, his physically exhausted and emotionally drained side faded to a 3–1 defeat in what amounted to a second-place shoot-out with Everton two days later. Many of the players realised they might never get closer to winning the league title – not in West Ham's colours anyway – but once the pain had subsided they were able to contextualise the events of that season and take great satisfaction from their endeavours.

'There was disappointment but I think we all felt a sense of achievement as well,' said Martin. 'In the end, we had too many games to play in such a short space of time while Liverpool had the experience.' Meanwhile, Tony Gale, who later scooped a champions medal with Blackburn in 1995, reflected, 'I will never forget those days as long as I live. That was a dream team – wonderful to play in and wonderful to watch. If we had today's saturation TV coverage at that time, the whole nation would have thrilled to the football we played. We were lucky with injuries, using only 13 players on a regular basis, but it's far and away the best side I ever played in. West Ham will be lucky if they ever get one so good again.'

•••••••••••••••••••

Baby Bentleys on the Skids

'Pathetic!' – veteran journalist Brian Glanville, January 2007

ALAN CURBISHLEY is frequently given great credit for keeping West Ham in the Premier League following his arrival midway through the 2006–07 season. Seven wins in the final nine league games to secure a miraculous survival is something any manager would proudly highlight on his CV in luminous yellow. Yet it mustn't be forgotten that the former Charlton boss was partly – some might say largely

– responsible for the mess the Hammers found themselves in as the campaign entered the final straight.

When Curbishley succeeded Alan Pardew at Upton Park, West Ham were sitting third from bottom with 14 points from 17 games, so there were clearly problems that needed addressing. After a shock 1–0 home success against Manchester United – who were unbeaten in their previous dozen league outings – just a few days after the new manager's arrival, the Hammers embarked on a suicidal run of 11 Premier League games without a win.

It was a nightmarish sequence that saw West Ham collect a meagre three points and, if the home FA Cup embarrassment at the hands of struggling Watford is also taken into account, a run of six successive defeats. The three most distressing results suggested the Hammers were beyond all hope in the early part of 2007 – each one was like a savage blow to the head that left them bloodied, bruised and beaten.

The first came on New Year's Day, when West Ham crashed to a humiliating 6–0 defeat at Premier League new boys Reading – their biggest loss since a 7–1 collapse at Blackburn in October 2001. Headers from Brynjar Gunnarsson and Stephen Hunt, plus an own goal by Anton Ferdinand and a close-range conversion by Kevin Doyle, put Reading out of sight before the half-time whistle had even arrived, while Leroy Lita and Doyle's second of the day completed a thoroughly regal romp by the Royals.

'You're not fit to wear the shirt!' chanted the disgusted West Ham fans in the Madejski Stadium, while Curbishley left his players in no doubt about his feelings during a lengthy post-match inquest. When he eventually appeared to meet the media, he spoke of how the opposition had displayed the 'newly promoted hunger' that West Ham had done in securing a top-half finish the previous season and admitted, 'Reading had everything that we didn't – enthusiasm, pace, shape, aggression and, above all, hunger. They have the commitment and desire of wanting to be in the Premiership and driving the Baby Bentley. If Reading come ninth this year, they won't be going around in an open-top bus, they'll just be looking forward to the next season. At Charlton I was used to getting in that position and seeing the same hunger and spirit in the team.'

There was no doubt that Curbishley believed his players were getting too big for their boots, yet the manager, amazingly, accused the press of distorting his words after they focused on his 'Baby Bentley' jibe. 'I was talking about the Baby Bentley in terms of Reading but it was spun around so that it looked as though I was having a go at my own players,' he complained.

Indirectly, that's exactly what he had done and it suggested some naivety on his part, having enjoyed a relatively sheltered existence in his 15 years at Charlton, that he failed to anticipate how the media would interpret his comments. A similar example took place when he pointed out that many of the new signings the previous summer, such as Carlos Tevez, John Pantsil, Tyrone Mears, Javier Mascherano and Jonathan Spector, had not established themselves as regular starters. The papers referred to them as 'flops' to send Curbishley into a rage. So while the following weekend's 3–0 FA Cup win against Brighton should have been used to positive effect, Curbishley opted to attack the press instead. 'I'm loyal to my players so I'm very disappointed that some of them think I've had a go at them,' he said before storming out of the media room in a huff. 'Pathetic!' muttered veteran journalist Brian Glanville as the manager whizzed past him.

Curbishley had never scored an own goal as a West Ham player but he had certainly done so as boss, with the media subsequently accusing him of 'throwing his toys out of his pram' and lacking 'media savvy'. Another inquest took place when playmaker Yossi Benayoun was quoted as saying the team had 'played like a bunch of drunks' when being hit for six at Reading, a result that assistant boss Mervyn Day claimed 'killed us' in terms of trying to recruit good new players in the January transfer window. No wonder they ended up with Luis Boa Morte and Nigel Quashie.

Injury-hit West Ham looked no less inebriated when they visited Curbishley's former club Charlton – now managed by Pardew, with the two men having effectively completed a job swap – for a classic relegation six-pointer. The Hammers were five points adrift of fourth-bottom Wigan, while Charlton had joined them on twenty points from twenty-seven games. The media's build-up to the clash focused on the contrasting styles of the two managers, with Pardew's enthusiasm having improved his new outfit's prospects after they had looked doomed, while Curbishley's downbeat demeanour was questioned. 'You can't expect me to be happy when I've won one game in ten,' he argued.

The poor results were evidence of serious discontent behind the scenes. Morale was low among the players – many of whom were suspicious of the new management team who were struggling to win their trust – and cliques were dividing the squad. Argentine pair Tevez and Mascherano were feeling marginalised because of a lack of involvement, while Curbishley had fall-outs with senior men such as Benayoun, Teddy Sheringham and Christian Dailly among others. It was no surprise that one insider described the mood as 'awful', while Day later admitted there was 'resistance' to Curbishley's ideas and a host of problems to resolve. 'We were fire-fighting for the first two months,' he revealed.

Goalkeeper Robert Green, meanwhile, believed he was being made a scapegoat when he was dropped for six games after the Reading debacle (a one-game penalty for every goal conceded, perhaps) but would maybe have wished for a longer spell out of the side if he'd known how events would turn out at Charlton on 24 February.

The Addicks were boosted by the presence of Darren Bent following a two-month injury absence and the striker celebrated his return by scoring Charlton's third shortly before half-time, after goals by Darren Ambrose and Jerome Thomas had made it obvious which way the points were heading. Thomas completed the 4–0 rout – which also saw the hosts hit the woodwork twice – and Curbishley's embarrassment was compounded when the West Ham fans joined his old Charlton supporters in chanting the name of his rival Pardew. 'That was obviously very hurtful for Alan,' said Day. 'That was the point where I started to think we might not make it,' he added. Even former Hammers defender and Sky pundit Tony Gale was forced to put aside his usual optimism and admit, 'I just can't see them getting out of trouble.'

That looked ever more the case after Tottenham's visit to Upton

Park eight days later. It had all looked so promising when Mark Noble put West Ham ahead on his first league start of the season and Tevez brilliantly curled home a free-kick off the underside of the bar to finally open his account for the club in his 20th appearance. His 1,141-minute wait for a goal was over and he duly ripped off his shirt before jumping into the lower tier of the Dr Martens Stand to celebrate with his ecstatic supporters. Despite a 2–0 half-time lead it was still a case of hope rather than expectation for home fans and when a penalty by former Hammer Jermain Defoe – after Lee Bowyer brought down Aaron Lennon – and a volley from Teemu Tainio brought the scores level just past the hour mark, they were entitled to fear the worst.

But when substitute Bobby Zamora made an instant impact by heading West Ham into a 3–2 lead with just five minutes remaining, a first win in 11 games looked not just possible but likely . . . until Spurs unbelievably hit back with two goals in the dying moments. Dimitar Berbatov curled an 89th-minute free-kick into the top left-hand corner and, with the Hammers pushing forward in a desperate bid to win the game, they got caught on the break. Green could only parry Defoe's shot and Paul Stalteri was on hand to put the ball into the empty net and claim an unlikely, not to mention undeserved, 4–3 win for Tottenham.

It was a devastating moment and one that had surely banged the final nail into West Ham's coffin. Noble left the field in floods of tears while Curbishley accused his players of being 'naive'. The result dumped the Hammers to the bottom of the table for the first time that season and left them a massive ten points adrift of fourth-bottom Manchester City who had two games in hand. With just nine matches remaining, fans were already mapping their routes to Barnsley, Plymouth and Colchester – and who could blame them?

Bonds is the Name, Bonds are to Blame

'When the Bond Scheme came in all hell broke loose'
– Billy Bonds, May 1992

WEST HAM have been accused of shooting themselves in the foot on many an occasion during their history, but the launch of the infamous Hammers Bond – commonly known as the Bond Scheme – in the early part of the 1991–92 season ranks as one of the most calamitous examples.

Having won promotion back to the First Division at the second time of asking under Billy Bonds during the previous campaign, it was imperative that the Hammers could rely upon the full backing of their tremendously loyal supporters if they were going to stand a decent chance of consolidating their position among the big boys. Instead, in what appeared to be one of the most misguided moves of club ownership ever, West Ham conjured up a concept that would alienate their fan base in the worst possible way and inspire a bitter backlash as the campaign disintegrated into riots and eventual relegation. Never mind Billy Bonds, this was a case of silly bonds as far as most observers were concerned.

English football was still reeling from the Hillsborough Disaster, which saw 96 people tragically killed during the FA Cup semi-final between Liverpool and Nottingham Forest on 15 April 1989. With the subsequent Taylor Report recommending that all clubs in the top two divisions should have all-seater stadiums by the start of the 1994–95 season, a financial burden was placed on the directors of West Ham, who calculated that it would cost in excess of £15 million to redevelop the Boleyn Ground to the required standard.

A cunning plan was devised that the dim-witted Baldrick character of *Blackadder* fame would have been proud of: West Ham would re-build the ground . . . and the fans would pay for it. Indeed, as the scheme's 12-page launch brochure proudly boasted: 'It is hoped the Hammers Bond will raise £15.1 million towards the total costs of the project (£15.5m excluding VAT). The balance will be funded by the club from other sources.' Some 19,301 bonds were made available at three different price levels – £500, £750 and £975 – and, in return for that initial outlay, supporters were told they would then be allowed 'the exclusive right for not less than 50 years to buy a season ticket for your own named seat . . . Only those supporters who buy a bond will be guaranteed the right to buy a season ticket,' the brochure stressed.

In other words, if fans didn't buy a bond, they couldn't buy a season ticket. And if they couldn't buy a season ticket, they would be left to fight for the 6,199 seats not allocated to bondholders, with the planned redevelopment of the Boleyn Ground based on a new restricted capacity of 25,500. Even the club realised that their anticipated exploitation of loyalty would probably not be enough to entice enough supporters to accept this wonderfully generous offer, so they applied extra pressure by leaving the fan base in fear of the consequences. According to the launch brochure (entitled *We Shall Not Be Moved*), the only alternatives to the Hammers Bond were: 'closing the ground and moving to another purpose-built stadium'; 'sharing another club's ground'; 'selling key players'; 'a share flotation on the Stock Exchange'; and 'approaching banks to increase our borrowing from the current level of over £2m'. 'These options were rejected,' the brochure stated, before warning: 'If the Hammers Bond is not a success, the club will be unable to proceed with the full redevelopment. The capacity could fall to as little as 12,500. Many loyal fans would be denied the opportunity to watch West Ham. Money would have to be borrowed to finance such work and the fewer seats available would mean less revenue. This could condemn the club to second-rate status.'

New managing director Peter Storrie added, 'If we still have terraces in August 1994 we won't be allowed to admit our supporters onto them and our capacity could be reduced to approximately 12,600. With an average home league gate so far this season of 22,822 such an event could mean that many supporters would be turned away.'

In a somewhat cynical act to tug on supporters' emotions, the club persuaded West Ham hero Trevor Brooking to endorse the scheme and the former midfielder said, 'If everyone clubs together, we can make Upton Park one of the best football grounds in Britain.'

Needless to say, the vast majority of fans were in no mood to 'club together' – as if they were having a whip-round in the Boleyn Tavern on the corner of Green Street – and with fanzines such as *Fortune's Always Hiding* leading the way in galvanising the fans against the scheme, it quickly became clear that West Ham's propaganda had fooled nobody. Moreover, the timing of the launch could not have been any worse, with West Ham recovering from a poor start of just two wins in their first thirteen league games, to beat Tottenham and Arsenal in successive weekends and take a point from Liverpool, before the feeling of negativity began to take hold. 'We were doing OK,' said Billy Bonds, 'but when the Bond Scheme came in all hell broke loose.'

A succession of home games became the focal point for fan protests and, with the team sliding back to the bottom of the table as a result of six defeats in seven league outings, the embarrassing 1–1 FA Cup draw with non-league Farnborough sparked the first of several pitch invasions during the early part of 1992. The club attempted lamely to polish up the Bond Scheme by offering ten-year discounts of up to £100 per season against the cost of season tickets but very few were buying it . . . literally.

The visit of Everton to Upton Park on 29 February (which ended in a 2–0 defeat) saw one fan grab a corner flag and plant it in the centre circle as he staged a one-man sit-down protest. Skipper Julian Dicks was the first on the scene to retrieve the flag and he remembered, 'I picked it up and pretended to stab him with it. I asked the guy what he was doing and he said he opposed the Bond Scheme. A few more fans came on the pitch after that and one of them came up to me and said, "I f**king love you." I just said, "Oh cheers!" They had every right to protest but not when the game's going on. Everyone's concentration goes.'

Dicks spoke out against the Bond Scheme after the game and the entire squad was subsequently called together during training two days later. 'Obviously I disagreed with the idea,' says Dicks, 'because they were asking people to fork out £975 to watch a load of crap. And then Peter Storrie and Billy Bonds called us all in and said, "You just get on with your football and leave the rest to us." The thing is, they spent around £2 million advertising the thing and they could have bought two good players for that.'

Not that two good players would have been enough to rescue the Hammers from relegation that season once the revolt against the Bond Scheme was in full swing. 'Bumbling West Ham only have themselves to blame,' wrote one reporter. 'They have scored their biggest ever own goal – the wretched and reviled Bond Scheme.'

Manager Bonds certainly believed the club destroyed their own chances of survival, answering 'in a nutshell, yes', when later asked if the Bond Scheme was directly responsible for the 1992 relegation. 'I never backed the Bond Scheme either,' he admitted. 'I couldn't say anything against it because it was something the club was doing. I just had to sit on the fence and say nothing. I refused to do certain things for the Bond Scheme that the board had asked for. I thought it was a diabolical liberty.'

West Ham finished bottom of the table with 38 points from 42 games and relegation could not have been more poorly timed, with the club missing out on the huge increase in revenue a place in the newly formed Premier League would have provided. However, director and future chairman Terence Brown later defended the club's decision to launch the Bond Scheme and insisted it had been necessary, despite only 808 fans taking part and the obligation being scrapped, to secure the loans of £11.5 million that funded the eventual construction of the Bobby Moore Stand (opened in February 1994) and the Centenary Stand (opened in January 1995). Brown said, 'The scheme played a fundamental part in regenerating the club. Sadly our supporters have never really understood the importance of the underwriting agreement with the banks. It is a shame that such a financially advantageous arrangement, from the club's point of view, is so misunderstood.'

The problem, of course, was that while it was 'financially advantageous' for the club, it wasn't for the fans. And that's something they had no problem understanding. Today, even the official West Ham website refers to the Bond Scheme as 'a public relations disaster' and acknowledges the 'hostility' it generated. Its very mention will forever be synonymous with a campaign of controversy, conflict and crisis.

····················

Video Killed the Rotterdam Star

'Not like it said in the brochure, if you like'
– Harry Redknapp, 1998

MARCO BOOGERS' achievements in English football were rather closer to dilapidated old caravan than five-star hotel but the Dutch striker did manage one enviable feat on these shores. By pole-axing Manchester United's Gary Neville, Boogers lived the dream of all those Liverpool and Manchester City fans who utterly despise the United skipper.

It's clutching straws but at least it's pure fact, which is more than can be said for the vast majority of column inches written about Boogers this side of the North Sea. For rarely has the Premier League career of a foreign player led to such mirth and myth.

There were three main strands to The Legend of Mad Marco, so which were 'true' and which were *'onwaar'* (that's 'false' in Dutch)?

- *After fleeing from West Ham back to Holland, he lived in a caravan: onwaar.*
- *He suffered a mental breakdown: technically onwaar.*
- *He was signed on video evidence alone: True . . . but then again, perhaps onwaar.*

That the last of these is open to conjecture is a situation not helped by Harry Redknapp. The manager who signed the 28 year old for the Hammers in the summer of 1995 seemed to delight in giving contrasting definitions of the detail relating to Boogers' signing.

53

Adding spice to the tale is perhaps Harry's own typically tongue-in-cheek way of deflecting attention from the fact that he was responsible for one of the most calamitous transfers in the history of the club.

To illustrate: soon after things started to go Edam-shaped for Boogers at Upton Park, Redknapp revealed how incensed he was by all the rot being written about his £800,000 acquisition from Sparta Rotterdam. By that stage, Boogers had made just two sub appearances and been banned for four games for the Neville tackle. 'Of course he's the kind of player I expected,' said Harry. 'I knew exactly what I was getting. Suddenly people have been telling me that I hadn't seen him play and I bought him off a video. I don't know who dreamt that one up. I had seen him play, once, but I did watch a video as well. Then I get silly letters written to me and people dreaming up ideas that I didn't know who he was. What a load of nonsense!'

Yet three years later in his autobiography, Redknapp revealed: 'I admit for the first time in my life I signed a player purely on video evidence. Someone sent me a tape of Boogers in action and urged me to watch it. I was very impressed. I took the risk and signed him. He could play a bit but certainly he was nowhere near as impressive as the video had made out. Not like it said in the brochure, if you like.'

If Gary Neville had also gone into Boogers' background a little more closely and researched his favourite films, he would probably have chosen to wear full body armour when West Ham's second game of the 1995–96 season took them to Old Trafford. In a Q&A soon after arriving in England, Boogers revealed that he liked 'the gory type of movies with lots of blood. My favourite actors are Bruce Willis, Jean-Claude Van Damme and Sylvester Stallone.' It was his finely observed interpretation of one of Van Damme's martial arts moves which sent Neville sprawling, although Boogers insisted the wet grass was to blame for his dramatic contribution as a second-half substitute. Either way 'Horror tackle!' headlines accompanied the striker's first substantial appearance on the UK's back pages.

By the time of the United game, frustration at an underwhelming start to his career in England was already beginning to nag at a striker who, just the previous season, had been ranked the third-best player in Holland and who boasted a good record of 103 goals in 238 league games for Dordrecht, Utrecht, RKC Waalwijk, Fortuna Sittard and Sparta.

Bristol Rovers' Marcus Stewart had been Redknapp's desired target that summer but at £1.5 million West Ham were out-priced. So while London neighbours Arsenal could afford to splash £7.5 million on Dennis Bergkamp and Chelsea had Ruud Gullit, Hammers gambled on a relatively undiscovered Dutch master, reportedly pipping a clutch of top clubs to his signature. 'I could have gone to Napoli or Everton, and Borussia Dortmund wanted me as well,' Boogers claimed in an interview in Holland. 'But suddenly West Ham United came in. That was a beautiful club to me, with the famous colours alone. So I chose West Ham.'

Pre-season didn't augur too well. Boogers missed a sackful of chances against TSV Munich but did manage to open his account against Bournemouth. He later opined that English players seemed to spend more time playing golf than they did honing their football skills, while Redknapp suggested that Boogers was stuck in the rough from the moment he started training at Chadwell Heath. 'Right from the word go Boogers' attitude stank,' Harry said in his autobiography. 'He didn't want to work, he was lazy and the players all took an instant dislike to him. He didn't fancy the physical side of the game. He didn't take to the English style of football, hated training and said his wife couldn't settle.'

Little surprise then that the 6 ft 1 in. forward was restricted to an appearance from the bench in the first game of the season, a 2–1 home loss to Leeds United. The frustration of another 45 minutes getting splinters at Old Trafford resulted in Neville being left flat on his back, Boogers feeling flatter than his flat-top hairstyle and, most controversial of all, the flat landscape of the Netherlands beckoning Marco home – there to go off his rocker in a caravan . . . a charge he always flatly denied!

'I read the craziest stuff. What kind of rubbish is this?' the attacker later asked. Answer? The kind of 'rubbish' that *The Sun* revelled in dishing out under its 'Barmy Boogers' headlines. In fairness to the tabloid, the root of the misunderstanding lay partly, by his own admission, at the feet of West Ham's former PA announcer and travel arranger Bill Prosser.

Fully eight years after the caravan/mental breakdown tale first started doing the rounds, and with Redknapp fuelling the myth in his autobiography – 'We eventually found him hiding out in a caravan in Holland and only got him back by reading the riot act' – Prosser attempted to clear the matter up in an interview with *The Guardian*: 'Marco was depressed after being sent off . . . and disappeared for a few days. West Ham's *Clubcall* reporter phoned me and said he was trying to find Boogers for an interview but could not reach him. He asked if I had booked any flights for him. I told him I hadn't but added, "If he has gone back to Holland, he's probably gone by car again." The reporter misheard me and stated on *Clubcall* that I had said, "If he's gone back to Holland, he's probably gone to his caravan." The legend endures and Marco Boogers never played for West Ham again. I feel a bit responsible for his misfortune.'

In fact, Boogers did play for West Ham again. Returning from Holland – allegedly with a doctor's note confirming that he had been 'psychologically unfit to play football' – to have another stab at his three-year contract, he made two further substitute appearances, successfully negotiating early baths against both Aston Villa and Blackburn but completing a miserable Hammers playing record of four sub appearances in four defeats (eleven goals conceded).

The one and only positive moment in Boogers' stint at the Boleyn came when he played in Alvin Martin's second testimonial in a team featuring Chris Waddle, Jamie Redknapp and Steve McManaman. The Dutchman smacked home the first goal in a 3–3 draw with Chelsea at Upton Park, as if to prove to Redknapp Sr that video had not, in fact, killed the Rotterdam star.

Tony Cottee and Iain Dowie, both in their second spells at the club, were by now firmly established as Redknapp's favoured strike partnership and, to rub salt into Boogers' clogs, in December he suffered cartilage damage during training. After emergency surgery on his knee, he was allowed to return to Holland once again for the three-month recuperation. Only the birth of his son three days after

Christmas made up for the abject misery of his first half-season in English football.

There was to be no second half. With all parties acknowledging that the West Ham/Boogers marriage was simply never meant to be, he was allowed to go out on loan to FC Groningen, inevitably making a permanent return to Dutch football. He rounded off his playing career at his first club FC Dordrecht, where after retiring he turned his hand to coaching.

It took Boogers four sub appearances, three urban myths, two trips back home, one video and no goals to go from being the third best player in Holland to being ranked number nineteen in *The Times'* list of the worst players ever to play in the Premier League.

No other player has given supporters of opposing teams such licence to take the mickey out of West Ham. Perhaps funniest, or most tragic, of all is that Boogers comes directly after Bonds in the alphabetical list of players who have appeared for West Ham. From the sublime to the ridiculous. There's nothing *onwaar* about that.

■■■■■■■■■■■■■■■■■■■

The Great Escape

'Seven wins out of nine is unbelievable'
– Alan Curbishley, May 2007

FORMER SHEFFIELD United boss Neil Warnock attempted to rewrite history when claiming in his autobiography that Carlos Tevez – 'football's equivalent of a murderer out on bail', as he affectionately describes the striker – is the man who 'scored the goal for West Ham that kept them up and put us down'. Not for the first time when talking about the Tevez affair he is sorely mistaken, because if you take the Argentina international's strike out of the 1–0 win at Manchester United on 13 May 2007, the Hammers still keep their place in the Premier League and Sheffield United still lose theirs.

The fact is that West Ham headed to Old Trafford on the dramatic final day of the 2006–07 season knowing a draw would be good enough to guarantee survival, irrespective of whether the Blades lost at home to fellow strugglers Wigan or not. However, if Warnock wants to distort events to vindicate his sense of paranoia and injustice, the majority of West Ham fans won't argue with him. After all, it makes for a much better memory – probably the very best in recent Hammers history.

Once it came to light that West Ham had breached FA rules in relation to the third-party ownership of Tevez and former team-mate Javier Mascherano – for which the club was hit with a record £5.5 million fine – there was always going to be heavy scrutiny of any role that either of them might play in helping the club to avoid the drop. Inevitably, he was involved from start to finish as the Hammers launched arguably the greatest escape act of all time.

Ten points adrift of fourth-bottom Manchester City – who had two games in hand – and eleven behind Sheffield United, it was time for West Ham to get out the prayer mats. In fact, a little divine intervention did occur when aptly named assistant referee Jim Devine kindly ruled that Bobby Zamora's shot at Blackburn, on 17 March, was a legitimate goal when it was obvious that strike-partner Tevez had accidentally blocked the ball on the line. Not just that but Lee Bowyer had appeared to handle in the build-up. With Tevez earlier being awarded a hotly disputed penalty and picking himself up to wipe out Christopher Samba's opener for the hosts, there's little doubt West Ham got the rub of the green for once. 'We've had a bit of luck but I'm not complaining,' relieved boss Alan Curbishley said after his side's first away win of the season. It didn't take long for a fearful Warnock to put in his twopenn'orth, the Sheffield United boss claiming, 'If West Ham stay up now, they ought to give Mr Devine life presidency of the club.'

Zamora and Tevez were both on target again in a comfortable 2–0 home win against Middlesbrough next time out, with the latter bagging his third goal in as many games after being handed four successive starts. 'He hadn't scored but the crowd kept singing his name and that put a bit of pressure on us,' explained Curbishley as to why he had finally decided to give Tevez a run in the side. If the fans could recognise that the South American was a special talent, it's somewhat bewildering that the management couldn't. As his assistant Mervyn Day admitted, 'We were wondering why the crowd loved him so much.'

The victory against Boro – only the second time the team had secured back-to-back wins all season – closed the gap on fourth-bottom Sheffield United to five points with seven games to play. As if things weren't bad enough, however, the Hammers still had to face five of the top seven clubs while the Blades were playing five of the bottom seven. One of the most daunting prospects was a trip to Arsenal but it was appropriate that West Ham should become the first visiting side to win at the new Emirates Stadium given they had been the last one to claim victory at Highbury before its closure. Zamora lobbed Jens Lehmann in first-half stoppage time to claim a shock 1–0 win that saw Hammers goalkeeper Robert Green play the game of his life to keep the Gunners – who had at least 25 goal efforts – at bay. 'The penny has now dropped about how hard we have to work,' said Curbishley, inferring that the players had not been shaking much of a leg for him until recent times.

Sadly, the team's new-found industry couldn't stop them from collapsing to a 3–0 defeat at Sheffield United that seemed to have dropped them back to square one. 'You've got to pick up points against the teams around you and we haven't done that,' conceded Curbishley. A 4–1 home defeat by second-placed Chelsea made it a bad four days for the Hammers and even former boss Harry Redknapp was left to admit, 'West Ham are dead and buried now.'

Yet Zamora claimed his fifth goal in seven games to earn a 1–0 home win against an in-form Everton on the weekend that bottom outfit Watford were relegated. What was particularly remarkable about West Ham's recent revival – four wins out of six at that point – was that it had begun under the huge cloud of a potential points deduction for the misdemeanours relating to the Tevez and Mascherano signings. So there was a mammoth sigh of relief on 27 April when it was announced that a heavy fine would be imposed instead, much to the annoyance of strugglers such as Wigan and Sheffield United, who had been hoping that the Premier League inquiry panel would help save their bacon by sending the Hammers down.

Fittingly, a buoyant West Ham visited Wigan the following day and romped to a 3–0 victory thanks to goals from Luis Boa Morte, Yossi Benayoun and Marlon Harewood. Wigan chairman Dave Whelan was furious. 'We were never going to win that match,' he whinged. 'West Ham were on fire and why not? They had just got away with murder.' There's that word again. And he was in a bigger flap the following weekend when the Hammers' 3–1 home success against Bolton – thanks to two Tevez goals and one from Mark Noble – lifted them level with Sheffield United (albeit with a slightly inferior goal difference) and dumped Wigan into the bottom three with just one game left to play.

West Ham were out of the drop zone for the first time in five long months and could not have hoped for a better scenario for their final-day visit to Manchester United. With the Premier League title already won, it was a meaningless game for the Red Devils who were expected to rest key players in preparation for the following weekend's FA Cup final against Chelsea, although manager Sir Alex Ferguson pledged to name a 'strong' side. The Hammers could afford to lose at Old Trafford as long as Wigan – three points behind them – failed to win at Sheffield United but with both northern clubs feeling a sense of injustice over the Tevez affair, the conspiracy theories began to circulate before the big day. If West Ham were losing heavily, Sheffield United could afford a modest defeat in the knowledge that both they and Wigan would survive.

Curbishley dismissed such ideas, insisting, 'I don't see any other outcome than everybody trying their hardest to win.' His assistant Day, however, later revealed his concern. 'The fear we had was that if we were 4–0 down at half-time, Sheffield might psychologically relax because they wouldn't feel under any pressure,' he said. 'It wasn't about conspiracy theories, it was about trying not to give Sheffield an edge.'

A skip-load of rubbish has since been written about the team Ferguson named to face West Ham, with one *News of the World* columnist in 2010 remembering it as a 'second string' line-up when it was nothing of the sort. Indeed, Edwin van der Sar, Wayne Rooney and Michael Carrick were actually restored to the side that had played out a goalless draw at Chelsea in midweek, although Hammers fans were naturally pleased to see that Cristiano Ronaldo, Ryan Giggs and Paul Scholes were only on the bench. If anything, it was the less established players who provided most commitment during the game while Rooney shrugged off wayward shots with uncharacteristic good humour – not that John O'Shea, Kieron Richardson and Darren Fletcher could be considered novices with 113 appearances between them that season.

After a quarter of an hour, it came through that Wigan had gone in front through Paul Scharner – at which point Sheffield United were in the bottom three, although it would only take a Manchester United goal to put West Ham there instead. And they had their chances, with Alan Smith and Richardson being denied by Benayoun on the line as the home fans chanted, 'Send them down! Send them down!'

'Staying up! Staying up!' came the reply from the visiting end when it was discovered that Sheffield United had levelled ten minutes before the break to restore the table to its earlier order. That belief solidified when Tevez put the Hammers ahead in first-half stoppage time with his seventh goal in ten games – and surely his most memorable. The Argentinian played the ball to Zamora and bulldozed his way through the home defence to collect the return as it dropped, before slotting home from a tight angle.

Yet Curbishley and Day were quickly brought back down to earth when they returned to the dressing-room to discover that Wigan had gone in front again through a David Unsworth penalty. Day said, 'We were up and down like a yo-yo in that first half. I was still worried because I knew that Manchester United were the type of team who if they got one goal could easily score two, three or four.'

Ronaldo, Giggs and Scholes were all brought on with half an hour to play and United duly stepped up a gear, with Green being forced to make several good saves in the later stages of the game. Day admitted he could have 'killed the fourth official' when he displayed three minutes of added time but when the final whistle blew, the Old Trafford party began – with both sets of fans among the 75,927 crowd trying to out-celebrate each other. In financial terms, however, West Ham's survival was worth far more than Manchester United's title triumph.

Curbishley was left to reflect on his side's 'incredible achievement' after they had been a massive 66–1 *on* to be relegated at one stage. 'Seven wins out of nine is unbelievable when you look at the opposition we've played,' he said. 'Tevez has been tremendous but there have been some magnificent performances throughout the side over the past two months.' On that all were agreed, although some fans still credit midfield misfit Nigel Quashie for sparking West Ham's recovery, as the team never looked back once he suffered the ankle injury against Tottenham that ended his season.

Meanwhile, relegated Warnock complained that he'd been 'sold a dummy' by Ferguson, who naturally defended his team selection. 'I feel for Sheffield United,' he said, 'but I think I played the right team and West Ham have been in championship-winning form.' It wasn't the fault of Ferguson – or Tevez, for that matter – that the Blades couldn't even force a draw against a ten-man Wigan side after the dismissal of Lee McCulloch. It wasn't anybody else's fault that Phil Jagielka handled to give Wigan the spot-kick that won the game. But that's Warnock – once again trying to rewrite history.

....

We're All Going on a European Tour

'Don't do that, you'll only inflame the situation'
– John Ball, August 1999

A WEST HAM fan says *'Moi, sina olet kaunis'* to the attractive, blonde hotel receptionist. 'Oh, thank you very much,' she blushes, clearly grateful for the compliment without realising the Londoner has been telling every Helsinki girl he's clapped eyes on that they are indeed very beautiful. In Metz, a boisterous Hammers supporter is showered with fire extinguisher foam as he clings on to perimeter fencing during the game. 'Don't do that, you'll only inflame the situation,' says West Ham security officer John Ball to the gendarme responsible, without any hint of irony. In Osijek, a group of drunken journalists stagger out of a nightclub as dawn breaks and throw wads of cash at a cab driver to give them a tour of nearby Vukuvar, a city devastated during the Croatian War of Independence in 1991. 'My father was killed here. My brother was killed over there,' says the guide at a particular stop as one of his ailing passengers sneaks behind a tree and throws up.

None of these random events would have taken place had West Ham not qualified for European competition via the league for the very first time in their history in 1999, with their fifth-place finish – their second highest ever – taking them into the Intertoto Cup. With the team coming eighth the previous year, the platform for further success was there although the 1998–99 campaign was certainly not without its problems – particularly in attack. Manager Harry Redknapp had swooped for Arsenal legend Ian Wright but, despite hitting the winner on his debut at Sheffield Wednesday on the opening day of the season, the anticipated glut of goals from the 34 year old never really materialised, with injury restricting him to just 25 appearances that term.

The fact that his nine league goals proved enough to make Wright the Hammers' top scorer for the season says much about the team's lack of a cutting edge, with his former Gunners partner John Hartson scoring just four times in twenty outings before being allowed to join Wimbledon in a £7.5 million deal in January. While the huge fee was a surprise, his departure perhaps wasn't, with the Welshman having recently been fined for kicking team-mate Eyal Berkovic in the face during a training-ground clash. Hartson's sale allowed Redknapp to splash the cash on three players, with the £1.75 million spent on Paolo Di Canio providing far more of a return than the club-record £4.5 million invested in Cameroon midfielder Marc-Vivien Foé, or £1 million wing-back Scott Minto.

Di Canio was an outcast at Sheffield Wednesday after famously pushing over referee Paul Alcock during a match against Arsenal and collecting an 11-game ban. And although the Italian's four goals in thirteen appearances looked modest on paper, his mercurial presence was enough to help inspire the Hammers to seven wins in their final fourteen games. He later joked that he thought he'd entered a 'lunatic asylum' when arriving at Upton Park but described crazy characters such as Wright, Neil Ruddock and John Moncur as 'the heart and soul of the dressing-room'. Ruddock had been signed at the start of the season along with fellow defender Javier Margas, although the latter subsequently spent more time in his Chilean homeland than he did in the chilly East End as he struggled with injury and a homesick wife.

Margas had looked uncomfortable with certain aspects of British football, not least the aerial bombardment provided by Wimbledon as they somehow recovered from a 3–0 deficit at the Boleyn Ground to claim a shock 4–3 win. Incredibly, that was the first of eight occasions that season in which the Hammers would concede four goals or more, including two of the final three games. The dismissal of three West Ham players – Wright, goalkeeper Shaka Hislop and midfielder Steve Lomas – by card-happy referee Rob Harris resulted in a 5–1 defeat by Leeds in the penultimate match at Upton Park.

'The passion inside me will always be the same but I hope I can be forgiven,' pleaded Wright after doing something very wrong when rearranging the items in the referee's changing-room following his red card. The FA failed to show the clemency Wright was looking for and dished out a £17,500 fine and three-game ban. There were no excuses for the 6–0 spanking at Everton the following weekend but a 4–0 home win against Middlesbrough proved enough for West Ham to finish above Aston Villa and Liverpool in fifth place.

Trevor Sinclair, Frank Lampard, Marc Keller and Berkovic had chipped in with twenty-one goals from midfield but the team's total of forty-six in the league was ten fewer than the previous campaign, yet earned a point more despite a goal difference of minus seven. Go figure . . .

Redknapp declared his side's qualification for the Intertoto Cup 'a tremendous achievement', although it's worth noting that fifth place would generally have taken a team directly into the UEFA Cup without the need for an early start to competitive action. Indeed, the

Hammers kicked off their European campaign with a third-round first-leg home tie against Finnish part-timers FC Jokerit on 17 July, a full three weeks before the start of the Premier League. Paul Kitson scored the only goal of the game, in front of just 11,908 fans, to send West Ham across to Helsinki's Olympic Stadium a week later with a slender advantage that they managed to protect thanks to Lampard's second-half equaliser in a 1–1 draw.

The midfielder was on target again as the Hammers secured another 1–0 home win against Heerenveen in the next round just four days later, with just 7,485 fans bothering to show their faces this time. New £3.5 million signing Paulo Wanchope scored his first West Ham goal when bagging the winner in Holland to wrap up a 2–0 aggregate victory. The three wins then helped the Hammers to hit the ground running when the league season began, with Lampard scoring in the 1–0 home success against Tottenham that commenced a sequence of four victories and one draw in the opening five games.

However, when Louis Saha gave Metz a 1–0 win at Upton Park, during which Lampard missed a penalty, it seemed that West Ham's European aspirations were all but over. Not so – the Hammers produced a stunning display in the return leg at the Stade Saint-Symphorien two weeks later, with Sinclair and Lampard both netting before half-time, ahead of Nenad Jestrovic setting up a tense finish with the 68th-minute strike that levelled the aggregate score. Two away goals in France would still have been enough to take West Ham through, but with Metz in the ascendancy nothing could be taken for granted – especially with troublesome scenes on the terraces proving a heavy distraction after a firecracker was thrown into the away end. Fortunately, Wanchope delivered the knockout blow just six minutes later when rounding goalkeeper Lionel Letizi to poke home, although whether it was seen by the West Ham fans whose view was now obscured by a mountain of fire extinguisher foam is debatable.

As one of three Intertoto Cup winners that summer the Hammers were duly presented with what can only be described as a generously sized egg cup, but the major prize was qualifying for the UEFA Cup for the very first time. Wanchope, Di Canio and Lampard gave West Ham a comfortable 3–0 home win against NK Osijek in a first-round first-leg game that saw Igor Stimac make his second appearance for the club, following a £600,000 move from Derby. However, when the Croatian defender returned to his home country and collected a booking in the second leg – with Kitson, Ruddock and Foé on target in a 3–1 win – it came to UEFA's attention that Stimac should not have been playing in European competition at all, having yet to serve a two-game ban picked up during his Hajduk Split days. Thankfully, UEFA admitted their negligence in failing to advise all parties of the suspension and threw out Osijek's efforts to be reinstated at the Hammers' expense.

What it did mean, however, was that Stimac was unavailable for the second-round games against Steaua Bucharest, which appeared to represent West Ham's toughest test so far. And so it proved, with Laurentiu Rosu and Sabin Ilue scoring the two first-leg goals for the Romanians in what travelling supporters would consider one of the most corrupt cities on the planet. Police confiscated beer from fans and happily sold it back to them inside the Stadionul Ghencea, while one uniformed local's chief source of revenue seemed to stem from demanding evidence of identity and running off with people's wallets.

The manager of an expensive four-star hotel also enjoyed a profitable sideline by knocking on doors with three girls in tow and asking, 'You like ladies?' The gang of headbanging Hammers fans who suddenly disappeared from the dance floor of the basement disco along with the erotically gyrating females who had joined them clearly did. The next morning, a prankster from Grays jumped behind the wheel of a coach outside the hotel and promptly smashed it into the vehicle in front, causing £4,000 worth of damage and collecting a £1,900 fine.

A fortnight later, West Ham duly crashed out of European action themselves as their second leg against Steaua at Upton Park fizzled out in a frustrating goalless stalemate. Redknapp was left to reflect on 'one of those nights' that he would not wish to remember, while the more boisterous Hammers followers stored away memories of several evenings' 'entertainment' they would be unable to forget.

Sinking in the Rain

'Few people have taken more criticism during my time as West Ham manager than Iain' – Harry Redknapp, 1998

IAIN DOWIE and George Best were both strikers for Northern Ireland. And there the similarities come to a shuddering halt – other than to say that each was responsible for putting an unforgettable Cheshire Cat grin on the faces of the fun-starved denizens of Edgeley Park.

Best achieved the feat in 1975 when, to the astonishment of those still convinced he should be exhibiting his lavish skills in the highest echelons, he made three appearances for Stockport County. Dowie did it in more concentrated form, simply by jumping in the air and connecting his head with the ball. The hapless centre-forward was, by this point, so unfamiliar with the knack of scoring that he did so at the wrong end of the pitch, broke his ankle, helped to inflict a grim cup giant-killing on his own team and carved his name high on the list of the most ridiculed Hammers players of all time.

List-makers seem to have a thing for Dowie. *The Sun* awarded him top spot in its list of the ugliest footballers ever, decrying: 'Imagine the rest of our top ten ugly footballers all photo-shopped into one mess and what do you get? Iain Dowie. With Dirk Kuyt's sloth-like eyes, David Hopkin's big ears, Robert Prosinecki's baldness and Peter Beardsley's slobbering mouth, Dowie would have scared the living daylights out of most opponents during his 13-year career.'

Meanwhile, *The Times* had him ranked at number 28 in its list of the worst footballers of all time, chiding that 'It's Iain Wow-ie!' was a headline highly unlikely ever to be attributed to his talents.

In fairness to Dowie, both of these charts are not just cruel but contentious. Yet it takes an enormous leap of faith to imagine that anyone will ever outrank him on a list of the most sensational own goals, given the shocker he netted in a televised Coca-Cola Cup tie at a rain-sodden Stockport the week before Christmas in 1996.

The Hatfield-born former non-league player was in his second spell at the Hammers, having initially joined from Luton Town in March 1991 for £480,000. Just twelve appearances and four goals later he was sold to Southampton for a £20,000 profit, presumably with manager Billy Bonds unmoved by Dowie's agricultural style, in spite of a one-in-three strike rate.

In stark contrast, in the close season of 1995 Bonds' successor Harry Redknapp saw Dowie as the ideal recruit for a squad that had left it late the previous season to pull away from the relegation zone. Redknapp returned Dowie to a wholly underwhelmed Upton Park from Crystal Palace for £250,000. 'Everybody at the club said I was a fool, because the fans hated him,' Redknapp revealed in his autobiography. 'The chairman even said he and I would be a laughing stock if he returned. But I liked what I saw. Dowie was an honest pro who I could see doing a job for us.'

'H' had the sceptics nibbling on a small slice of humble pie in 1995–96, Dowie's nine goals and robust endeavour impressing the supporters enough to vote him as runner-up to Julian Dicks in the Hammer-of-the-Year poll. He even struck up an unlikely forward partnership with Portuguese wonder kid Dani, whose pop star looks had the sports pages coining 'Beauty and the Beast' headlines in the pair's honour.

Unfortunately, when the players scored in tandem, in a 4–2 home thumping of Manchester City, in March 1996, it proved to be the end, rather than the start of the fairytale. Neither would net again in the Premiership in West Ham colours. Loanee Dani's anxieties lasted just a few more weeks before he was packed off back to Sporting Lisbon. For Dowie, the agony lasted a mind-melting 40 games. Only in the League Cup did the mechanical engineering graduate ever again manage to get the ball-to-onion bag equation right. And it was the same competition which effectively sealed Dowie's Hammers fate.

In season 1996–97, victories over Barnet and, thanks largely to a Dowie brace, Nottingham Forest, had pushed West Ham to round four of a competition which was providing a smidgeon of relief in an otherwise faith-sapping campaign marred by ill-fated foreign signings, poor league form and too few goals. Second Division Stockport County were next up, a tie at Upton Park in the November.

An inept performance under the lights, with Hammers scraping a 1–1 draw thanks to Romanian misfit Florin Raducioiu, didn't augur well for the replay three weeks later, although in the interim Dowie managed to locate his shooting boots again, this time for Northern Ireland in a World Cup qualifier.

So to Stockport on a Wednesday night when all those 'grim up north' clichés about dark satanic mills and northern rain coming down like rods of iron came true . . . and then some.

With Raducioiu gone AWOL on an infamous West End shopping trip with his wife, Redknapp was forced to play his compatriot midfielder Ilie Dumitrescu up front alongside Dowie. In the 21st minute, from Dumi's corner Dicks headed in to put Hammers 1–0 up, seemingly dampening any chance of a giant-killing in the south Manchester mud.

Looking comfortable at 1–0 has never really been part of the West Ham psyche and, sure enough, two minutes later Dowie pulled out all the stops to maintain the tradition. A County corner was half-cleared by the shaven head of captain Dicks. The sopping wet heads of two Stockport players propelled it back into the air. Then came horror header number four.

In what one must assume was an attempt to nod the ball over his own bar, the leaping Dowie, neck muscles bulging, somehow contrived to nut the ball perfectly beyond the reach of goalkeeper Ludo Miklosko and into the bottom right-hand corner of the net. Andy Gray, Alan Parry's co-commentator on Sky, sounded as shocked as the drenched, dumbstruck Irons fans in front of whom Dowie had just lodged the OG of the century. 'That's incredible!' exclaimed Gray. 'What a response from Stockport. Exactly the sort they would have wanted, but not from the man they thought was going to get them the equaliser!'

The camera panned to Dowie, drained of colour, blinking and wincing in the glare of the floodlights and the relentless downpour. If only those 10,000 holes the Beatles sang about were in Stockport rather than up the road in Blackburn. With West Ham still reeling from this self-inflicted body blow, just three minutes later yet another header, this one from Brett Angell, provided the conclusive goal. The game was effectively over by half-time. So, too, was Dowie's season, the villain of the piece hobbling off with a fractured ankle. As he would later recall, 'I can remember seeing the vitriol and anger on the faces of the West Ham fans. They are passionate people and I felt that I'd let them down.'

The pain from that injury was about to be compounded by a horrendous amount of stick from all quarters – including his own supporters – which turned this honest, hardworking journeyman into little more than a figure of fun. With the arrival of Paul Kitson and John Hartson among others, Dowie had fallen well down the striker pecking order by the time he recovered from his injury. He was eventually offloaded to QPR in January 1998, but not before the club magazine offered him the chance to reflect on what by any standards had been a nightmare 18 months, during which he had sadly lost his father. Dowie said, 'I played in the team when confidence was very low and we had a lot of problems, but throughout that time I always gave my all. I saw people come and go who didn't want to play for West Ham and they weren't bothered about wearing the shirt. I didn't score as many goals as I would like to have done, but I like to think that I earned the respect of the fans through my efforts.'

The jury would always be out on that one, except where boss Redknapp was concerned. Always his own man, with his own unique view of the world, Redknapp insists that Dowie was one of his best-ever Hammers signings.

The really sad part of Dowie's West Ham tale is that he had been an Irons supporter since childhood. He used to dream of emulating his heroes, such as fellow striker David Cross – later his assistant boss at Oldham Athletic – by playing on the Upton Park pitch, scoring lots of goals and becoming a fans' favourite.

Well, one out of three ain't bad.

Entering the Ice Age

'My vision is to challenge for the highest honours'
– Eggert Magnusson, November 2006

PERHAPS 'EGGY POP' would have been a more appropriate introduction for the wrinkly-faced 59 year old as he marched out in front of the crowd and saluted the cheering thousands. Eggert Magnusson was the person milking the applause while 'The Passenger' – to quote one of Iggy's best-known song titles – was his young grandson, who was carried onto the pitch ahead of West Ham's game with Sheffield United on 25 November 2006.

It was the kind of reception generally reserved for those with an established place in people's affections; not a man who, just a few weeks earlier, had been totally unknown to them. Yet Magnusson – the public face of that week's Icelandic takeover – represented somebody who might just possibly ensure that fortune would not always be hiding at Upton Park.

To put the supporters' feelings of excitement, anticipation and relief into context, it's important to understand the sequence of events during the autumn of that year as speculation about West Ham's potential change of ownership developed. Chairman Terence Brown, who owned around 36 per cent of the club's shares, had fought off a challenge from a rebel shareholder group known as 'Whistle' in 2003. Having brought the Hammers back from the financial brink following relegation, he was presumed to be no more willing to sell now that the club had enjoyed a successful first season back in the Premier League. The reality was that, with a top-half finish in the league and an epic FA Cup final display against Liverpool fresh in people's minds, the value of the club had been hugely enhanced; it was suddenly a very good time to consider offers.

The general public first became aware that West Ham was on the market when the club issued a statement to the London Stock Exchange on 1 September 2006, to confirm that discussions regarding a possible sale had begun. The interested party was Iranian businessman Kia Joorabchian – the man whose Media Sports Investment Ltd group (MSI) owned the economic rights of Argentina internationals Carlos Tevez and Javier Mascherano, who had just arrived at Upton Park in somewhat unconventional circumstances.

Joorabchian had made an unsuccessful attempt to buy the Hammers after they had won promotion in 2005, but was reassured by Brown's claim that 'any serious proposition will be studied carefully'. The chairman added, 'I am not about protecting my position; I know I am a mere custodian of the club.' The fact that the price would now reportedly exceed £70 million did not appear to put Joorabchian off. Indeed, he told the media that he planned to plough £200 million into the club, with half of that being spent on players. 'There is no point buying West Ham unless you are going to invest in turning them into one of the top teams in the country,' he said.

However, there was huge conjecture as to who funded the activities of MSI, with Joorabchian saying no more than to confirm the company was 'backed by a diverse group of powerful men with interests in oil, the media and entertainment'. The speculation was that these men included Russian oligarch Boris Berezovsky and Georgian businessman Badri Patarkatsishvili, although Joorabchian would deny having any direct business involvement with either of them. Berezovsky, formerly the richest man in Russia before being forced to seek exile in London following accusations of fraud and embezzlement, had sold his oil firm Sibnet to Roman Abramovich. His relationship with the Chelsea owner, who had spent around £300 million on building a team to win the Premier League title in 2005 and 2006, inevitably prompted stories of another rouble-funded revolution at an English football club. Ian King, editor of *The Sun*'s financial pages, said, 'If this takeover goes through, it will mean three Premiership clubs [including Chelsea and Portsmouth] are directly or indirectly backed by Russian money.'

Joorabchian won a certain amount of support by talking of the great potential at Upton Park. 'West Ham can be bigger than Chelsea,' he said. 'What is so impressive about the club is that when they have hit bad times, the passion and loyalty of the fans has seen them through thick and thin. Sometimes when I look at Chelsea, despite their recent success, it's all a bit cold. They talk more about the brand than the football club.'

However, this didn't prevent suspicions developing about the concept of billionaire businessmen using football clubs for their own ends. The *Evening Standard* ran a detailed article warning of 'an impending cataclysm in the world's favourite sport' and suggesting that Berezovsky and Patarkatsishvili were 'the architects of a scheme to revolutionise the way football is run'.

The evidence that a plan existed to 'control an international soccer network' was 'circumstantial but compelling' they claimed. It didn't help that reports emerged that MSI was being investigated in relation to suspected money-laundering activities in Brazil (with the authorities later seeking to quiz Berezovsky about the company's £20 million stake in Corinthians football club), although such allegations were fiercely denied. Meanwhile, British sports minister Richard Caborn entered the debate by insisting the mystery backers of MSI should reveal themselves. 'Those involved should be as open and transparent as possible,' he said. 'The Premiership is not a millionaires' playground.'

The idea of the Hammers falling under corporate foreign ownership sparked hysteria in some quarters, with the *Daily Express* referring to signs of 'a dramatic reshaping of West Ham's precious soul'. Other papers echoed the theme, with the *Daily Mirror* talking of West Ham being 'the most traditional of clubs, working class through and through, where Cockney folktale memories of the Blitz spirit sit hand in hand with the tales of the Boys of 86'. As a postscript, they added, 'Something has changed at Upton Park and it will never be the same again.' Meanwhile, Hammers boss Alan Pardew, who had earlier claimed he could 'do a lot with £100 million', insisted that 'whoever comes in will have a wall up against them' because it was his job 'to protect the integrity and history of this club'.

It wasn't long before Berezovsky's name was back in the news – on the front pages this time – after former KGB agent Alexander Litvinenko was murdered in London having been poisoned with polonium-210. Litvinenko had once been assigned the task of protecting Berezovsky and later went public with the claim that he had been ordered to assassinate him – while also seeking political asylum in Britain. In March 2010, Berezovsky, who had by now been sentenced to two lengthy jail terms if he returned to Moscow, was awarded £150,000 in damages after winning a libel case against Russian TV channel RTR Planeta, for alleging that he was involved in Litvinenko's death.

If the potential link between Green Street and Red Square was not grim enough, Patarkatsishvili, who had once been quoted as saying he was 'not involved in any possible bid for West Ham' but was 'thinking about it', died suspiciously of a heart attack in his Surrey home in 2008 after claiming there were forces looking to kill him.

As discussions about an Upton Park takeover continued in the autumn of 2007, 'super agent' – in football terms rather than espionage – Pinhas Zahavi was forced to deny he was a potential investor in the Hammers through MSI. It then emerged that another Israeli, property developer Eli Papouchado, was considering the idea of helping Joorabchian raise the funds he needed, although it was feared his primary interest was the land the Boleyn Ground was sitting on rather than the football played inside it.

Meanwhile, West Ham were struggling at the foot of the table and the question was whether the takeover talks were undermining the team's performances, or vice versa. There was, naturally, huge pressure on Pardew to reduce the threat of relegation if Brown was to secure the figures he was looking for, but he was forced to do so while stories circulated about which new manager might replace him if Joorabchian won his battle. Former England boss Sven-Göran Eriksson was one name that refused to go away and Pardew admitted, 'The sooner the takeover talks are over, the better it will be for everyone. I even heard people outside my office discussing whether I was staying.'

News of the World journalist Martin Samuel was particularly scathing of the Hammers hierarchy for allowing the uncertainty to rumble on, accusing Brown of 'wrecking three years of hard work by destabilising Pardew while holding out for the £29 million that would be his share of Joorabchian's takeover'. The chairman, who succeeded Martin Cearns in 1992, was no stranger to criticism. Taking into account his defence of the despised Bond Scheme, the controversial departures of managers Billy Bonds and Harry Redknapp, the appointment of the inadequately experienced Glenn Roeder and subsequent relegation, the sale of the club's best young players, his reported generous salary and the perceived lack of investment, the fans had plenty of reasons to question Brown's performance. The chairman himself admitted that the 'belt tightening' in 2002 had 'maybe not been the right move' as he accepted some responsibility for West Ham's drop out of the top flight.

Yet Brown could point to the club's recent promotion – the second under his chairmanship – the redevelopment of the Boleyn Ground, the successful youth scheme, two European qualifications and the breaking of the club's transfer record when offering his defence. 'The club was on its knees when I joined,' he said. However, Brown, a qualified accountant who had previously run a holiday homes firm in Sussex, was a private individual who suffered from his attempts to keep a low profile. Even manager Pardew admitted that the chairman 'wasn't particularly good with the media', adding, 'The fans hammer him but he has held his hands up to some of those criticisms.' Indeed, after watching West Ham secure their place back in the Premier League in 2005, Brown said, 'I hope Alan has shut up his critics, but I doubt that I've silenced all of mine.'

The accounts for the year up to 31 May 2006 provided evidence of West Ham's recent progress, with pre-tax profits of £6 million announced against a virtual doubling of turnover to £60.1 million.

On 12 October, West Ham issued a second statement to the Stock Exchange in which they revealed they had held 'initial discussions' regarding a possible buyout with a different party, fronted by Icelandic businessman Magnusson. Joorabchian, who was still haggling over the price by querying the club's debt figures, insisted the Icelandic interest was a 'red herring'. However, Magnusson hit back by insisting, 'If there are any red herrings, it is the other bids. We are looking at this very seriously.'

Magnusson, dubbed a 'biscuit baron' by the media because of his past ownership of a bread and biscuit manufacturing company, had impressive sporting credentials, having been president of the

Football Association of Iceland since 1989 following a five-year period as president of Valur Reykjavik, and also holding a seat on UEFA's executive committee. Although he made no bold promises at that early stage, the fans certainly seemed to favour his move for West Ham ahead of Joorabchian and MSI. There were no reported links with Russian oligarchs or Israeli property developers, no stories of expensive Swedes coming in to manage and no suspicions about the Icelander's possible motives for wanting to buy the club.

Magnusson was soon allowed to inspect the club's accounts while Pardew said he was 'enthused' after holding a meeting with the prospective new chairman. 'I am all ears because I want to take this club forward and hopefully into the Champions League,' he said.

The first Icelandic bid was rejected but any doubts about there being sufficient funds were dismissed when it was revealed that billionaire financier Björgólfur Guðmundsson was backing the initiative. Guðmundsson was the chairman of Icelandic bank Landsbanki, had business interests in a number of different environments and had football credentials himself, having played for his country's oldest club KR in Reykjavik, where he later became chairman. And with the potential buyout not dependent on mysterious outside investors, it was beginning to look increasingly more attractive to all those with West Ham's best interests at heart.

By mid November, negotiations had taken the price up to an eyebrow-raising £85 million – plus responsibility for the club's £22.5 million debt – and on the 21st of the month the Icelandic bid was formally accepted, with Magnusson securing agreements to purchase 83 per cent of the club's 20,202,352 ordinary shares (the West Ham directors' beneficial holdings representing 45 per cent and the remaining 38 per cent coming from other shareholders) at a price of 421p each, with a recommendation being made to the remaining stakeholders to accept the offer. 'The offer reflects fair value for West Ham, considering its significant history, recent performance and prospects, and its position as a leading London club,' stated Brown. As anticipated, Magnusson would succeed Brown as chairman, who would stay on as a non-executive deputy vice-chairman, while fellow consortium members Thor

Kristjansson and Gudmundur J. Oddsson would also join the board. Guðmundsson was handed the position of honorary life president while outgoing directors Charles Warner and Martin Cearns would become associate members to 'ensure the traditions of the club are preserved'.

Brown was adamant that the club was being 'passed into good hands' and added, 'I think Eggert will be tremendous for West Ham.' Meanwhile, Olafur Gardarsson, an Icelandic agent and lawyer who had known Magnusson for nearly a decade, insisted, 'Eggert will make West Ham successful. It's difficult to stop him once he gets involved in a project.' Indeed, once Magnusson took charge, he wasted little time in stating his grandiose ambitions. 'My vision is for the team to challenge for the highest honours in English football, as well as getting into Europe,' he said, while also revealing plans to relocate the club to the new Olympic Stadium in 2012.

After being awarded the warmest of welcomes by the Upton Park faithful, he watched the Hammers secure a 1–0 win against Sheffield United, which gave their survival prospects a vital boost. 'I'm not going to let these people down,' he promised.

●●●●●●●●●●●●●●●●●●●

Careers on a Knife Edge

'You probably saved my life' – Calum Davenport,
September 2009

THE FICTION and screen writers might dictate that no grittily realistic East End tale would be complete without some form of knife crime, but it's taking the stereotype a bit far when two West Ham players are found collapsed, with blood pouring from their wounds after being stabbed. Trevor Morley and Calum Davenport were victims of separate violent clashes nearly 20 years apart that saw them requiring emergency hospital treatment – and with one in danger of losing rather more than just his playing career.

Morley scored seventy goals in six seasons for the Hammers following his arrival from Manchester City at the tail end of 1989, but the sad fact is that, to the football fan at large, the busy striker will be remembered less for hitting the back of the net and more for the controversial incident at his Waltham Abbey home in March 1991, that left him nursing a nasty stomach injury and having to fend off speculation about his sexuality. Morley had racked up 16 goals as West Ham put themselves on course for promotion from the Second Division and the later stages of the FA Cup that season. However, everything was suddenly put into jeopardy – not least the striker's health – when it came to light that the 29 year old had been hurt in an incident involving a knife.

Reports revealed that Morley's Norwegian wife Monica had been detained and questioned by police for some 12 hours while her husband was tended to at Harlow's Princess Alexandra Hospital, where his condition was described as 'comfortable'. With no other information available about what the police labelled a 'domestic incident', it was perhaps little surprise that wild rumours began to circulate as to how and why West Ham's top scorer had ended up in a hospital bed.

The wicked whisper that inevitably captured most people's imagination was that a row had developed after Morley was found in a compromising position with team-mate Ian Bishop (with whom he had travelled down from Manchester hand-in-hand – metaphorically speaking – to sign for the Hammers). 'The biggest mistake I made was not commenting on it because the newspaper people accused me of all sorts of stuff,' admitted Morley in Steve Blowers' *Nearly Reached The Sky* chronicle. 'The fact is that the wound was caused by a drunken accident – but the papers wanted a story. They said my wife caught me in bed with another woman but I wouldn't comment because I'd been advised not to. Then they came up with the line that one of my kids had done it or had caught me in bed with another woman. Eventually it came round to "your wife caught you in bed with another man" and me and Bish being together.'

Fans were relieved to see Morley fully recovered and back in time to play in the FA Cup semi-final against Nottingham Forest after he had missed nine games, but the gay gossip persisted. Morley said: 'Nothing like that was reported in the media so how did those stories spread so quickly? I have to say, I didn't handle it well. The rumours about me being gay killed me for a while and ruined my football. I'd go out onto the field and hide.'

Bishop admitted the speculation put a strain on his relationship with Morley during that period. 'It ruined our friendship for a bit,' revealed the midfielder. 'We'd be in some pub and would hear people whispering things about us. Sometimes we'd go across to have a go at them – we were lucky not to get our heads kicked in.'

Yet the pair also proved they could eventually see the funny side, with Bishop sending himself up by suggestively putting his arm around Morley's waist as they defended a free-kick. Julian Dicks remembers how Trevor wandered into physio John Green's room to see a 'skeleton with all these knives stuck in it'. He added, 'He wasn't too happy but laughed about it later.' When the club magazine asked Morley which celebrity he'd like to swap places with, he'd clearly forgotten about the supporters' suspicions, choosing George Michael!

If Morley's injuries were the result of a spontaneous incident, there was something much more sinister about the serious attack on Davenport in 2009 that left the Hammers defender in intensive care for six days. Reports appeared on 22 August that the player was having urgent surgery at the Bedford South Wing Hospital after being stabbed in both legs during the early hours of that morning. Furthermore, his 49-year-old mother, Kim Stupple, was also wounded in the altercation, which took place at her Kempston home. Several neighbours in Springfield Avenue were woken by the 5 a.m. disturbance and one passer-by told the *Daily Mirror*: 'A woman was crying uncontrollably and a man was screaming at the top of his voice. He was standing over another man, who was just lying there motionless. There was blood everywhere but the man kept punching him in the head while screaming, "This is what you get when you f**k with us." I thought he was dead.'

Just two days later, a 25-year-old man – named as Worrell Whitehurst from Derby – appeared in front of Bedford magistrates and was remanded in custody after being charged with causing grievous bodily harm with intent. Whitehurst, who happened to be the boyfriend of Davenport's sister Cara, was also charged with causing actual bodily harm to Stupple and driving while disqualified. Being accused of knifing your girlfriend's brother and mother probably isn't the best way of being welcomed into a new family, yet it didn't appear to do Worrell too much harm with Cara. Having revealed that she was pregnant, she was seen to mouth the words 'I love you' to him as she provided moral support in court.

Meanwhile, Davenport remained in intensive care and, although his condition was declared as stable, it was speculated that his playing career could be over – even if he was to walk again. The 26 year old, a £3 million signing from Tottenham in 2007, might have been out of favour at West Ham after reportedly telling Gianfranco Zola 'I'm not f**king playing for you' during a dressing-room bust-up, but the manager was naturally quick to express his shock and sympathy. 'We're very sorry to hear what happened and it's a terrible story,' he said.

It was revealed that Davenport had lost 50 per cent of his blood in the vicious assault – clearly intended to destroy his livelihood – and the player issued some words of gratitude midway through September as he continued to recuperate in hospital. 'Thank you to everyone who has sent messages of support,' he said. 'I have quite a long way to go before I recover but I am feeling positive. I would also like to thank anyone who has ever donated blood – you probably saved my life.'

However, although his health was gradually improving, events elsewhere were taking a distinct turn for the worse with the police confirming on 28 October that Davenport was being charged with assaulting his sister on the evening he suffered his stab wounds. 'I am deeply shocked and disappointed at the decision and I deny any wrongdoing,' he responded, with reports suggesting that a row had broken out after Calum had told Cara he didn't approve of the company she was keeping. As he later surveyed the 15-inch scar on one of his legs, he might have been entitled to feel he'd had a point.

On 16 November, Whitehurst pleaded guilty at Luton Crown Court to all charges and was warned by Judge John Bevan QC that he faced a substantial prison term, although sentencing was adjourned until the charges against Davenport were dealt with. The player appeared at the same court on 25 January 2010, to deny the charge of causing actual bodily harm and was granted bail on the condition that he made no attempt to contact his sister – whom, it was alleged, he had headbutted after an evening's drinking. On 1 July 2010, Davenport was cleared of all charges of assault, while two weeks later Whitehurst was jailed for six years. Prior to this period, in March 2010 it was announced by West Ham that Davenport had left the club.

It was a disenchanting end for the player who made only an unlucky 13 appearances for the 'fantastic club' he'd been delighted to return to on a permanent basis, following a loan spell in 2004. 'I loved playing at Upton Park,' he said. 'I really felt at home there.'

....

Curb Your Enthusiasm

'I had no option but to leave' – Alan Curbishley,
September 2008

ALAN CURBISHLEY raises his glass and proposes a toast to a privileged group of journalists who have joined him for a special pre-Christmas lunch at the Boleyn Ground. The wine is flowing and so is the conversation, with the West Ham boss cracking jokes aplenty and reeling out a string of amusing anecdotes that draw on his many years in football and his brother Bill's rock 'n' roll adventures as manager of The Who, Robert Plant and Judas Priest. Curbishley is candid, colourful and charismatic – in stark contrast to the conservative and circumspect character the general public are familiar with when he is in front of the cameras.

Yet perhaps West Ham fans should not be too surprised to hear that Curbishley does not always conform to expectations. The 49 year old was considered to be the perfect candidate to take charge of the Hammers following the sacking of Alan Pardew in December

2006, having been developed by the club as a youngster. He made nearly 100 first-team appearances as a midfielder under John Lyall and was frequently linked with a return to his natural habitat after establishing himself as a top-flight manager at Charlton. With all that claret and blue blood running through his veins, it was a formality that he fully understood the club's traditions, philosophies and ethos for entertainment, so would always be fondly appreciated by the supporters during what would surely be a lengthy reign at Upton Park.

However, despite overseeing probably the greatest escape from relegation of all time and then lifting the team to a very respectable top-half finish, Curbishley would see his tenure at West Ham end in premature and bitter fashion – resulting in legal proceedings against the club. While fans were concerned about the circumstances of his departure, they were hardly crying into their beer over the idea of him having pinned his final team sheet to the dressing-room wall.

Matters came to a head at the start of the 2008–09 campaign when West Ham sold defenders Anton Ferdinand and George McCartney to Sunderland, in separate deals amounting to £14 million. Curbishley had insisted during the pre-season period that he always had 'the final word on who comes in and out of the club', but was then forced to admit that the decision to accept £8 million for Ferdinand had been 'taken out of my hands'. It was a generous offer for the centre-half, who had come on in leaps and bounds since emerging from the youth team in the shadow of older brother Rio, but the suspicion was that both Curbishley and the player watched the deal go through with a sense of regret.

Predictably, Hammers chief executive Scott Duxbury was quick to justify the sale of Ferdinand on the basis that the 23 year old had failed to accept the club's most recent contract offer. That personal decision appeared to have more to do with an inflated view of what he was worth than any deep-rooted desire to leave Upton Park, but Ferdinand allowed himself to become convinced that a change of scene might just make him a better player. 'The deal was the right one for the club, given we could not agree a new contract and that there were just two years left to run on the existing one,' said Duxbury. 'Our fans have a particular affinity with players that have come through the academy system, but we think this should help us to promote even more young talent through the ranks.'

In other words, West Ham were a bit thin on the ground for players and couldn't afford to buy quality replacements so would have to rely on more youngsters – such as the emerging James Tomkins – to bail them out. Curbishley had insisted he had 'the backing of the board' when he was listed as the bookmakers' 5–1 favourite to be the first Premier League manager to leave his post that term, but he also claimed that 'nothing surprises me any more'. It's fair to suggest that he was quickly proved wrong – on both accounts – as the Hammers hierarchy made a number of decisions that would convince Curbishley that his position with the club was no longer tenable.

If Ferdinand's departure left the West Ham defence weakened, it was looking shot to pieces just five days later when it was confirmed that McCartney was also heading to the Stadium of Light in a £6 million deal. Once again, the Hammers suggested they had little choice but to allow the full-back to rejoin the club he had left in a £1 million switch two years earlier, once he had demanded a move. 'It became clear after he handed in a written transfer request that he was desperate to move on for family reasons,' said Duxbury.

This was difficult for fans to accept given the Northern Ireland international, who had started all 38 league games for the Hammers the previous season, had signed a new five-year contract at Upton Park less than six weeks previously. He hardly seemed 'desperate to move on' when declaring, 'I have enjoyed my time at West Ham and have no desire to leave.' To appease supporters, West Ham issued a statement – credited to nobody in particular – in which they insisted the transfers of Ferdinand and McCartney 'were right for the club' and that 'decisions had to be taken based on our best long-term interest'. Yet by admitting that West Ham's annual wage bill had increased by £25 million and that owner Björgólfur Guðmundsson had pumped £30.5 million in 'to bolster the club's financial base', the communiqué simply confirmed fears that the club was losing money and needed to sacrifice key assets.

It was too much for Curbishley to stomach and, on 3 September 2008, he submitted his resignation, which the club confirmed was 'accepted in the best interests of both parties'. The former boss wasted little time in revealing why he had quit Upton Park. 'The selection of players is critical to the job of the manager and I had an agreement with the club that I alone would determine the composition of the squad,' he said. 'However, the club continued to make significant player decisions without involving me. In the end, such a breach of trust and confidence meant that I had no option but to leave.'

His stance was supported by the League Managers' Association (LMA), who said, 'The club's unilateral actions around player transfers, without reference to their manager, have created irreparable damage to Alan's working relationship with the directors. The LMA has been working with Alan in an attempt to resolve his grievances with his employers but, sadly, reconciliation was not possible in the circumstances.'

McCartney also backed his former manager, saying, 'Curbishley's views were that Anton and I weren't going anywhere but the club went behind his back and accepted the fees. I have seen on the West Ham website that I handed in a written transfer request when I never did anything of the sort. My family were quite unsettled in London but the manager said that I was staying at West Ham. Then I got a call saying a fee had been accepted. The club are just trying to cover their tracks with the supporters. These are strange times at West Ham.'

Not everyone was in Curbishley's corner, however, with businessman Kia Joorabchian – strangely credited as 'transfer adviser' – claiming the former manager had paid the price for a series of costly mistakes after being given funds to spend in the summer of 2007. Injury victims Freddie Ljungberg and Kieron Dyer had barely played and Joorabchian said, 'The players brought in were probably not the board's idea of taking the club forward.'

There were suggestions that Curbishley's knowledge of the global transfer market was not what it might have been; this was something the Hammers had sought to address with the appointment of Gianluca Nani as technical director, believing the Italian's knowledge of the European scene would prove a valuable asset.

While supporters were sympathetic to Curbishley after seeing his authority undermined by sales he hadn't authorised – with the vast majority believing the manager should always retain control of such matters – many took satisfaction from the likelihood that West Ham's football would become more enjoyable to watch under a different boss. It wasn't the fact that the Hammers had spent an entire season stuck in mid-table that bored fans to tears; indeed, a tenth-place finish was not to be sniffed at given the huge injury problems the side had to contend with. More, it was Curbishley's safety-first strategy in many games that was so difficult for fans to absorb, with the manager applying the cautious philosophies that had served him so well during his 15 years at Charlton – when generally the underdog – rather than the spirit of adventure demanded by the Boleyn faithful.

Curbishley later insisted that he had been forced to be pragmatic for much of his reign. 'The pleasing thing was that the squad stood up to the injury situation,' he said, 'but the disappointment was that no one really appreciated it. It was always: "Oh, we're tenth but we're going nowhere."'

It wasn't long after Curbishley's departure that it became public knowledge that he intended to pursue a claim for constructive dismissal against West Ham, having had 18 months remaining on his £1.5 million a year contract at the time of his resignation. The Hammers counterclaimed against their former boss in respect of the increased costs incurred by the appointment of successor Gianfranco Zola and his assistant Steve Clarke, but the odds always looked in favour of Curbishley, who insisted his contract allowed him to have the 'final say' on players. What was perhaps surprising was that any Premier League club would agree to any such clause when there will always be times when it makes financial sense to sell a player who the manager would prefer to hold on to.

Curbishley was linked to a number of management positions over the next year or so but admitted he was 'waiting for a Premier League job'. He added, 'I feel I've done my apprenticeship in the top flight.' Of course, remaining out of full-time employment wouldn't damage any compensation he might receive if his case was successful, and on 3 November 2009 it was adjudged by an FA Premier League arbitration tribunal that West Ham had indeed been in breach of contract when selling players over Curbishley's head. Needless to say, the Hammers' rather spurious efforts to mitigate the situation came to nothing when their counterclaim was thrown out.

With the club in serious financial trouble following the collapse of Guðmundsson's banking empire, and a reported £20 million compensation payment awarded to Sheffield United over the Carlos Tevez affair, it was yet another costly blow. Yet it was to the credit of new co-owner David Sullivan that he swiftly agreed a settlement with Curbishley, reported to be in the region of £2.2 million, as he began to mop up the mess left behind by the previous regime. 'This had to be dealt with from a moral and legal point of view as quickly as possible,' said Sullivan.

Curbishley had won his battle but, while feeling vindicated, he was still left with a deep sense of regret that he was unable to fully exploit the potential of managing West Ham. 'It was the job for me,' he confided, 'but I feel I didn't get the chance to fulfil what I was hoping to do. But in keeping the side up and finishing tenth, it wasn't a bad effort.'

....

What If in Cardiff?

'It was a fantastic spectacle for English football'
– Alan Pardew, May 2006

THEY SAY that 'if' is a much bigger word than its two letters suggest. It's somewhat appropriate, then, that it can be found in Cardiff – the city where West Ham were left to wonder what might have been, had certain key moments in the 2006 FA Cup final gone their way.

In taking Liverpool to a thrilling 3–3 draw and extra-time before losing on penalties, there is little doubt that West Ham played an integral part in one of the greatest FA Cup finals of all time. But what if Hammers right-back Lionel Scaloni hadn't 'sportingly' kicked the ball out of play to allow Liverpool's Djibril Cissé to receive treatment just moments before Steven Gerrard's injury-time equaliser? What if Gerrard hadn't taken out Marlon Harewood with a late challenge that rendered the West Ham striker a hobbling passenger during extra-time? Far more significantly, what if Gerrard hadn't shaken off a secret groin problem – one that Hammers boss Alan Pardew had been made aware of (among other things) by a Liverpool 'mole' in the build-up to the game?

The simple answer, as far as the supporters are concerned, is that West Ham would probably have confounded all expectations and won their first major trophy since 1980. Liverpool were the red-hot favourites, with the existing European champions on an electrifying run of form that had seen them win their previous 11 games. The Hammers, meanwhile, were a newly promoted side that had allowed Liverpool to do the double over them that season, although they could at least draw on recent experience, with the visit to the Millennium Stadium on 13 May being their third in the space of two years, following their brace of Championship play-off finals.

They were also without suspended midfielder Hayden Mullins following his harsh dismissal in a recent clash with the Reds, who had lost Spanish midfielder Luis Garcia for his involvement in the same incident. Yet the odds of 9–2 for West Ham to win the game seemed generous considering that only six places separated the two teams in the final Premier League table.

What the bookies were not aware of, however, is the amount of inside information Pardew had obtained from a source close to the Liverpool squad. As well as the niggling injury that Gerrard had been nursing – and was reluctant to reveal – it was also learned by the West Ham manager, via private correspondence, that 'angry' striker Fernando Morientes was unlikely to start and that manager Rafa Benitez planned to deploy 'a different system' than usual. Pardew was warned to anticipate 'unexpected changes' and that the belief among the Liverpool players was that they would 'destroy' the Hammers.

Pardew's big hope in the run-up to the game was that key Liverpool midfielder Xabi Alonso would fail to recover from an ankle injury, although doubts about the Spaniard's fitness made it more difficult for the West Ham chief to finalise his preparations. However, he worked on the assumption that both Alonso and Gerrard would be fit to start and planned for his players to put pressure on the latter to prevent the England midfielder from using what Pardew considered to be his biggest weapon – his right foot. He also believed that breaking Liverpool's offside trap was the key to success and planned to use Harewood to exploit space around defender Sami Hyypia that would be created by luring left-back John Arne Riise out of position. He hoped to take advantage of Liverpool's controversial zonal-marking system at set pieces and revealed to his source that beanpole striker Peter Crouch would be allowed to win his headers, but if in possession would find the Hammers to be 'very aggressive'.

Pardew also divulged that he had started a 'war of words' in the press to plant seeds of doubt in the opposition's minds in the belief that 'the psychology of the game' favoured West Ham. With the big event coming on the back of the Hammers beating Tottenham in their final league game, to deny their bitter London rivals a place in the Champions League, Pardew was adamant that his players' energy levels had 'peaked at the perfect time'.

As it transpired, the Hammers boss had been sold something of a dummy, with Liverpool naming eight of the ten outfield players – including Gerrard and Alonso – that had started at Portsmouth the previous weekend, although Morientes did indeed have to be satisfied with a place on the bench. Given Benitez's habit of squad rotation, maybe the lack of changes was the very surprise that Pardew had been warned about. Whatever, everything certainly seemed to go to plan for West Ham when the big day arrived as they raced into a two-goal lead within the opening half hour.

The first goal came after 21 minutes when Scaloni's cross from the right was diverted into his own net by Liverpool defender Jamie Carragher. The second followed seven minutes later, when Reds goalkeeper Pepe Reina fumbled a shot by Matthew Etherington and allowed Dean Ashton to force the ball home. For Hammers fans it all seemed too good to be true, but with Liverpool having recovered from a three-goal deficit against AC Milan to win the Champions League final the previous season, the general feeling was that it was far too early to consider victory a formality. So it proved, with Cissé meeting Gerrard's long ball and volleying past Hammers keeper Shaka Hislop to reduce the arrears after 32 minutes. Gerrard completed the comeback nine minutes after the break when he smashed home from distance after Crouch had nodded down Alonso's free-kick.

The momentum was firmly with Liverpool, but somehow the pendulum swung in West Ham's favour once again when Paul Konchesky's hopeful cross from the left sailed over Reina's head into the net with 62 minutes played. With all three of their goals coming via an element of good fortune, maybe the Hammers were destined to win the FA Cup for the first time in 26 years, in the season that former managers Ron Greenwood and John Lyall – who had claimed the trophy three times between them – had passed away.

But it was not to be. With just seconds remaining, Scaloni put the ball out of play when he saw Cissé go down with cramp. The Argentina full-back, who was on loan from Deportivo La Coruna, thought his ploy would help run down the clock knowing that Liverpool would have to throw the ball back to the Hammers. Yet his cunning plan backfired because when play resumed, Scaloni's rushed clearance simply returned possession to Liverpool and Gerrard broke West Ham hearts with a 30-yard thunderbolt that flew past Hislop into the back of the net.

Further misfortune befell the Hammers during the extra-time period when Harewood was caught by Gerrard – who went unpunished – which meant the striker was in no condition to take advantage when the ball rebounded in front of him after Reina had tipped Nigel Reo-Coker's header onto a post. Furthermore – and crucially – he was unable to participate in the subsequent penalty shoot-out, which Liverpool won 3–1 after Bobby Zamora, Konchesky and Anton Ferdinand failed to convert.

Nearly two-and-a-half hours of sensational drama were finally over and the disappointed West Ham fans remained behind in the stadium to pay tribute to their side's incredible efforts. For the first time since 1953, the FA Cup final had produced six goals and at no stage of the game were the Hammers ever behind, having held the lead for a total of 59 minutes. Boss Pardew knew he would probably never come closer to winning a major trophy, but was left to draw on the positives. 'I'm so proud of my team,' he said. 'We played our part in one of the greatest FA Cup finals ever. It was a fantastic spectacle for English football. I thought we'd won the game but a special player produced a special moment.'

Assistant boss Peter Grant took a different view, however. 'Even when we were 2–0 up I knew we didn't have the players to dictate the game. As a boxer we were putting our jabs in but we'd have needed to knock the opposition out because we never had the control.'

Yet he believed tiredness played a part in Liverpool's match-saving goal. 'Gerrard could hardly move his legs at the end of normal time and that's why he was so deep when the ball came to him for his second equaliser,' he said. 'It's disappointing not to have won the game, but the drama we helped produce is what everybody wants on cup final day.'

West Ham failed to lift the trophy but won plenty of new friends – and they could also take huge consolation from the fact that by reaching the final they had secured a place in the UEFA Cup, thanks to Liverpool having qualified for the Champions League. The prize of European football goes a long way to explaining why the celebrations after the 1–0 semi-final victory against Middlesbrough at Villa Park – courtesy of Harewood's fierce strike – were the type usually reserved for trophy-winning occasions. Pardew later complained that his side had been handed 'awful draws', with earlier ties against Blackburn, Bolton and Manchester City meaning the Hammers had been forced to play five Premier League outfits during their amazing FA Cup run.

The manager also claimed that West Ham faced a difficult task when they were paired with Palermo in the first round of the UEFA Cup at the start of the following campaign – and Pardew's frequent referral to them as 'Palmero' hardly inspired confidence. The Sicilian outfit had only finished eighth in Serie A the previous season, but were promoted into Europe when Lazio were banned for their role in Italy's match-fixing scandal.

It was appropriate that the Hammers were greeted by the imposing sight of Mount Etna as they flew towards the island for their second leg because their 1–0 defeat at Upton Park, two weeks earlier, had certainly left them with a mountain to climb. Andrea Caracciolo had scored a disputed goal just seconds before the break after the ball appeared to have gone out of play, and West Ham were unimpressed by the strong-arm tactics of Palermo in a game that witnessed a 20-man melee.

Rather more serious fighting was on the agenda when local youths stormed the Teatro Massimo to hurl missiles at Hammers fans who had travelled out to the Sicilian capital – a city whose constant battle against organised crime is reflected in the fact that the Falcone-Borsellino airport is named after two anti-Mafia investigators who were murdered in 1992. Twenty-six West Ham supporters were arrested and six injured, yet just one Italian was held – indicating that the masked perpetrators had long whizzed off on their Vespas by the time the *carabinieri* bothered to take an interest. The increased security that was promised for the following evening's game certainly didn't stop one group of English journalists from smuggling a ticketless friend into the Stadia Renzo Barbera, despite having to negotiate a series of heavily guarded gates.

Sadly, it proved far more difficult for West Ham to find their way past the Palermo team, whose fine form was in stark contrast to that of the visitors, who had lost Ashton to serious injury and were struggling to integrate the talents of Argentina stars Carlos Tevez and Javier Mascherano following their recent arrival. Indeed, the Hammers had lost their last three games and not won in six, so weren't exactly fancied to make further progress, although things could have been different had home goalkeeper Alberto Fontana not denied Tevez, Harewood, Carlton Cole and James Collins in the opening 30 minutes.

Two goals by Fábio Henrique Simplício and a further strike by future Hammer David Di Michele gave Palermo an emphatic win that hardly reflected the visitors' valiant efforts and left Pardew declaring, 'A 4–0 aggregate scoreline flatters Palermo but, after a result like that, I can't really claim we were the better team.' The 'Cockney Boys on

Tour' T-shirts were plentiful in the bars overlooking the sun-kissed Mondello beach a few miles along the coastline the following day, although in reality it was less a tour and more a trip – but one well worth having.

On a Whinge and a Prayer

'The Joey Beauchamp deal was a total disaster'
– Billy Bonds, October 1994

THE CLUE is in the surname. Beauchamp is an old French term meaning 'beautiful field'. And oh, how Joseph Daniel of that title pined for the wide open spaces and home comforts of Oxfordshire, the place of his birth, as he surveyed his new dwellings in the ugly metropolitan sprawl of London Town.

Like a character from a Dickens novel (Charles, not Alan), young Joey packed his new Pony-sponsored shirt into a spotty handkerchief on a stick and waved a forlorn farewell to life in the provinces. He was off to make his fortune in the place where the streets were paved in claret and blue. What he lacked in street wisdom he would make up for in talent, for this fine young athlete had it in spades. If he buckled down and saved up as much as he could of his meagre £2,000 weekly wage (plus bonuses and signing-on fee) over the coming months and years, he might go far.

Alas, for months and years see minutes and days. For unlike a character from a Dickens tome, our Joey's story didn't merit a whole book. Verily, with the summer sun of 1994 still a beating down and n'er a first-team appearance under his belt, the Cotswolds seized back this befuddled young fellow from the sinister clutches of England's cruel capital, leaving behind just a single, short chapter of pure farce.

Harry Redknapp, then assistant manager to Billy Bonds, recalled in his autobiography that the winger's woes became apparent on the very first day of pre-season training, following his June arrival from Oxford United for £850,000. Not that the nature of his problem was instantly crystal to Redknapp. When Beauchamp muttered to him that he 'should have gone to Swindon', Redknapp assumed that the player was idly chatting about getting confused on his route to London along the M4 that morning. It was only when Beauchamp added 'this is too far from home' that the penny dropped.

The previous spring Beauchamp, one of the brightest attacking stars outside the top flight, had been on the point of joining Swindon Town, before deciding to stick at the Manor Ground. But if he thought Redknapp or Bonds might care a damn about his West Country regrets rather than his West Ham ambitions, he was badly mistaken. Initially, Bonds opted for pragmatic diplomacy when asked about his homesick recruit's commute and suggestions that Beauchamp felt the club was 'too big for him'.

'He signed a three-year contract,' said Bonds. 'He's got to settle down. I was very shy when I first came to the club in the days when we had superstars but you have to grow up. Besides, we've got no superstars here now. There are no flash players. They are a good bunch of blokes and he should be finding it easy to settle in.'

But he wasn't and he didn't. As the full realisation sank in that 23-year-old Beauchamp was seemingly willing to jeopardise the chance of a lifetime largely because of heavy traffic on the M25, diplomacy turned to disgust. Bonds later fumed in *West Ham United: The Managers* that he should never have gone back on his first instincts. When initially approached about moving to Upton Park, Beauchamp had seemed unsure. Then he'd changed his mind – and would soon change it back again!

'The Joey Beauchamp deal was a total disaster,' Bonds said, confirming this as his worst-ever signing for West Ham. 'The boy was a total wimp. I just told him he'd better keep his nut down because the fans weren't going to be too happy with him either.'

One of the great frustrations about the whole tawdry saga for the fans was that fast, skilful left-sided wingers had proven so popular and effective down the years at the Boleyn. Redknapp inferred, however, that this one came with an 'h' after the 'w'. Beauchamp apparently hated the drive from Oxford, hated being away from his girlfriend – allegedly spending hours on end to her on the phone during a pre-season tour of Scotland – and, to put it frankly, appeared to hate everything about being at West Ham.

Redknapp said that, from day one, Beauchamp did nothing but sulk and show brass neck where money was concerned. He also believed that the Beauchamp fiasco was a significant contributory factor in Bonds' decision to quit in August 1994, although it's a suggestion the former manager refutes. Either way it was Harry who had to resolve the mess once he was installed as Bonds' successor.

Beauchamp belatedly got his 'dream move' to newly relegated second-tier Swindon Town, but not without more shoddy shenanigans that left Redknapp seething and culminated in the Professional Footballers' Association being called in to represent the player when relations between he and West Ham became irrevocably strained.

Despite his eagerness to leave the Hammers, Beauchamp's contract talks with Swindon dragged on for an eternity, to the point where the Robins looked like they too would have preferred to wash their hands of him. Eventually, a deal was struck whereby Swindon gave West Ham £200,000 plus defender Adrian Whitbread, who was valued at around £500,000. So, a net loss to Hammers of £150,000 but a hit worth taking in order to move on from an episode that had turned the club into a laughing stock.

Utterly unsurprisingly, after just a season with Swindon, Beauchamp's career came full circle when he rejoined his first love, Oxford United. Voted the club's 'Player of the Nineties', this was clearly a marriage made in heaven. At West Ham, however, his name will always be synonymous with the transfer from hell.

■■■■■■■■■■■■■■■■■■■■

Argy-bargy

'I'm sorry but I have no control over Tevez'
– Eggert Magnusson, March 2007

ON 10 MAY 2007, a letter from solicitor Herbert Smith was sent to a newspaper group to contest 'defamatory and extremely damaging' statements in relation to their client Terence Brown, the former West Ham chairman, in an article regarding the club's controversial signings of Carlos Tevez and Javier Mascherano the previous year. Needless to say, it was just one of many hundreds of pieces of correspondence seeking mitigation or threatening litigation as the legal profession – along with Sheffield United, of course – emerged as the big winners in what will forever be known as 'The Tevez Affair'.

Never has one topic in football provoked so much comment and debate, based on so many misunderstandings, misinterpretations and misjudgements. Even to this day, the general notion seems to be that West Ham were fined a record £5.5 million for having fielded an 'ineligible' player – or two – as a result of 'illegal' third-party ownership and hence retained their Premier League status at the expense of relegated Sheffield United by default. 'Cheats Prosper' and 'The Sickening Swindle' were just two of the damning headlines that appeared in May 2007, as the critics complained of a serious miscarriage of justice. 'Some of the things that have been written about us have been scandalous,' said assistant boss Mervyn Day as he reflected on the aftermath of his side's survival that year. 'People haven't understood the situation and failed to recognise that the registration of the players was valid all the way through.' Indeed, a Premier League spokesman insisted, 'This has never been a case of West Ham fielding an ineligible player. From the day they signed Tevez they owned his registration. The only problem we had was the existence of a clause in the agreement that would allow [economic-rights owners] MSI to sell the player. That was a breach of the rule which forbids any third party from influencing the policy of any team.'

If the initial financial penalty imposed on the Hammers caused massive shockwaves throughout football, then so did the actual signings of Tevez and Mascherano when the news broke on 31 August 2006. 'The Argentina World Cup stars have been signed on permanent contracts,' said a club statement before concluding, 'All other aspects of the transfers will remain confidential.' It was a stunning coup, with Tevez being dubbed 'the new Maradona' and Mascherano described by the Argentina legend himself as 'a monster of a player'. How on earth could West Ham afford the pair of 22 year olds, who were estimated to be worth a combined figure of at least £30 million?

The reality was that the economic rights of the two players were actually owned by four corporate entities – of which Media Sports Investment Ltd (MSI) was one – with MSI frontman Kia Joorabchian confirming only that the deals with West Ham were 'complex and involved many aspects'. Third-party ownership of players was common in territories such as South America but was an alien concept in Britain – although not an illegal one – and was difficult for many people to comprehend. Nevertheless, Hammers chairman Brown hailed 'a momentous day' for the club, while manager Alan Pardew beamed, 'This will give us a real chance to compete with the very best teams in Europe.'

As the two former Corinthians players were unveiled at Upton Park on 5 September, speculation was rife that the pair had been offered by Joorabchian as a short-term 'sweetener' to boost his chances of completing a prospective buyout of the club. However, Pardew insisted, 'I can assure you they will not be leaving in the next transfer window.' Indeed, coach Peter Grant later revealed, 'It was guaranteed to Alan that there were no get-out clauses in their contracts for a minimum of a year. And from a business point of view, as far as we were concerned, everything was above board.'

Sadly, Grant's faith would prove misplaced in both respects. In fact, the only declaration that could be relied upon was Pardew's insistence that he would 'never be forced to play either player', because neither of them was allowed to establish themselves in the team during the autumn period – despite West Ham's awful run of results. After Pardew was sacked by new chairman Eggert Magnusson in December, Mascherano complained, 'His manner with Tevez and me was not the same as with the rest of the team. I don't think he could accept our arrival.' Except their prospects didn't improve under new boss Alan Curbishley, whose assistant Day said of Mascherano, 'He was so low it was untrue and his situation was irretrievable by the time we arrived.'

Whether the Premier League would have taken a renewed interest in the contractual nature of the two Argentinians had Mascherano not joined Liverpool midway through the season – after a protracted delay – is unlikely, although there was the suspicion that they had been alerted by other means. On 2 February 2007, the club revealed that they were 'fully cooperating with the FA Premier League' regarding player registration and a month later it was confirmed that West Ham had been charged with two alleged rule breaches. A Premier League statement referred to rule E10, in respect of 'transfers that enabled third parties to acquire the ability to influence the club's policies' while West Ham's 'failure to disclose the third-party agreements' was considered to contravene rule B13, in relation to clubs behaving towards each other 'with the utmost good faith'.

West Ham declared their intention to 'vigorously defend' themselves but had submitted a guilty plea by the time of the two-day hearing in front of an independent, three-man panel in London at the end of April. By now Tevez was playing an active role in trying to keep the Hammers up, with Curbishley insisting it 'wasn't going to make the situation any worse', while Magnusson made no attempt to disguise the fact that he had little say in the striker's future. 'I'm sorry but I have no control over Tevez,' he said during a conversation in the club's trophy room.

At midday on 27 April, it was announced that West Ham had been fined an unprecedented £5.5 million for the two rule breaches, while a twenty-five-page Premier League report made for fascinating reading in terms of the specific terms of the player contracts, what the club was deemed guilty of and who was allegedly responsible. The problem with Tevez's four-year deal was that it allowed MSI to terminate the agreement in January 2007, upon payment of £2 million to the club –

a figure that would reduce to £100,000 in any other transfer window. Mascherano had a similar arrangement, with the club receiving £150,000 in the event of any transfer during his five-year contract. In both cases, neither West Ham nor the players themselves had the power to object to the moves and that is what contravened Premier League rules – as well as the fact that these clauses were hidden in 'side contracts' that had previously been kept under wraps. In their defence, West Ham argued correctly that such agreements were never legally enforceable and, although the commission acknowledged this, the club was punished because, it was insisted, they had entered into the deals in good faith.

Meanwhile, the report revealed the roles played by legal director Scott Duxbury and managing director Paul Aldridge in the signings, with the latter accused of telling Premier League chief executive Richard Scudamore 'a direct lie' – something he would bitterly contest, particularly as he had not been asked to submit testimony.

The commission acknowledged that a number of factors fell in West Ham's favour – such as their guilty plea, the change of ownership since the original indiscretions and their subsequent disclosure of the hidden documents – and therefore declared that 'a deduction of points would not be proportionate punishment', especially as such a penalty would have 'consigned the club to certain relegation'.

Inevitably, fellow strugglers Wigan, Sheffield United, Fulham and Charlton – disappointed not to see their own survival chances enhanced – expressed their discontent and became the 'Gang of Four' determined to fight the decision not to dock West Ham points. Wigan chairman Dave Whelan believed the Hammers had received preferential treatment because of their status in the game and complained, 'Had it been Wigan, Watford or a smaller club, it would have been a ten-point deduction, no question.' Whelan spoke of 'suing the Premier League or West Ham' in a bid to seek 'justice', while also questioning how Tevez was allowed to remain available for West Ham's final three games of the season.

The Hammers had satisfied the Premier League's demands in April by destroying the offending third-party agreements and Scudamore confirmed, 'We have a copy of the letter of termination.' He also acknowledged that the motives of the 'Gang of Four' were financially driven and fuelled by self-interest. 'The suggestion that we wanted to keep West Ham in the Premier League at the expense of the so-called smaller clubs is one of the most offensive things I've ever heard. With the league being as lucrative as it is, people are desperate to stay in it and people are hanging on by any means they can.'

Sheffield United chairman Kevin McCabe, however, insisted he was acting on a point of principle. 'We don't expect to get relegated but will support the club that does,' he said. Yet a closing run of 11 games, that saw the Blades win just twice and fatally lose at home to Wigan on the final day of the season, did indeed see them drop through the trapdoor as the Hammers survived. 'You get stuck into West Ham,' said Whelan when consoling McCabe after the final whistle at Bramall Lane. 'We're right behind you.'

On 16 May it was confirmed that Sheffield United had submitted a formal challenge to the independent commission's verdict, while McCabe laughably suggested his side should be reinstated into a 21-team Premier Division. 'It's a very simple solution,' he said. The Premier League warned all their members that any legal action 'would fly in the face of the disciplinary structure that the clubs themselves created', while Magnusson said, 'There have been all sorts of misinterpretations.'

However, on 22 May, it was announced that Sheffield United's claim would be referred to an arbitration panel in June, prompting the club's publicity machine to launch the 'Campaign for Fairness' that saw actor Sean Bean play a prominent role. This is the man who Blades boss Neil Warnock claimed confronted his wife with the accusation that her husband had 'got us relegated – he's a f**king wanker'. An allegation Bean denied.

Common sense prevailed on 3 July when the panel rejected the claim that the decision to simply fine West Ham was 'irrational or perverse', but they went beyond their jurisdiction when stating that 'this tribunal would, in all probability, have reached a different conclusion and docked points from West Ham'.

Their personal opinion was irrelevant but it encouraged Sheffield United – by now blinded by their own misleading propaganda as they continued to complain of Tevez's 'ineligibility' – to take the matter to the High Court and claim that the arbitration panel had made 'an error in law' by deciding against them. The appeal was rejected but the club's lawyers, who obviously benefited from remaining active, issued a statement to insist that 'Sheffield United are not precluded from taking further action against the Premier League or West Ham'.

As the close season progressed it became increasingly clear that Tevez was unlikely to stay at Upton Park, although MSI could not move him on to his chosen destination of Manchester United until West Ham – ever conscious of the Premier League watching over their shoulders – approved any deal, as they held the striker's registration. With Joorabchian claiming he still owned the player's economic rights, however, a month of wrangling saw FIFA recommend that the case be referred to the Court of Arbitration for Sport in Lausanne, Switzerland, while the Iranian businessman issued High Court proceedings against the Hammers for unilaterally terminating their contract with him.

News emerged of a 'secret document', allegedly signed by Duxbury on 1 December 2006, agreeing to the release of Tevez in the summer of 2007, but West Ham insisted this was no longer valid. Finally, on 3 August, it was announced that an out-of-court settlement had been agreed with Joorabchian, with the Hammers being paid £2 million to release the registration of Tevez, who promptly headed to Old Trafford on a two-year loan from MSI (with no clauses that could be interpreted as representing a third-party influence).

A fortnight later, Sheffield United, who had by now kicked off their Championship campaign against Colchester, announced that they intended to sue West Ham for losses suffered as a result of relegation and plucked a figure of £50 million out of thin Yorkshire air. Finally, the matter was referred to yet another FA arbitration process – unfortunately accepted by the Hammers to avoid the matter going through the law courts. However, the decision, on 23 September 2008, fell in the Blades' favour thanks to the testimony of Joorabchian's lawyer Graham Shear, who claimed that West Ham had made verbal agreements with MSI when terminating the third-party contracts that offended the Premier League. Panel chairman Lord Griffiths said, 'If the Premier League had known what Mr Duxbury for West Ham was saying to Mr Joorabchian's solicitor following the commission decision, we are confident that the Premier League would have suspended Mr Tevez's registration as a West Ham player.'

In the end, it wasn't what was written in a contract that doomed the Hammers to a costly legal defeat but what somebody allegedly said – a somewhat tenuous way for the whole sorry affair to be decided.

West Ham's attempts to take the matter to the Court of Arbitration for Sport came to nothing and, on 16 March 2009, it was announced that an out-of-court settlement had been reached with Sheffield United, with it being reported that a figure of around £20 million would be paid over several years to the Championship club. 'The time was right to draw a line under this whole episode,' insisted Duxbury, although sadly that was not the end of the story as Warnock, members of his old squad and various other parties came out of the woodwork to suggest they should also be compensated.

The FA then launched a new probe into the whole matter in the light of Lord Griffiths' findings before clearing West Ham of any further wrongdoing. In February 2010, it was reported that the Hammers' new owners, David Gold and David Sullivan, had launched a legal challenge to the advice given to the previous hierarchy, after inheriting a situation that represented a significant drain on their resources.

Tevez revealed his ongoing love for West Ham by giving the crossed hammers salute to fans when appearing for latest employer Manchester City at Upton Park on the final day of the 2009–10 season. Four years earlier, former chairman Brown had described his signing as 'the biggest in West Ham's history'. It's difficult to argue with him, because it certainly proved to be the most expensive . . .

■■■■■■■■■■■■■■■■■■■

What a Pair!

'Upton Park was filled with my kind of folks'
– Frank McAvennie, 2003

KEN ARMSTRONG sits high on the list of the most influential players during the most accomplished league campaign in West Ham's history. Ken who? In the first game of the 1985–86 season, a bruising collision between Armstrong, a moustached 6 ft 2 in. Birmingham City centre-half and West Ham striker Paul Goddard saw the latter depart early with a dislocated left shoulder. An injury to one of John Lyall's most reliable charges did not augur well for the new campaign.

However, as the saying goes, one man's misfortune is another man's gain. Or two men in this case. Pushed up front from his attacking midfield birth, new signing Frank McAvennie's understanding with Tony Cottee didn't seem wholly obvious that day at St Andrew's, as Armstrong & Co. beat West Ham 1–0 in a turgid affair in front of just 11,000 fans.

But by the time City were relegated nine months later, Cottee & McAvennie had become such a lethal strike partnership that their names became permanently conjoined. Previous Hammers pairings of Johnny Dick & Vic Keeble and Vic Watson & Jimmy Ruffell notched marginally more league goals between them in a single season, but Cottee & McAvennie did it in a campaign when the club finished higher than it had ever done in its history.

It was one of those very rare times when West Ham could say they were the envy of English football. Granted, Everton's Gary Lineker was the hottest property and Liverpool's Ian Rush and Kenny Dalglish were consistently the most ruthless combo around. But through a magical alchemy founded on McAvennie's charisma and skill and Cottee's pace and promise, it was West Ham's forward line that really caught the country's imagination in 1985–86, as they notched 54 goals between them in all competitions.

Cottee's understanding with fellow Londoner Goddard was itself more than half decent, the pair sharing 38 goals between them in the previous season. Stocky of build, nimble of foot, sensible of haircut, the similarities generally seemed to work in their favour. McAvennie was different from Cottee in many ways – from his flamboyance to his impenetrable Glaswegian accent – and it was these contrasts that provided the secret ingredient as West Ham found themselves in possession of not just a half-decent forward pairing, but the finished article. Their magic as a twosome only really lasted one season, but what a season! And what a pair – no Page-Three model or Stringfellows-related pun intended.

Lyall once attempted to explain how hours of hard work at Chadwell Heath helped perfect the chemistry. 'They both had terrific pace and we learned how to exploit it. Rather than play low passes to their feet, a situation that would have involved them in battles against bigger defenders, we were trying to play balls into the spaces between defenders. We had worked at this for weeks in training, with the midfield players running at the defence with the ball before sliding it between the centre-back and the full-back for Tony or Frank to chase.'

'It didn't happen by accident,' said Cottee. 'We both tried very hard to make it work as well as it did.' While early on the coaching and playing staff took time to fathom the best qualities of mystery man McAvennie, bought for £340,000 from St Mirren, partly on the recommendation of then-Aberdeen manager Alex Ferguson, Lyall knew everything there was to know about 20-year-old home-grown product Cottee. 'He had a thirst for goals that was quite extraordinary. Put the ball into a little space in the penalty area and he would deal with it clinically. When he was scoring he was as happy as a sandboy.'

Two goals from McAvennie on his home debut, a 3–1 win over QPR, were the first of 46 the pair shared that season in the league, the Scot coming out tops with 26. Frank, who had only taken up football full time six years earlier, also chose the game against the Hoops to prove that behind the happy-go-lucky persona, bleached blond hair and Colgate smile lay a bit of a tiger. Clattering a QPR defender right in front of the Chicken Run was the first of many personal PR masterstrokes that season.

Plaistow-born Cottee was forced to suffer the frustration of five more winless games before the 'sandboy' started to smile, with a 2–2 away draw against Sheffield Wednesday marking the first time he and McAvennie both featured on the scoresheet. It was during that winless sticky period, when questions were being asked not about Cottee's strike rate but his work rate, that a crisis meeting called by skipper Alvin Martin seemed to open a psychological lock for the whole team.

'There were no holds barred,' remembered McAvennie. 'Basically, Tony was told that he was a lazy little shit. To his credit Tony sat there and took it. I got it, everyone got it. The meeting really cleared the air.'

For Frank, the next game against Leicester City, a 3–0 home victory in which they again notched in tandem, represented the opening few bars of a beautiful symphony. 'That game spelt something for me – the beauty of Upton Park,' he wrote in his wryly titled book, *Scoring: An Expert's Guide*. 'Whatever the supporters felt you caught the gale of their emotions. I realised Upton Park was filled with my kind of folks.'

From the end of August to Boxing Day 1985, Hammers went 18 league games unbeaten. The strike pair's stats during that period read like something out of a Boleyn fairytale: McAvennie bagged five in four consecutive games at the start of the run; Cottee duly followed with five in five; they bagged two each in a 4–1 win over Aston Villa; Cottee scored in both legs of the Milk Cup second-round game against Swansea City; McAvennie got both goals in a 2–1 win over title rivals Everton.

With broadcasting contractual wrangles meaning no *Match of the Day* until the second half of the season, there was scant opportunity for people outside Upton Park to see the deadly duo in action – unless you count man-of-the-moment McAvennie's appearance on the *Wogan* chat show. When West Ham did make it onto ITV's *Big Match* or a live cup game, the pair's energy and artistry caught the eye, but both were always at pains to point out that their success was as much about provider as finisher.

For a while, the fierce winter weather that marked the start of 1986 seemed to freeze the pair's progress – except in the FA Cup, in which Cottee netted in all but the fifth round as they made it as far as the quarter-finals.

In the league, the turning point was a 1–0 win over Sheffield Wednesday in March, the Hammers embarking on a ten-game period in which either Cottee or McAvennie failed to score on just two occasions. Ironically, it was during that period that defender Martin achieved a feat neither striker managed all season – a hat-trick, in the 8–1 home thrashing of Newcastle United.

Sadly, in the end their Herculean efforts didn't quite prove enough to propel West Ham to their first-ever First Division title. Kenny Dalglish, McAvennie's hero as a boyhood Celtic fan, ruined the script with a winner for Liverpool at Chelsea on the last Saturday of the season.

Major consolation for Frank in that incredible campaign came with a scoring debut for Scotland in which he played alongside his idol, subsequently booking himself a place in the squad for the 1986 Mexico World Cup finals. Under-21 starlet Cottee didn't quite make it onto England's plane, but he did walk away with the PFA Young Player-of-the-Year award to go with a Hammer-of-the-Year award that he was convinced should have gone to his strike partner. 'I was absolutely staggered,' said Cottee in *Boys of '86*. 'I had spells where I was as good as him and individual games where I'd done better, but Frank had been so consistent. He was our best player that season, without a doubt.'

The following campaign – a crushingly disappointing one in which Hammers slid back to mid-table mediocrity – belonged to Cottee, who scored twenty-two league goals to McAvennie's seven. In reviewing their careers overall, few would argue that TC's contribution to the club wasn't the more impressive. In 335 appearances he hit 145 goals, putting him 5th on the all-time scorers chart. McAvennie is back in 19th, his 57 goals coming in 188 appearances. Cottee made the better start to his Irons career, scoring on his debut against Spurs in 1983 as a 17 year old. McAvennie made the better finish, signing off with a sensational second-half hat-trick against Nottingham Forest on the last day of the 1991–92 season.

Both played for their countries and both had two spells at West Ham; McAvennie returning from Celtic in 1989, Cottee coming home from Everton in 1994. Frank's unique appeal worked in his favour when it came to *Hammers News* magazine's chart of the 50 Greatest All-Time Hammers, compiled in 1998 and based on reader opinion. The Scot was ranked at number nine, with Cottee two places back. Trevor Brooking came top of that poll and it was in his capacity as an expert contributor to *Match of the Day* magazine that Brooking put Cottee/McAvennie at number nine in the publication's Top 20 All-time Strike Partnerships, commenting, 'The great West Ham philosophy was passing and moving and then it was running off the ball, which was the great strength of that pairing.'

Post-playing days, the similarities are once again few and far between. Cottee has gone about establishing a media career for himself in the diligent, respectable way one would have expected. McAvennie has admitted to excessive drinking and occasional drug use, spent a month on remand in Durham prison on a charge of conspiracy to supply drugs (later found not guilty) and, as recently as January 2009, was given a four-month suspended sentence for his part in a bar brawl on the Isle of Man.

To the public at large, McAvennie's reputation as a footballer has long been in danger of being superseded by his penchant for the booze and the 'burds'. To West Ham fans, especially those old enough to recall the 1985–86 campaign, it will always be the other way round.

When the back pages couldn't get enough of the pair as they banged in goals for fun, a silly story did the rounds suggesting they didn't get on. It was lazy journalism at its finest, the assumption being that just because they were different characters they didn't like each other.

If ultimate proof were needed that opposites attract, the pair appeared on stage together in *The Tony Cottee & Frank McAvennie Show*, a Hammers nostalgia-fest at Thameside Theatre, Grays, in 2009. The night would be remembered for Frank and Tony giving it their best as stand-up comedians, but Cottee & McAvennie's greatest legacy as entertainers is the time their peculiar chemistry pushed West Ham seriously close to being the best team in the land. No joke.

Shout to the Top

'It sounds cocky, but we knew a long time ago we would win promotion' – Ian Bishop, April 1991

'SOME PEOPLE are on the pitch! They think it's all over!' Kenneth Wolstenholme's immortal words might have coincided with a glorious moment in West Ham's history as Geoff Hurst claimed his hat-trick to wrap up England's World Cup final win against West Germany in 1966. But they could also have been used to describe a moment that fans would rather forget, namely the final minutes of the 1990–91 season as the Hammers battled against Notts County in pursuit of the Second Division title.

West Ham's 2–1 defeat was a disappointing way to end a promotion-winning campaign, but they would still be champions as long as closest rivals Oldham failed to win their home fixture against third-placed Sheffield Wednesday – and they were being held to a 2–2 draw as the final whistle blew at Upton Park. It was celebration time and the jubilant claret and blue faithful flooded the pitch in anticipation of manager Billy Bonds appearing in the upper tier of the West Stand with the trophy in his hands.

'Champions!' Champions!' chanted the ecstatic crowd. Suddenly confusion spread about the final score at Boundary Park, with murmurs that Oldham had somehow grabbed a late winner – to complete their recovery having been two goals down – as their game had overrun by several minutes. Eventually, confirmation came through that the Latics had indeed snatched victory with an injury-time penalty to rip that valuable piece of silverware out of West Ham's grasp.

'When I heard the truth I broke down in tears,' admitted winger Stuart Slater as his emotions in the Hammers dressing-room got the better of him. Bonds believed it was a 'cruel' turn of events given his players' outstanding efforts throughout the campaign, but insisted, 'We have still had a very successful season. Promotion has always been the priority and to achieve that with five games to play was better than we could have expected.'

West Ham's place at football's top table after two years dining with less engaging company had been secured with a 2–0 home win against Swindon, courtesy of goals from George Parris and Iain Dowie, back on 20 April. It was no more than they deserved after setting a new club record of 21 unbeaten league games at the start of the season as the momentum of the previous campaign, in which they had won 11 of their final 17 outings under new boss Bonds, carried through. The sequence that provided the platform for promotion included a 7–1 thrashing of Hull City, which is remembered not so much for the huge scoreline but the fact that defender Steve Potts managed to score the only goal of his 506-game career at the club. 'Disgraceful!' he has since quipped about his miniscule goal tally.

As the promotion campaign gathered momentum, comparisons were inevitably made with the Hammers side that had stormed to the Second Division title ten years earlier, but Bonds was eager to play things down. 'No one is kidding themselves that the job is done,' he said. 'There are a lot of very difficult games to come.' Whether a trip to Barnsley came into that category or not is debatable but the Yorkshire outfit, who would finish eighth that term, proved good enough to sneak a 1–0 win three days before Christmas and bring an end to West Ham's fantastic unbeaten league run.

However, it had been an emphatic statement of intent, with a number of players establishing their pedigree during their first full seasons at the club. Among them were Czech goalkeeper Ludek Miklosko and stylish midfielder Ian Bishop, who both won praise from veteran defender Alvin Martin midway through the campaign. 'Ludo has been a revelation and is a First Division keeper, there's no two ways about it,' he said. 'And what I like about Bish is that he's very honest when he plays. He knows it's not just about flair, creativity and looking the part. He picks up runners and helps his team-mates.'

Bishop had been handed the captain's armband in the enforced absence of Julian Dicks, who had damaged his left knee in a 1–1 draw at Bristol City in October. Typically of the man known as 'the Terminator', the full-back continued to rampage forward for another two games before being advised that he had suffered torn ligaments and required major surgery that would rule him out for a year. Chris Hughton arrived from Tottenham to fill the big hole at left-back while Tim Breacker had recently been signed from Luton in a £600,000 deal to play in the other full-back position. Meanwhile, Colin Foster – another player recruited by former boss Lou Macari the previous term – formed solid central defensive relationships with both Martin and Tony Gale. In attack, the previous season's joint-top scorer Jimmy Quinn and a fit-again Frank McAvennie (following a broken leg) both did well as partners for 17-goal striker Trevor Morley.

Defeat at Oakwell had cost West Ham their place at the top of the league table but that was restored following a 2–0 victory against Oldham on Boxing Day. However, a seven-game period that produced just one win during February and March saw them lose momentum before Bishop's winner at Port Vale put them back in pole position, until that final-day disaster against Notts County. Trophy or no trophy, the main thing was that West Ham were back where they belonged. 'I know it sounds a bit cocky,' reflected Bishop at the season's (anti) climax, 'but we all realised a long time ago that we were good enough to win promotion and that we would do it.'

Maybe the Hammers would not have bothered if they had been aware of the horrors that faced them during the 1991–92 'Bond Scheme' campaign that saw them sink back from whence they came in embarrassing fashion. Managing director Peter Storrie admitted the club was 'at an all-time low' at that point so it is to the immense credit of Bonds that he was able to oversee a second promotion campaign in three years. Harry Redknapp was now beside him as assistant manager, joining in the summer of 1992 following a nine-year period in charge of Bournemouth. Harry claimed that 'what I first saw at Upton Park shook me to the core' and would later relay a story about Foster failing to turn up for training, simply because his sponsored car had been reclaimed, as an example of the poor attitude and discipline at the club. 'The poison of the rotten apples was beginning to spread,' he complained.

Redknapp was so clearly disillusioned by the atmosphere at the club that defender Gale took it upon himself to inform Bonds' side-kick what everybody else had been thinking. 'We'd heard that you were bright and chirpy but you've been a miserable bastard,' he told him. 'You haven't stopped moaning since you've been here.'

Redknapp responded by painting on a smile and trying to lift spirits in the camp. Dicks later claimed that Harry 'took most of the coaching' while the assistant boss quickly got involved in player recruitment, lining up modest deals for Peter Butler, Mattie Holmes and Mark Robson from Southend, Bournemouth and Tottenham respectively, for a combined outlay of £215,000. 'They turned out to be terrific signings,' said Redknapp. Indeed, their contributions in the middle of the park and on the flanks proved invaluable as West Ham recovered from two defeats in their opening three games to quickly establish themselves as genuine promotion contenders.

Bristol City were thrashed 5–1 on their own turf in September, while Sunderland were hit for six with no reply the following month. However, with season-ticket sales down by 8,000 and the attendance of 10,326 against the Wearsiders representing the lowest league gate at Upton Park since 1957, it was clear that the damaging impact of the Bond Scheme and subsequent relegation was going to demand considerable powers of recovery.

Morley and Clive Allen eventually struck up an incredible 36-goal partnership during the 1992–93 season as the Hammers racked up the points in pursuit of runaway leaders Newcastle. It says something about the supporters' deep understanding of football that they should elect quietly efficient defender Potts as their Hammer of the Year. In fact, Potts ended the campaign wearing the skipper's armband after a fit-again Dicks had been stripped of the captaincy as a result of his continued ill-discipline, which saw him miss 13 games due to suspension. Midfielder Martin 'Mad Dog' Allen was also no shrinking violet, receiving 13 yellow cards and winning the accolade of being the first player to amass 41 disciplinary points – for which he was fined heavily and banned.

Bonds was understandably aggrieved because he feared the tenacious twosome would undermine his side's hopes of winning promotion. 'Their records could cost us dearly,' he said, although Dicks later insisted, 'Martin and I had done far more to get us promotion than risk costing it.' Given the manager's concerns, it's ironic that he should recruit famously fiery striker David Speedie on loan for the season's run-in, not least because the Scot had an immediate fight on his hands winning over the fans following his five-year spell at rivals Chelsea.

Bonds complained that the abuse thrown at Speedie after one typically erratic performance was 'disgusting', but his signing proved to be an astute one and four goals in eleven games would ultimately play a big part in helping West Ham cross the finishing line. Automatic promotion had looked assured until Portsmouth embarked on an astonishing run of eleven wins from twelve games to turn up the heat and it eventually resulted in a dramatic final-day shoot-out for second spot, with the Hammers ahead by virtue of having scored just one goal more.

With Pompey at home to mid-table Grimsby, it meant West Ham had to match their result against Cambridge – who needed a win to avoid relegation – and hope they scored no more than one fewer goal in doing so. Speedie scored two minutes into the second half to become one of the unlikeliest Hammers heroes, but when it was discovered that Portsmouth were leading 2–1 it meant that one more goal for the south coast side would be enough to lift them into second place. The tension was palpable on and off the Upton Park pitch but, thankfully, Dicks resisted the temptation to shoot from a tight angle in the dying seconds and crossed for Clive Allen to poke home and spark scenes of bedlam. 'Some people are on the pitch! They think it's all over!' It was now . . .

■■■■■■■■■■■■■■■■■■■

Castigated After Castilla

'I wonder what the game is coming to' – John Lyall,
September 1980

GERRY IS a West Ham fan. He lives in the south of France, spends his mornings collecting walnuts that have dropped off a neighbour's tree and makes the residents in his tiny village laugh so much that he won six votes in their local elections despite never being listed as a candidate. He misses watching the Hammers – which he did as a season-ticket holder for 30 years – but has an abundance of good memories to reflect on. Bad memories, too, the most disturbing of which relate to the events of 17 September 1980, when West Ham visited the Santiago Bernabéu Stadium to take on Real Madrid's nursery side Castilla in the first round of the European Cup Winners' Cup.

'The day was dominated by the police,' he recalls. 'They would stop their cars when they saw our fans and threaten them with batons but if the fans gave them money they would let them go. I saw this happen many times so I hid my West Ham colours. The Bernabéu was a concrete marvel compared to English grounds. Our official group of fans was in the upper tier at one end but others could pay on the door and go anywhere.

'The terrace was made of large steps that we could sit on and I positioned myself about six rows back from the staircase entrance at one end. There was lots of space and we were all relaxed and happy. One fan, wrapped in a Union Jack flag, stood up and sang "Rule Britannia" so the police took him out. Before the game started, about 100 West Ham fans appeared to our right in the upper tier near the halfway line and started singing. When David Cross scored to put us 1–0 up, we celebrated as usual and the police left us alone.

'I can't remember exactly when the trouble began but the Spanish supporters in the lower stand underneath the unofficial group of West Ham fans started making a noise and moving about. Later, I heard stories that people had been urinating on them from above. Then a group of police, having heard that West Ham fans somewhere were causing trouble, appeared at my level and started hitting people on the back of the heads or in the face with their rubber batons. They hit women and children without mercy and I saw one ten-year-old boy hit from behind. People were crying and the scenes seemed to disturb our players as they conceded three late goals.

'After the game, I wanted to get back into the city centre as quickly as possible. The main route from the stadium was a wide grassy central reservation that the West Ham fans were using with four rows of very slow traffic to our right. On the other side of the cars were the Spanish supporters who were celebrating and taunting us. The Spaniards started throwing bricks, which our fans then returned. I rushed to get away and joined three lads who were doing the same. One of them was a quiet young man called Frank and, as we walked away from the trouble behind us, we exchanged a few words about the game.

'The central reservation ended with a barrier above an underpass that went beneath us. To the right was a narrow path next to the traffic and the three lads went that way, while I chose a wider path to my left. Then I saw a coach pass by and suddenly the lads were dropping onto the road below. One of them appeared to have leg injuries and a friend of Frank's shouted, "Get help, he's really hurt." I looked around and saw a police car heading towards us with its lights flashing. I tried to make it stop but it rushed by. I had no idea that the coach had crushed one of the lads against the barrier and that Frank was fatally injured, so I walked on looking for help but gave up as I got into town. The next day, when I boarded the coach home, I was told that Frank had died. He was killed trying to avoid the trouble and I still ask myself, "Why him?"'

It was, in the words of one newspaper headline the following day, the 'Night of Havoc!' News of Frank Sait's death had yet to emerge, with the reports of West Ham's 3–1 defeat against the Spanish second-division side focusing on the behaviour of the English supporters. 'West Ham fans created havoc in Europe last night as the Londoners' defence, which had not conceded a goal for six matches, disintegrated dramatically,' wrote John Parsons in the *Daily Express*. 'Yet if the result was damaging enough, the trouble on the terraces could have even more serious repercussions.'

The paper referred to 'incidents' requiring the intervention of riot police inside the ground, with allegations of 'beer and other rubbish' being dropped onto Spanish fans, while it was claimed that two arrests had been made outside the Bernabéu before kick-off. Angry Hammers boss John Lyall admitted after the match, 'I wonder what the game is coming to. This sort of behaviour just lowers all the standards. We took every precaution possible and then this happens.'

Indeed, West Ham had restricted ticket sales to fans travelling with officially recognised groups, but reports confirmed that independent supporters could also purchase tickets at the ground before the game. 'The incidents on the terraces certainly didn't help us,' added Lyall. 'We had a nightmare 15 minutes.' Skipper Billy Bonds, who had written an open letter asking fans to behave, complained, 'Whatever we do, still some of them don't listen. The players were aware of what was going on but I can't offer that as an excuse.' Paco had levelled for Castilla in the first-leg clash after West Ham conceded a free-kick midway through the second half, while blunders from Bonds and Geoff Pike allowed Valin and Cidon to send the majority of the 40,000 crowd home happy.

The following day, it was confirmed that a West Ham supporter had been killed after being hit by a bus after the game and that eight further arrests had been made inside the ground. The *Daily Express* reported: 'Frank Sait, an 18-year-old carpenter, was run over by a coach as fighting British fans spilled out of the stadium. Witnesses said that British youths hurled beer bottles onto the pitch and spat and urinated on Spanish fans below. Some British fans, however, alleged that the trouble started when Spanish supporters spat at them. And Yorkshire language teacher, 31-year-old Stephen Drake-Jones, who works in Madrid, claimed the Spanish police over-reacted and behaved brutally. He said: "I was knocked down with a police baton because I went to try to help a West Ham fan who was being beaten."'

It was claimed that Sait's family, who lived in Stepney, were trying to raise £1,200 to bring his body back home. Frank's eldest brother

Patrick insisted, 'He was a devoted West Ham fan and would not have wanted to get involved in any trouble.

Madrid newspaper *AS* was quick to criticise the travelling West Ham fans, stating, 'Britain is a country rich in culture but its [soccer] envoys abroad are worse than the barbarous hordes headed by Attila.'

As speculation grew that the Hammers would pay a heavy price for the disturbances, David Miller of the *Daily Express* wrote: 'West Ham, the happy entertainers of English soccer, face a ban from Europe over Wednesday's disgrace in Spain. For 20 years, British clubs and travel agents have transported drunken mobs across Europe in the name of sport without a care.'

He added, 'Drunken British hooligans are now marked men. Continental police do not ask questions first.'

With fingers of accusation being pointed in all directions amid the media hysteria, West Ham's commercial manager Brian Blower remained in Madrid to establish the facts of what had taken place. Manager Lyall later insisted 'the information he gathered from official sources showed earlier reports to be grossly exaggerated'. Yet that didn't stop governing body UEFA from announcing that the Hammers would be banned from playing their next two European home games – including the second leg against Castilla – within 300 kilometres (187 miles) of Upton Park. However, with the club, which was also fined £7,700, having had no opportunity to defend its position, West Ham launched an appeal against the judgment.

West Ham secretary Eddie Chapman said, 'We would have liked to put evidence to UEFA.' Rene Eberle, UEFA's disciplinary secretary, hit back, 'That was not technically possible because of the time involved. We are determined to clamp down on the problems of English supporters.' Meanwhile, Hammers Supporters' Club chairman Tom Jenkinson warned, 'It won't matter if they play 1,000 miles from Upton Park, our lads will get there. Everyone blames the Spanish fans for starting the trouble and I think they should be banned from coming over.'

With Sunderland's Roker Park seeming the likely venue for Castilla's visit to England, a four-man delegation from West Ham –

including Lyall and Blower – flew to UEFA's headquarters in Zurich to argue their case: that the club could only be held responsible for legitimate fans who had obtained their tickets through them. Accepting the club's plea but wanting to send a message out to unruly fans, UEFA scrapped the original penalties and declared that the Castilla game could indeed take place at Upton Park – behind closed doors. 'At least our players will be in familiar surroundings,' shrugged Chapman, although there would be nothing familiar about the ghostly atmosphere at the Boleyn Ground on 1 October.

It was estimated that West Ham would lose around £60,000 in gate receipts from a game that would be watched by just 262 people, with each club being restricted to 70 officials and the extras being made up of official observers, reporters, photographers, ballboys and a handful of policemen. One switchboard operator, eager to see the game, joked, 'I said I'd hide in the ladies but they've threatened to flush everyone out.'

More worrying than the financial losses was how on earth the Hammers could be inspired to overturn a 3–1 deficit without the traditional roar of the Upton Park crowd. Lyall set up two full-scale practice matches, telling the reserves to 'tackle, chase and harry' the first-team players in a bid to create the spirit of competitive action in isolated surroundings. Meanwhile, the ballboys were instructed to keep on their toes as it would suit Castilla to see time wasted with the ball stuck under empty seats.

With Brooking ignoring medical advice to take a two-week rest with a groin problem, West Ham displayed their superior class to score three first-half goals through Pike, Cross and Paul Goddard. Although Miguel Bernal's long-range strike for the Spaniards took the game into extra-time, two further goals by Cross – as he claimed a historic hat-trick – saw the Hammers win 6–4 on aggregate. 'Football without the crowd and the atmosphere is unthinkable – like Jimmy Hill without a beard,' reported Gordon Ogilvie.

Lyall reflected on the episode by describing UEFA's idea to play the game behind closed doors as 'absolutely brilliant', believing it served as a strong deterrent to hooliganism. 'Soccer has got to win this fight,' he said. 'There is not the slightest doubt in my mind that

Wednesday night at Upton Park was a triumph for football.'

West Ham's European adventure continued with a 4–1 aggregate victory against Romanian outfit Poli Timisoara in the second round, while 34,957 fans at the Boleyn Ground gave a standing ovation to Dynamo Tblisi after a stunning display of technical football in their 4–1 first-leg win. The Hammers claimed a surprise 1–0 success in the Soviet Union as they said goodbye to the competition, yet it's their two games against Castilla that will, sadly, always be remembered for making the headlines during the Cup Winners' Cup campaign.

Getting Shirty

'I really didn't know what was right and wrong'
– Paul Ince, November 1997

THE WEST HAM dream team from the last 30 years has some dead certs – Trevor Brooking, Alan Devonshire, Paolo Di Canio, Rio Ferdinand, Julian Dicks, Alvin Martin; some very probables – Tony Cottee, Joe Cole, Billy Bonds; and some contentious pub argument fodder – Phil Parkes or Ludek Miklosko, Ray Stewart or Tim Breacker, John Hartson or Frank McAvennie?

One area of the pitch, above all, presents some serious head scratching for those for whom scribbling a dream team on the back of an envelope is a periodic guilty pleasure. Who's going to do the ball winning for the other midfielders to do their Academy creative stuff? Billy Bonds was a centre-back during this era so can't really be considered; Scott Parker, although Hammer of the Year twice running, arguably needs another season or two to cement his name into the annals; Geoff Pike, John Moncur or Steve Lomas? Not quite up to the mark. Nigel Reo-Coker? Er, nope.

There is a contender who has a cast-iron case for his hyper-competitiveness, his ferocious spirit, his intelligent passing and big-game goals. Yet to contemplate scribbling his name down would be seen not so much as guilty pleasure as an outrageous act of treason.

In 1988, Paul Ince exploded into the sporting headlines with two goals for West Ham in a 4–1 Littlewoods Cup win over Liverpool, the Reds' biggest cup defeat in fifty years. Yet it was an incendiary display of an altogether different kind just a few months later that marked Ince out as the most reviled man ever to play for the club. Overnight, he became the original Upton Park anti-hero, the man who set the bar at a height only Frank Lampard Jnr has ever come close to reaching.

Long after his playing career came to an end, Ince continues to get grown men in a lather for posing in a Manchester United shirt in a national newspaper while still a West Ham player. To a significant majority of supporters he will always be the 'Boleyn Betrayer', 'the Guv'nor Grotesque of Green Street', 'the Arrogant Arch-Villain of Upton Park'. Or, to cut to the chase . . . 'Judas'.

That the picture being painted is pantomime-esque reflects the fact that more than 20 years have elapsed since Ince's error of judgement par excellence. The abuse he suffered on his latter visits as a player for Wolves and manager for Blackburn was, in the main, closer to 'boo-ya-hiss' than the kind of unprintable vitriol and threats he endured on his earlier returns to E13 with Manchester United.

Chucking insults at Ince has become a rite of passage, passed on from father to son, mother to daughter. It may not be pretty, but allowing your passions to run away with you is the essence of modern football, something Ince knows all about from hundreds of overzealous tackles and spats with opponents and referees, during an illustrious career with United, Inter Milan, Liverpool, Middlesbrough, Wolves, England . . . and West Ham.

In keeping with Tony Carr, the coach who developed him and who rates Ince as his best ever youth product, and the manager who nurtured him, John Lyall, West Ham fans should, in theory, be immensely proud that Ince went on to captain England and become the first black manager of a Premier League team – however short-lived his tenure at Ewood Park. Yet unlike the players and management who knew him personally and could, therefore, be philosophical about his messy departure from Upton Park in September 1989, for the supporters he was an idol, a home-grown gem of immense potential who, through accident or not, ended up committing a major indiscretion against the shirt they could only ever fantasise about wearing.

For many, the gravest insult was that Ince took so long to apologise for his misdemeanour. It wasn't until November 1997, in an expansive interview with Tony McDonald in the club magazine, that Ilford's most infamous son finally expressed sorrow. 'I was young and it's something I regret. I just hope that the fans accept now that people make mistakes. It was a long time ago . . . '

Ince insisted that naivety and misunderstanding, rather than calculation and arrogance, were to blame for the Man Utd shirt pose that was published in the *Daily Express* soon after the Hammers were relegated at the end of the 1988–89 season. Lyall, a mentor to the 21 year old, had been sacked and unhappy Ince was receiving tentative overtures from Old Trafford.

A holiday in the sun set one of football's greatest fiascos rolling. It was apparently suggested by his advisers that as he was going away for a few weeks, Ince should have his picture taken wearing a Manchester United shirt, just in case a deal was completed between the two clubs during the holiday.

'I didn't really want to have the photo taken but I went along with it,' claimed Ince. 'People forget that I was still very young at the time. I really didn't know what was right and wrong.'

Lawrence Lustig of the *Daily Star* took the exclusive picture, the snapper being instructed that if the move to United didn't come about, then it must not be released. With the *Daily Express* sharing the same photo library a colossal mix-up ensued, according to Ince. 'That's how it came to appear in the *Express* . . . and it caused murders!'

With his protracted move to Old Trafford not even out of the starting blocks, Ince returned from holiday as both a West Ham player and Public Enemy No. 1. 'I can understand the fans' reactions, because it wasn't a nice thing [for me] to do,' he continued. 'When the pre-season friendlies started, half the Hammers fans were telling me "don't go", while the other half were saying "piss off!"' Or words to that effect.

To add to the youngster's troubles, new West Ham boss Lou Macari also effectively told Ince to piss off when the player approached him about a pay rise he claimed had been agreed with Lyall before he'd gone on holiday and which would have quadrupled his £250 per week wage. In 2010, Ince revealed in the *News of the World* that he could hold a grudge as long as any West Ham fan. 'I had no respect for him then and absolutely nothing has changed . . . he can go rot' – seemingly also suggesting that it was Macari and not Lyall's sacking, the lure of Old Trafford or the rabid derision of thousands of Hammers fans, which prompted his exit from the club.

As expected, in the first game of the 1989–90 season, away to Stoke City, Ince suffered a torrent of abuse and Macari decided it was unwise to play him in the cauldron of Upton Park for the subsequent home game against Bradford City. The scowl that so often featured on the marauding midfielder's face as he tore around the pitch now transposed itself onto the back pages with a dig about the fans that had turned on him. In describing a section of the support as 'morons' Ince seemed to be going out of his way to alienate himself, although he insisted that his comment was entirely justified given the abuse his wife Claire received when she attended a match at the Boleyn.

A matter of weeks later, Ince's 91-game, 11-goal West Ham career came to its inevitable end – with an extra dose of controversy. When Manchester United raised concerns about a previous injury apparently evident on X-rays, they offered to pay a mere £800,000 of a £1.7 million fee, the balance being met on a £5,000 pay-as-you-play basis. With Ince's position at Upton Park virtually untenable, United had West Ham over a barrel and hence the unsatisfactory deal was accepted.

Ince's first return as a United player came four seasons later in February 1994. 'Bubbles' didn't get much of a look-in that day as minds and voices were focused on giving Ince an atypical East End welcome home. As the script demanded, he got the equaliser in a 2–2 draw, while West Ham fans got castigated by some parts of the media for racially abusing the player. Not to forgive the mindless minority, but like so many elements of the whole ugly saga, ambiguity, exaggeration and contradiction won the day.

Subsequent appearances against the Hammers for a variety of clubs rarely passed without some incident worthy of media note, whether it be rich language from the terraces or fruity tackles on or by Ince.

The sense of betrayal still hangs heavy and, while the vitriol may have become a little more diluted with the passage of time, it doesn't take much to create heated argument between Ince's accusers and apologists.

The last word on the matter must surely go to the fans that share centre stage with the man himself in this curious panto. In the same issue of *Hammers News* in which Ince chose to express his feelings, supporters were given two pages to express theirs. While a couple said it was time to bury the hatchet, most were adamant that Ince should always remain a despised figure.

As Ian from east London put it: 'My kid might not even know why Ince gets stick, but I'll make sure he finds out. There are ways of leaving the club and whether it was bad advice or he was just a fool, he shouldn't have done it.'

Tony from Harrow perhaps located consensus best by saying, 'No, it's not time to forgive and forget. You don't wear the shirt of someone else while you're still with another club, it's as simple as that.'

The Class of '99

'There's quality oozing from every pore of every player!'
– Martin Tyler, May 1999

WHILE A host of multimillionaire household names milked the adoration during youth-team guru Tony Carr's testimonial game at Upton Park in May 2010, out in football's less glamorous reaches a certain bunch of modestly talented footballers could have been excused a wry chuckle.

West Ham's record-breaking FA Youth Cup final side of 1999 contained only two players, Joe Cole and Michael Carrick, who went on to truly fulfil their potential; the game's familiar potholes of injury, competition, poor decision making and sheer bad luck did for most of the others. Yet, every member of the Class of '99 can proudly boast that it was their collective heroics that gave Carr his highest high in 30 years as Academy boss.

The Hammers' performance against Coventry City, especially in the second leg of a televised final that they won by a 9–0 margin was, quite simply, electrifying. 'It was the pinnacle of my achievements as the youth-team manager,' stated Carr. 'I remember Frank Lampard Snr (then assistant manager to Harry Redknapp) saying to me after the game, "Enjoy the moment, it won't get much better than that!" He wasn't far wrong.'

The dazzling artistry and panache of Carr's kids even got to Sky Sports commentator Martin Tyler, who at one point exclaimed, 'There's quality oozing from every pore of every player!'

With the cushion of a 3–0 win at Highfield Road from the first leg, West Ham completed the 6–0 slaughter a week later at an Upton Park rocking with anticipation. The tie had to be delayed by fifteen minutes as only three sides of the ground had been opened and fans kept pouring in off Green Street to swell the crowd to 24,000. 'There was a realisation in east London that this game had to be seen,' said Tyler. 'The theatre of it was fantastic.'

Sam Taylor, Hammers' left wing-back on the night, concurred. 'We were sitting in the changing rooms before the game and you could hear the turnstiles in the West Stand going Bang! Bang! Bang! Tony just said to us, "Listen to that, boys. These people are coming to watch you."'

While the star attraction was undoubtedly Cole, the prodigiously gifted wonder-kid who had already appeared nine times for the first team, Carr insists that the side's terrific camaraderie was the secret of its success. In spite of a glittering career at Chelsea, Cole still rates the youth cup up there with his finest achievements. 'It's the best feeling ever because it's with all your mates. In the first team, the players come from all over the world but we had been together since we were ten. I was used to the big stadiums, but the lads, the excitement leading up to it . . . we ripped it.'

Drawn away in every round, Hammers saw off Stockport County, Walsall, York City, ever-precocious Arsenal and Everton, who had won the 1998 trophy. In the first leg of the final at Highfield Road, three second-half goals through defender Stevland Angus, striker Bertie Brayley, plus a stupendous chip from Adam Newton – arguably the best player over the two games – put the writing on the wall.

Game two and West Ham continued where they left off, Newton providing for Brayley to score after just three minutes. Twenty minutes later, on-fire Cole caused audible gasps in the crowd as he bamboozled his man-marker and fed Newton, who curled a beauty in off both posts. 'We were buzzing,' said Taylor. 'As soon as we went a couple of goals up, Coley and Carrick were wiping the floor with them.'

Before the break, Richard Garcia added a penalty, thereby notching a goal in every round. Carr remembered, 'At half-time I sat them down and told them, "You've won the FA Youth Cup, it's in the bag. They are not going to score six goals. What you need to do now is put on a five-star performance and show 24,000 people how good you really are."'

Acting on the gaffer's orders, West Ham's youngsters gleefully played 'keep ball', not through arrogance but because punch-drunk Coventry simply couldn't get the damn thing off them. 'All the lads were really good mates and most of us lived together,' said Carrick, one of the residents of the club's 'House of the Rising Sons' in Romford. 'We were just having a laugh on the pitch, everyone was playing brilliantly.'

In the 50th minute, Brayley latched on to a cute Carrick cut-back to bag three in the final overall. 'Ah, everything about that night . . . the atmosphere was unreal and the football was superb. It's a nice thing to have on my CV,' said Brayley. 'We were a tight-knit bunch, taught to play Total Football. Tony was a phenomenal coach and he was blessed to work with some talented players. Joey was always going to be a star. You felt Carrick was going to be a good player too. Adam Newton stood out with his pace, while at the back you had Stev Angus, our captain Izzy Iriekpen and Terrell Forbes – very athletic boys who could play football. It was like men v. boys.'

With fifteen minutes left, Geordie import Carrick, by now wearing a grin as wide as the Tyne Bridge, strode effortlessly past deflated Coventry defenders to make it five, then played a defence-splitting pass for Garcia to round things off and leave Cov keeper Chris Kirkland staring wistfully in the direction of the M1.

From his vantage point up in the gantry, Tyler was in no doubt that he had just witnessed something rather special. 'I've seen some fantastic players in Youth Cup finals over the years, but this was the most emphatic game.'

The final word has to go to Carr, who is adamant that West Ham finished the twentieth century with the best bunch of young players in the country. 'You get very few nights like that in your lifetime. I'm still trying to emulate it and I can't get anywhere near it . . . but there's still time yet.'

End of an Era

'John Lyall ran the club as if he was spending his own money'
– Alvin Martin, 2002

IT WAS typical of John Lyall's compassion for people that, when West Ham were relegated in 1989, his concern was more for others than himself. 'Relegation is such a disappointment because it affects so many people's lives,' he said. 'Managers, coaches and players can end up leaving the club and, when you take into account their families, it can create a tremendous amount of problems for people.'

Lyall was one of them, suffering the consequences after the Hammers dropped out of the top flight by being bluntly informed that his 34-year association with the club – as office boy, player, coach and manager – was over when the directors decided not to renew his contract. One of the first things he did following his dismissal was write a letter of gratitude to his players for their efforts. 'You get close to players and it's just nice to say thanks for what they did and that I was grateful,' he said. One such recipient was Julian Dicks – whose first full season at Upton Park coincided with the drop – and the full-back was appreciative of the gesture. 'I thought that was very nice because he didn't have to do that,' says Dicks. 'I spoke to John a few times on the phone and he said, "If you ever need advice, just ring me."'

It was another example of Lyall's selflessness that he chose to put talks about his own future on hold during the 1988–89 campaign in order to concentrate on West Ham's survival efforts. His faith in the club's board proved misplaced; equally, Lyall's loyalty to underachieving players undermined his efforts and eventually cost him the position he had cherished so much since taking charge in 1974.

Lyall showed great determination to succeed but a more self-seeking person would have cared less about a tug-of-war developing over his services and accepted a double-your-money offer to take charge at QPR in 1984. A manager with no concerns about the financial welfare of his club would have pressured his directors into spending big money when they were reluctant to do so. A man with little regard for his players as human beings would have denied them the chance to further their careers elsewhere if it was not in his club's best interest to let them go. A coach with less patience would have discarded some of his recruits as soon as they misplaced a pass or mistimed a tackle. And a boss preoccupied with his personal prospects would have pushed for a new contract while he still had substantial bargaining power.

In many respects, the beginning of the end of Lyall's reign at Upton Park – or certainly the start of the decline – came in the summer of 1986, after the Hammers had pushed Liverpool all the way for the league title and finished third. The club might have believed there was no need to fix something that wasn't broken, but in standing still they were always going to slip backwards; their failure to strengthen the squad at that time was a disastrous oversight. It was an ideal opportunity to exploit the club's success, but Lyall fought off the clamour for new signings by insisting, 'There's no point in buying players of a similar calibre to the ones we already have.'

With Tony Cottee and Frank McAvennie hogging the two striking positions, Lyall generously allowed Paul Goddard to make a £425,000 move to Newcastle to find the regular first-team football he deserved. Ultimately, it did West Ham few favours, especially when McAvennie's form deteriorated – not least because of his hedonistic lifestyle – to the extent that the previously prolific Scot scored just two goals in one 26-game period and the team eventually finished the 1986–87 season in a disappointing 15th place.

With McAvennie failing to score in nine outings at the start of the following campaign, Lyall allowed the striker to join his boyhood idols Celtic for a £750,000 fee in September 1987 while explaining, 'I didn't feel I could deny him the chance to fulfil an ambition.' A run of one win in the opening 12 games, including a 5–2 home defeat by Barnsley in the Littlewoods Cup, had the tabloids talking of a 'crisis', with images of the club's cracked crest splashed all over their pages. With Cottee forced to operate as a lone striker until Leroy Rosenior was signed from Fulham for £275,000 in March 1988, another season of struggle was inevitable. Thankfully, a memorable 4–1 home win against Chelsea in the penultimate game proved enough to see the Hammers finish 16th and avoid the relegation play-off spot on goal difference.

The warning lights were flashing, however, and they were no less dimmed when legendary skipper Billy Bonds retired and West Ham accepted a British record £2.2 million bid from Everton for a disillusioned Cottee, who naturally wanted to play for a club with more obvious ambition. With Walsall's David Kelly signed as a £600,000 replacement, it meant the Hammers were pinning their hopes on two strikers who had spent most of the previous season playing in the Third Division. It was a recipe for disaster and, with just three league wins to their name by Christmas, it was no surprise that West Ham found themselves at the bottom of the table. 'It's time John Lyall stepped aside,' insisted former Hammer John Bond. 'There are too many old faces at the place and changes need to be made.'

The problem, particularly in light of several key injuries, was the contribution of some of the new faces, with low-grade signings such as Gary Strodder (£100,000, Lincoln), Tommy McQueen (£150,000,

Aberdeen) and Allen McKnight (£250,000, Celtic) proving woefully inadequate, while injury-plagued midfielder Stewart Robson represented an expensive flop after his £700,000 arrival from Arsenal. It was McKnight and Kelly who incurred the fury of the fans as West Ham plunged towards relegation, while the papers conjured up the term 'McKnightmare' for the error-prone goalkeeper.

Dicks, a £300,000 signing from Birmingham, was a rare success (along with Arsenal legend Liam Brady after his £100,000 arrival from Ascoli), but he admits it wasn't easy for some of the other new recruits. 'McKnight came in for a lot of stick,' he says. 'For us to be bottom we were all making mistakes, but he got singled out and took a lot of the blame for the position we were in. It would have been better if John Lyall had changed things sooner rather than later, but he gave McKnight more games and he got worse and worse. I liked Kelly but he was another one who got hammered.'

Kelly and Rosenior mustered just 13 league goals between them during the 1988–89 season but Lyall later defended the club's transfer policy. 'That's the way that West Ham had to do it,' he said. 'With people like Mark Ward and Frank McAvennie, we bought them cheap and they became more valuable. Kelly and Rosenior were replacing two international footballers – it's not easy to replace Geoff Hurst, is it? We did lose some very important players but you can't just say you're going to spend X amount to replace them. It has to be done over time.'

Yet time was not on West Ham's side and, although a whopping £1.25 million was spent on bringing McAvennie back from Celtic in March in a late act of desperation, it was asking too much to rescue a side that went into their final ten games that many points adrift of safety. With Rosenior and Alan Dickens scoring vital goals, however, the Hammers dug incredibly deep to win five games out of six and keep their necks above water, so the last thing they needed was a final-day trip to title-chasing Liverpool. Rosenior wiped out John Aldridge's opener but, with the Hammers pushing forward for the winner they needed, Liverpool exploited the space at the back to win 5–1 and send West Ham down. 'We found the form too late,' reflected Lyall. 'The biggest disappointment was the Liverpool game. You fight so hard to try and succeed and when you fail it's very difficult to accept.'

West Ham had remained loyal to Lyall when relegated in 1978, as they had done when injury cruelly ended his promising playing career in 1964, but with his deal about to expire his future looked less secure this time around. Chairman Len Cearns had claimed Lyall's fate did not depend on survival, saying, 'Whether we stay up or not will not alter our consideration about John's contract.' That would indicate the club had already decided to make changes because, on Monday, 5 June 1989, the manager was summoned to the chairman's house in Chigwell and told that 'a majority decision' had been taken to let him go. 'Fair enough, Mr Len,' said Lyall, who rejected the offer of a second testimonial. 'I felt the supporters of West Ham had done enough for me,' he said.

The Hammers duly issued a statement to confirm the 49 year old's departure saying, 'The directors would like to thank John Lyall for his loyal service to the club. The vacant position will be advertised.' In recognition of his efforts, which included two FA Cup successes, runners-up campaigns in the European Cup Winners' Cup and League Cup, as well as promotion and the club's highest ever finish, Lyall received a £100,000 golden handshake and was allowed to keep his company Mercedes. John later admitted that he was 'upset but not angry' by what had taken place. 'There was no bitterness, just a feeling of sadness. I have no regrets,' he said.

Defender Alvin Martin was particularly shocked by the club's decision to dispense with Lyall's vast knowledge and experience. 'Everyone assumed John would remain at the club and end up stepping up to the board in years to come,' he said. 'I phoned him but didn't know what to say apart from that I was devastated.' Martin does not blame Lyall for failing to build on the 'Boys of '86' side that came so close to winning the league title. 'I wouldn't accept any criticism of John,' he said. 'You have to understand the restrictions he had. West Ham never had the finance to pay for the best. To his credit, John ran the club as if he was spending his own money. Another manager would have demanded millions to spend or been off, but John was never going to do that.'

Lyall returned to management at Ipswich Town in 1990 and guided the Suffolk side to the Division Two title and promotion, before taking the 'upstairs role' at Portman Road that many believe he should have been offered at Upton Park. Goalkeeper Phil Parkes, who joined Lyall at Ipswich for a short period, described him as 'the best manager I ever played under', while former Hammers team-mate Ray Stewart shares his respect. 'John was a great manager and I learned a lot from him,' he said. 'A lot of people who left West Ham to join other clubs were made more professional in their outlook because of what they learned from John. It was all about keeping good habits.'

Poker in the Rear

'The gambling did get a bit out of hand'
– Matthew Etherington, February 2010

WEST HAM had enough players on their treatment table in the autumn of 2008 without worrying about one of their stars getting his legs broken owing to unpaid gambling debts. So it came to light that the club had advanced a figure of £300,000 to Matthew Etherington after the winger revealed he had the heavies breathing down his neck. A Hammers source was reported as saying, 'The club decided it had no choice but to help Matthew. He's been a very worried young man.'

The figure amounted to around fifteen weeks' wages for the former Hammer of the Year, whose extremes of form during his five years at Upton Park suggested he often had more than football on his mind. Never mind the next right-back he was up against, it was beating the bookmaker that generally proved his biggest problem. If that wasn't disturbing enough, he was also handing over fistfuls of cash to his team-mates prior to kick-off as the squad's pre-match entertainment on journeys up and down the country included several rounds of poker. West Ham had stopped short of emblazoning the team bus with the slogan 'liquor in the front, poker in the rear', but there were some hedonistic habits taking place behind those dark-tinted windows.

As Etherington admitted, 'It did get a bit out of hand. You could win or lose 20 grand on a single journey, which is ludicrous.' It was just as well that FA rules prevented players from betting on their own matches, because the Hammers would have lost a fortune if they were backing themselves to win, with the card schools doing little to improve either the mood of individuals or the relationships between them. 'How can you prepare for a game when you are playing cards on the bus with lots of money changing hands?' said Etherington. 'If you're losing money, you're going to resent the person taking it from you.'

Alans Pardew and Curbishley both attempted to remove the threat posed to the reputation and spirit of the club by the gambling culture. The first headlines to indicate that a problem existed appeared in November 2006, when second-choice goalkeeper Roy Carroll was admitted to London's £4,000-a-week Capio Nightingale Hospital. Seeking to get his drinking and gambling excesses under control, the Northern Irishman still found time to display his sense of humour by checking in under the name of Jonathan (Johnnie) Walker.

Pardew was sympathetic to the keeper, insisting, 'We fully support Roy – he has gone about tackling his issues in the right way.' However, the manager was also concerned about the wider issues, with it being alleged that Carroll owed a big-name team-mate £30,000 – peanuts to top-flight footballers but a year's salary for most of the people who watched them. 'What has come out of Roy's problem is that there is gambling going on within the group and I have to sort it out before it becomes a bigger issue,' declared Pardew.

Just weeks later, with a string of poor results suggesting considerable disharmony within the camp, Pardew was handed his cards. The task of getting to grips with the problem fell to successor Curbishley, who could have been forgiven for thinking he had taken over at a millionaire's borstal rather than a football club. One player, who preferred to remain unnamed when referring to the gambling epidemic, claimed, 'The atmosphere is dreadful and people don't talk to one another – it's one big mess here.' Within a few months of the new manager's arrival it was reported that a second West Ham player was undergoing treatment, with Etherington spending time at the Sporting Chance Clinic, the Hampshire-based organisation founded by former Arsenal and England captain Tony Adams, to help sports people deal with their compulsions. 'As anyone who has suffered an addiction illness will know, this is not a problem that will disappear overnight,' said the winger. Prophetic words, for as he later admitted, 'Within six to nine months I was gambling again.'

Etherington later revealed he owed 'about £800,000' at one stage, although he calculated that his total gambling losses – thanks to dogs, horses, card schools and online poker – amounted to at least £1.5 million. It was small beer by comparison, but being hit with a £2,000 fine by Harlow magistrates for a drink-driving offence can't have improved his mood. It's safe to say that his transfer fee to Stoke City in January 2009, when it was decided a change of environment would help him, was not much more than the estimated amount of money he'd spent in pursuit of the buzz that football failed to provide. 'The illness will always be there,' he stated in February 2010, 'and I know it is waiting for me to get complacent.'

His former boss Curbishley had done everything he could to change the culture at Upton Park by imposing a ban on card schools while the players were under his supervision, but he could exert little influence over their post-training activities and it was reported that the manager fell out with one senior player after he took nearly £40,000 from a team-mate during one afternoon's session of poker.

Gambling was just one of several cancers eating away at the club as Curbishley tried to lift West Ham away from relegation danger in the early months of 2007. A number of unsavoury stories – with booze flowing as an undercurrent – hit the headlines during a season of struggle, to suggest that the players had lost their focus and badly needed bringing back into line.

Defender Anton Ferdinand brought the issue of player discipline firmly into the spotlight when it was revealed that he had broken a club curfew during the campaign to fly to the United States to celebrate his 22nd birthday. To make matters worse, he had allegedly told West Ham he had simply gone to the Isle of Wight to visit his sick grandmother, when the reality was that he'd taken a 9,000-mile round-trip to South Carolina. The defender might have got away with his unauthorised jaunt had he not been recognised by a Hammers fan – in a club called Knock Knock – who broke the story of his partying to the *News of the World*. 'I've made a stupid mistake,' admitted a contrite Ferdinand after being hit in the pocket to the tune of a fortnight's wages.

It was hardly the kind of publicity Ferdinand – the younger brother of former Hammers star Rio – needed, coming just a few months after being arrested and charged with assault occasioning actual bodily harm following an incident outside Ilford's Faces nightclub. He was cleared unanimously of any wrongdoing after a jury accepted that his actions had been in self-defence. He was also worried about the safety of his £64,000 watch – as anyone would be.

Ferdinand was perhaps right to be nervous, having – along with team-mate Nigel Reo-Coker – seen around £37,000 worth of watches, jewellery and mobile phones stolen from them the previous season following an alleged dispute over a girl's telephone number outside a south London club called Escapades. A 23-year-old semi-professional footballer playing for Croydon Athletic was subsequently jailed for two years.

The gambling and nightclubbing of West Ham's players did little to boost the image of the club around this time, but the honour of the biggest indiscretion surely goes to Shaun Newton, who won himself a seven-month ban from football in 2006 for taking cocaine.

The winger, a £125,000 signing from Wolves, failed a random drugs test after the 1–0 FA Cup semi-final win against Middlesbrough on 23 April 2006 – although the matter only entered the public domain when an FA disciplinary hearing took place three months later. It was duly announced that his ineligibility began on 20 May, the date on which Newton had been charged. Many felt the punishment was too lenient given that half the suspension would be eaten up by the close-season period – and was one month shorter than Manchester United defender Rio Ferdinand's ban for missing a drugs test in 2003.

An apologetic Newton insisted it was 'an isolated incident' that came about as a result of 'going through a difficult time personally'.

He added, 'I have let down the gaffer who is also a friend of mine.' Some suspected that had Newton's relationship with Pardew not been so strong – the two played together at Charlton in the mid 1990s – the outcome might have been different. Pardew admitted the episode had 'put a stain on our achievements', adding, 'We will stand by Shaun at this difficult time.' The attitude was in stark contrast to London rivals Chelsea, who sacked £16 million striker Adrian Mutu and goalkeeper Mark Bosnich when they failed drug tests after powdering their noses.

West Ham's head of technical support Niall Clark insisted the club could not 'condone the taking of performance-enhancing drugs or stimulants' but one joker quipped that if cocaine was performance enhancing then Newton should have complained because it clearly hadn't been working. Upon his return in January 2007, the 30 year old made just five appearances – four as substitute – before joining Leicester City on a free transfer.

Cynics suggested that West Ham were careful not to establish a dangerous precedent in case more valuable commodities ever found themselves in such a position. Indeed, former Hammers striker Jimmy Greaves said, 'It begs the question of how many other players enjoy a sniff and a puff . . . '

■■■■■■■■■■■■■■■■■■■

Pard Luck Story

'There were reasons why I had to do it' – Eggert Magnusson,
December 2006

ALAN PARDEW'S face was almost as grey as his hair as he stepped onto the pitch in the freezing cold air after West Ham's Carling Cup defeat at Chesterfield in October 2006. If any game suggested that the manager had lost the plot it was this one, with an ill-conceived team selection playing into the hands of the struggling League One outfit, who took full advantage to add another tale of horror to the

Hammers history books. It was as if Pardew knew it as well, as he offered little in the post-match press inquest to suggest he might be able to figure out how to dig West Ham out of the deep hole they found themselves in after eight successive defeats – a club record in one season. Yet, contrary to popular opinion, it seemed that it wasn't just bad results that ultimately cost the boss his job at Upton Park.

Pardew had first acknowledged his neck was on the line during the 2006–07 season after watching his side lose 2–0 at Portsmouth on 14 October, a result that dropped West Ham into the relegation zone and set a new club record of failing to score in a run of six successive defeats. Prior to the visit to Fratton Park, the Hammers had been knocked out of the UEFA Cup over two legs by Palermo and beaten by Newcastle, Manchester City and Reading in the Premier League.

'I think any manager who has lost six successive games has to have a certain amount of fear for his job,' he admitted. His prospects only looked bleaker when a 1–0 defeat at Tottenham the following weekend meant that West Ham had collected just five points from their opening nine games – three less than in the 2002–03 campaign when they were eventually relegated.

It was all such a far cry from the end of the previous season, when everybody was singing the club's praises for finishing ninth upon their return to the Premier League and taking Liverpool to a penalty shoot-out in one of the most scintillating FA Cup finals ever. The media focused on two likely causes for the sudden decline – the difficulty of integrating Argentina internationals Carlos Tevez and Javier Mascherano into the squad, following their shock and unorthodox arrival, and the prolonged speculation regarding a club takeover – but the reality was that it was more a case of two groups of reasons; those publicised and those not.

The absence of striker Dean Ashton, who had broken his ankle while on England duty, was always going to undermine the West Ham attack. As assistant boss Peter Grant admitted, 'We were playing quite well but the natural instinct to put the ball in the back of the net wasn't there. And as we lost games the confidence started to drain.'

Other players such as Danny Gabbidon, Yossi Benayoun, Anton Ferdinand and Matthew Etherington saw their preparations for the season undermined by injury, while it's also fair to say the Hammers didn't enjoy much in the way of luck during the opening months. The defeat at Spurs typified their misfortune, with Mido scoring in the third minute of first-half injury time when only 60 seconds had been signalled and former Hammer Jermain Defoe somehow avoiding a red card despite clearly biting Mascherano on the arm – a bizarre incident that even made the front pages.

Pardew complained that games were always going to be an uphill struggle if the team kept conceding the opening goal, as they did in ten of their first eleven outings, but suspicions were growing that the manager's constant shuffling of his cards – in a desperate bid to find a winning hand – was proving counterproductive. This was particularly apparent in attack, where he deployed five strikers in an astonishing eleven different permutations (including substitutions) in as many games.

If this was disorientating for supporters, it was no less confusing for forwards Tevez, Marlon Harewood, Bobby Zamora, Carlton Cole and Teddy Sheringham, who didn't know if they were coming or going. 'I've got to try and find the right formula but it's difficult,' admitted Pardew, while Tevez complained, 'I'm here to help but playing out of my role puts me under pressure.'

The poor form of Nigel Reo-Coker was another factor, with the captain's head appearing to drop after the Hammers ignored interest from bigger clubs for his services. Meanwhile, a culture of complacency had developed since the success of the previous season with too many players believing they had already established themselves as Premier League stars. Defender Gabbidon, one of the most candid men in the squad, admitted, 'Maybe the players thought we were better than we really were. We definitely haven't worked as hard as a team. The hunger we had last season hasn't been as evident and maybe there was a complacency there.' Experienced team-mate Christian Dailly could only concur. 'There's no doubt that some of the boys took their foot off the gas,' he said. 'If you begin to ease up, then you can end up in trouble.'

The autumn departure of assistant boss Grant, who took charge of Championship outfit Norwich City, probably had a greater effect than outsiders might have realised, but all the focus was on Pardew, who some believed had also become consumed by the increased acclaim and adulation in recent times. It was reported that he shocked his squad by arriving for training in a Ferrari – understandable for the players, but less appropriate for a manager who needed to retain authority. It was also alleged that he'd put a few noses out of joint by referring to his wealthy status (having reportedly earned over £1.5 million including bonuses over the previous year or so) when berating the team after one home defeat. With the *Daily Mirror* later referring to 'Internet rumours' unsettling the dressing-room at that time, it would appear that Pardew possibly had things on his mind other than where West Ham's next goal was coming from.

A lack of focus might be one reason why the West Ham teamsheet for the cup game at Chesterfield on 24 October had such a cockeyed look to it. With Kyel Reid, 18, being handed his first and only start of the season and full-back George McCartney making his debut, the left side of the team had an untried and untested feel, while Reo-Coker's deployment on the right ignored the fact he had looked unhappy in the role at Tottenham a few days beforehand. With defender Dailly being named alongside holding midfielder Hayden Mullins in the middle of the park, it was no surprise that there was little attacking thrust from the core of the team – although Harewood did end the club's 672-minute goal drought to put the Hammers ahead in the fourth minute.

However, goals by Colin Larkin and Caleb Folan saw the Spireites secure a famous victory to leave a nation of live TV viewers chuckling once again at West Ham's misery. Hammers chairman Terence Brown denied that he had accused his players of performing 'like a pub team' when visiting the dressing-room – not that he'd have been wrong in doing so – and insisted he'd wrapped a comforting arm around Pardew's shoulder and told him that 'everything will be fine'.

The newspapers inevitably speculated that the manager would be collecting his P45 if West Ham failed to avoid defeat against

Blackburn at home in their next game, but the reality was that, with a takeover of the club becoming a probability rather than a possibility, Pardew's position was always going to be preserved until such time that the owner's keys changed hands. The Hammers duly beat Rovers 2–1 to register their first victory in a dozen outings and followed that up with a 1–0 home win against Arsenal that was overshadowed by a touchline spat between Pardew and rival boss Arsene Wenger, who seemed to resent the idea of anybody celebrating Harewood's last-minute strike.

The two wins represented a false dawn, however, with West Ham losing four of their next five matches – the lone success being a 1–0 home win against Sheffield United, on 25 November, that marked the arrival of new owner Björgólfur Guðmundsson and chairman Eggert Magnusson. The latter had described Pardew as 'a great manager' – understandable given his previous achievements – and added, 'I fully believe he will help me take West Ham to the next stage.' Indeed, it had been stated in the official sale agreement of the club that the new owners' intention was 'to retain Alan Pardew as manager' – a pledge that had won the approval of the outgoing directors. Yet it would be just a matter of weeks before Magnusson broke his word, having found reason to revise his view.

Events came to a head after an injury-hit Hammers side – with McCartney partnering James Collins in central defence – collapsed to a 4–0 defeat at Bolton on 9 December. Kevin Davies scored twice before further goals by El-Hadji Diouf and Nicolas Anelka prompted home fans to regale Pardew with chants of 'you're getting sacked in the morning' – yes, that old chestnut. The debacle saw West Ham set a new club record of ten successive away defeats in a single season, and Pardew's usual bullishness in adversity was noticeably absent after the game. Although he insisted 'we're a lot better than we're suggesting', it effectively amounted to an admission that he was failing to get the best out of his players.

The result gave Magnusson the perfect opportunity to take action and Pardew was summoned to a meeting at Upton Park two days later, when he was told his services were no longer required. 'We can say you're leaving by mutual consent,' suggested Magnusson, but

Pardew rejected the offer in the belief that it would look like he had thrown in the towel. 'I wasn't going to accept that because I thought I could turn things around,' he later revealed. A severance package, reported to be worth around £1 million, was subsequently agreed on the remaining three-and-a-half years of his contract.

West Ham issued a statement on the afternoon of 11 December to confirm the manager's departure. 'The chairman and board have been concerned by the performances of recent weeks and feel it's the right time to make a change in the best interests of the club,' it said. At the same time, Pardew took the opportunity to draw attention to his achievements in his three years at the club, but later admitted, 'I felt aggrieved that I left West Ham too early. I felt there was no situation where they would get relegated.' That might have been the case, but the fact was that he had lost 13 of his last 16 games and few managers survive that kind of statistic.

The club's new Icelandic owners were accused of panicking about the financial impact of relegation, with the new £1.7 billion Sky-Setanta deal being worth around £40 million to each Premier League club every year. John Barnwell, the chief executive of the League Managers' Association, believed the decision to sack Pardew was 'worrying', while Reading chairman John Madejski, his old boss, went as far as to describe the culling as 'brutal'. Former assistant Grant was also very disappointed to hear the news. 'It left a bitter taste in my mouth,' he said. 'And it seemed the change had been made without looking at the full picture, which was rather strange.'

However, it appears there could have been unpublicised reasons as to why Pardew had lost the support of Guðmundsson and Magnusson so quickly. Up in the Boleyn Ground's trophy room, Magnusson admitted he could not reveal his full motives for making the change, which saw Alan Curbishley quickly arrive as Pardew's successor. 'There were reasons why I had to do it and I will keep those to myself,' he said. 'You have an obligation to make the change if things are not right.'

Perfect Ten

'It went like a blur, but it was absolutely fascinating'
– Trevor Brooking, April 2009

THE SIGN of a true superhero is when even their mistakes seem touched with genius. 'It's end-to-end stuff, but from side to side,' is one of Trevor Brooking's howlers from his days as a BBC co-commentator, yet even this gaffe has a gentlemanly creative quality to it that brings a tear to the eye of anyone who watched West Ham between 1967 and 1984.

For a club where so much seems to go wrong, Brooking was, and remains, a shining beacon of 'rightness'. Ordinarily, such a squeaky clean persona might begin to grate, but not where Sir Trev is concerned. His presence on a football field was such a unique delight, his influence on West Ham so wide-ranging, that he can be forgiven most anything.

There is no doubt that, to the man in the street, Brooking the player is defined by the header which allowed West Ham to slay mighty Arsenal in 1980. Frankly, that encapsulation is laughable, not to say irksome, to Hammers supporters. The FA Cup final header has huge significance in the history of the club, the lack of success since merely adding to its magnificence. Nevertheless, it was the freakish balance he possessed in his feet, hips and torso which did so much to turn Upton Park into a venue for true entertainment, not just sport, in the 1970s and early 1980s. Brooking always said it was important to let the ball do the work. Boy, did that ball work some magic in 635 games in the First Division, Second Division, FA Cup, League Cup and European Cup Winners' Cup.

At international level – where his 47 caps also seem laughable and irksome when compared to, say, Phil Neville's 59 – Brooking's great attacking understanding was with Kevin Keegan. At club level, it was with Alan Devonshire. Dev, with his pace and skill, and Trev, with his vision and control, complemented one another perfectly and, for the first four years of the time period covered by this book, the pair gave many West Ham fans their most memorable thrills. As someone who shared his ESP, Devonshire neatly sums up Brooking's talents. 'The amazing thing about Trevor was that opponents knew exactly what he was going to do, yet were powerless to do anything about it. They found it impossible to stop him.'

Those who take on the mantle of 'caretaker boss' are usually powerless to prevent an inevitable personal slide into, at best, the backroom, or worse, unpopularity and oblivion. Brooking being Brooking, he managed to emerge from two short spells at the West Ham helm in 2003 with his reputation not just intact but enhanced . . . and one of those spells ended in relegation!

Supporters and colleagues had long mused about the possibility of the former midfield maestro one day managing the club. Instead, his post-playing days had been dominated by *Match of the Day* punditry, chairing the funding body Sport England and running Colbrook Plastics Ltd, the company he had the typical foresight to form in 1970 when he was still trying to establish himself in the Hammers first team.

The closest he had come to an official role back at Upton Park was as a non-executive director, but that all changed when Hammers boss Glenn Roeder suffered a brain tumour in April 2003. In his three games in charge, Brooking achieved an away win over Manchester City, a sensational home victory against Chelsea, courtesy of a goal from back-in-favour Paolo Di Canio, and a 2–2 draw with Birmingham. Brooking later enthused, 'It was two and a half weeks of my life I will never forget. It went like a blur but it was absolutely fascinating. You can rabbit on in the TV studio all you want but when the decisions are down to you . . . well, you appreciate more about what the job demands. As soon as you finish one game your mind immediately drifts to the next one. It consumes you.'

His efforts were not enough to keep the Hammers up, but the passion shown on the pitch – and on the sidelines in the form of an uncharacteristically animated Brooking – stirred the soul of the Boleyn faithful. After the Man City game, his opposite number Kevin Keegan satisfied the press's curiosity about Brooking the boss, saying his old England buddy had been 'a nightmare' on the bench, frequently jumping up to appeal for fouls. 'Everybody has got passion and emotion in them. It just comes out in different ways – though I never heard Trevor swear.'

During his second spell in charge, after Roeder's sacking at the start of the new season, Brooking got well and truly into the gaffer groove, delighting the travelling fans at Gillingham with a blasphemous tirade after some sloppy West Ham play. Once again his record was impeccable – seven wins and just one defeat in eleven games – but taking on the job full-time was never an option, neither then nor six years later after Gianfranco Zola's sacking, when Brooking told the BBC, 'No, my family were never keen . . . they always said it would end up going sour at some stage. I enjoyed the spells but no, I think I shall wisely keep out of that and trundle off to watch the World Cup instead.'

Brooking attended South Africa 2010 in his capacity as director of football development with the FA, a role he had held since December 2003, just after his second stint as Hammers' caretaker boss. His remit, in a nutshell, is to guide the evolution of English football from grass roots to international level. As a technically gifted player himself, much of Brooking's work has focused on encouraging those who run junior football to work to a structure where skills and enjoyment are paramount, with the hope that these traits are carried through to Academy level and beyond. While some progress is evident, bickering between the various bodies involved in the administration and coaching of young footballers has resulted in Brooking both giving and taking criticism for the time it is taking for change to occur for the better.

What can never be in doubt about Brooking's philosophy towards playing, managing, coaching or administration is that he desperately wants football to live up to its reputation as 'the beautiful game'. His overall services to football were rewarded with a knighthood in 2004. 'This is a wonderful honour,' he said. 'My whole life has been about sport and my parents would have been chuffed to bits.' And back at Upton Park prior to the start of the 2009–10 season, the Centenary Stand – previously the 'North Bank', in front of which he had scored so many of his 102 club goals – was renamed The Sir Trevor Brooking Stand. 'This is my club, it will be my club forever,' he said in an emotional speech at the renaming ceremony.

For those who thrilled to Trevor's many achievements for West Ham – those who in one magazine poll rated him above even Bobby Moore as the all-time best Hammer and those who go weak at the knees watching replays of the goal he scored for England, when the ball miraculously wedged itself into the stanchion – former West Ham CEO Scott Duxbury has come closest to pinpointing The Meaning of Trev: 'He is not just one of our greatest ever players but also one of the country's best – and he continues to give so much back to the game in England.'

Billy Gets the Goat

'Harry keeps calling me a friend, but I don't see him as one'
– Billy Bonds, 1998

'CLOSURE' IS the kind of American-English jargon that is unlikely to ever trip from the tongue of Billy Bonds. With his socks rolled down, Bonds would no doubt be metaphorically tempted to kick such psychobabble into Row Z.

Roughly translated, closure is 'a feeling that an emotional or traumatic experience has been resolved'. To achieve it, it helps to talk through the offending experience with those involved, but Bonds has refused to speak to Harry Redknapp per se since the late summer of 1994, when the latter controversially replaced him as manager of West Ham.

Much as he appears to have lost respect for his old pal, Bonds stops short of blaming Redknapp for bringing a premature end to his illustrious 27-year association with the club. Instead, he blames himself for being 'a bad judge of character'. For his part, Redknapp swears blind that he did nothing to manipulate the circumstances that led to him being elevated from Bonds' assistant to the top job. 'I'd rather be out of work than have people saying I've stitched up my own mate.'

So the two main protagonists in this tale continue to stand at opposite ends of a bridge under which it appears too much water has flowed to imagine they will ever kiss and make up.

One of the saddest aspects of the saga is that, just 18 months after the death of Bobby Moore in 1993, following which the club was accused of neglecting its duties towards its greatest ever captain, its second greatest ever captain also found himself unsatisfactorily cut adrift from the place where he had contributed so much as a leader of men.

Managers come and managers go, but given his credentials as a player, Bonds parting from West Ham was always destined to cause emotional havoc of some kind or another. His name is woven so deeply into the fabric of the club that Bonds' roots as a Charlton Athletic player have effectively been erased from the minds of all those with West Ham associations.

As a fist-pumping warrior of a right-back, midfielder and finally centre-back, Bonds notched up a club record 793 senior appearances, his take-no-prisoners style always strangely at odds with West Ham's pushover reputation.

He played until he was 41 – and regrets not playing on into his mid forties, summing up the joy of football thus: 'There was no better feeling than that of battling with people to the point where they became deflated. I loved that side of the game . . . all you could say about me was that I got the job done.'

'Bonzo' led the side to two FA Cup triumphs and four major final appearances. He top-scored in season 1973–74 with 13 First Division goals. He twice came within one of his own mud-soaked whiskers of earning a full England cap and is widely recognised as the finest player never to achieve this honour. He was Hammer of the Year four times, was the first person to be awarded two testimonials by the club and was recognised with an MBE in 1988.

John Lyall once said of Bonds, 'He just keeps amazing me. He is the nearest thing I have seen to a football machine.' Alan Devonshire added, quite simply, 'There has never been a better professional.'

Courage and loyalty were bywords for the Woolwich-born player, and supporters of other teams often cited Bonds, ahead of Trevor Brooking, as the West Ham player they most coveted for their side. But behind the passionate playing style lay an unassuming personality, a family man who left others to bask in the limelight he did so much to create.

This intensely private streak in his character partly explains why, two years into his tenure as West Ham manager in 1992, he felt the need to appoint an ebullient personality like Redknapp as his right-hand man. Having experienced a relegation, a promotion, another relegation and the horrors of the Bond Scheme since replacing Lou Macari in February 1990, Bonds was in need of someone to come in and reinvigorate both the club and himself. With his tall, athletic frame hunched in the dugout, he seemed a beleaguered man at times. Who better, then, to help him tackle the ever-widening remit of the job than his former team-mate and best man at his wedding, Harry Redknapp, for whom things had gone stale at Bournemouth?

Despite West Ham being hot favourites to continue the yo-yo trend, the pair masterminded a return to the top flight in 1992–93 and achieved a respectable 13th-place finish, above Chelsea and Tottenham, in the following campaign. In August 1994, a pre-season tour of Scotland should have provided the perfect opportunity to galvanise the players and sow the seeds for Premiership consolidation in the months ahead. Yet, with the amount of intrigue, accusation and mistrust that was about to ensue, perhaps Ancient Rome would have been a better destination than Scotland.

Redknapp, who still lived in Dorset, had been approached by a consortium looking to invest in his former club Bournemouth; they were willing to offer him a huge financial stake as well as the manager's job. It was a tempting offer, but when Redknapp informed Bonds of his dilemma, Bonds apparently replied that if he was going to lose Harry, he might as well quit too. This is a version of events – one of many – that Bonds categorically refutes.

When Hammers chairman Terence Brown and managing director Peter Storrie – with whom Redknapp had established a good

Geoff Pike and Paul Allen lead the 1980 FA Cup final celebrations.

Cheat storm: John Lyall has an exchange of views with referee
Clive Thomas at the 1981 League Cup final.

The Bond Scheme: how not to win friends and influence people.

David Cross scores all four on a glorious night at White Hart Lane in 1981.

Behind the confrontational demeanour, Julian Dicks possessed great touch and technique.

Bobby Moore's death saw the Upton Park forecourt become
the focus for an outpouring of grief and respect.

Just what the doctor ordered: promotion left a sweet taste for Billy Bonds
and Harry Redknapp but a year later their relationship turned decidedly sour.

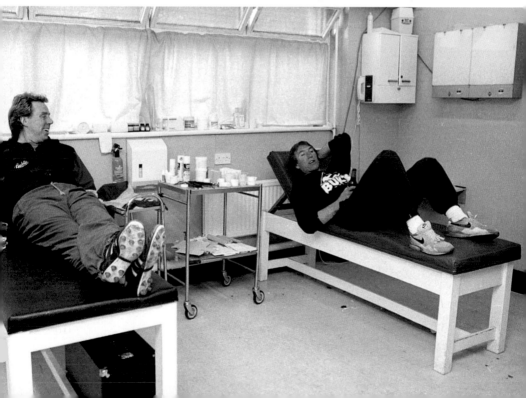

Dutch disaster Marco Boogers blew his big chance with West Ham in spectacular style.

How does it feel to get one of the mos glittering squads in the club's history relegated? Glenn Roeder' expression says it all

It's a love thing: passion was Paolo Di Canio's trademark during his four-year Hammers career.

Goal hero Bobby Zamora does the honours after victory in the
2005 play-off final at Cardiff's Millennium Stadium.

Alan Pardew's gifted young side take
he bus back to the Premier League.

Nigel Reo-Coker and Lionel Scaloni
celebrate but the 2006 FA Cup
final ended in disappointment.

If it's too good to be true, it probably is:
Alan Pardew unveils Carlos Tevez and Javier Mascherano.

Eggert Magnusson shows Björgólfur Guðmundsson how to wave to the crowd after the
Icelandic takeover in 2006. Social etiquette soon became the least of their worries.

Seven goals in the last ten games of the 2006–07 campaign, including a brilliant final-day strike versus Manchester United, ensured lasting idolatry for Carlos Tevez.

Tell me when it's all over: Alan Curbishley's reign as boss ended in September 2008 but the legal wrangling was far from finished.

Crowd trouble during a Carling Cup tie against Millwall in 2009 had Fleet Street's finest rushing to find a bandwagon.

Gianfranco Zola feels the strain
during a difficult tenure as manager.

Saviours: David Sullivan and
David Gold rescued the club from
financial meltdown in 2010

Robert Green's smile was rudely erased as he, Matthew Upson and
England experienced a calamitous World Cup in South Africa.

friendship – got wind of the Bournemouth offer, they drew up a plan which ultimately ensured Redknapp stayed at Upton Park. Having become aware that his role as assistant manager had expanded to the extent that Redknapp was overseeing much of the training, as well as the wheeler-dealing in the transfer market he so enjoyed, the West Ham board deduced that he was simply too good an asset to lose. Or to put it another way, they appeared to have decided that Harry's loss would be more damaging to the club than Billy's.

In Scotland, aware that news of the Bournemouth offer had been 'leaked' to the papers, a meeting was arranged by the Hammers hierarchy to clarify the options. Redknapp recalls in his autobiography that it was Bonds who said they had better go and see Brown and Storrie in Brown's hotel room. However Bonds, in *West Ham United: The Managers*, remembers a less spontaneous course of events: 'When I got to the room at six on the dot, everyone – the board members, Storrie and Harry – was already sat in the room. It stunk. I'm not a mug and I got the strong vibe that they had already discussed everything.'

Redknapp maintains in his autobiography that when Brown then raised the subject of him becoming manager and Bonds being appointed director of football, it was a bolt out of the blue. 'Things were getting very uncomfortable. This wasn't what I expected when I mentioned the offer from Bournemouth. In fact it was the last thing I wanted.' With Bonds' pride hurt badly – 'I didn't feel needed any more' – a decidedly frosty meeting finished with ambiguity hanging heavy in the air.

As if things weren't tense enough, at the same time Bonds was having to deal with the fall-out from the Joey Beauchamp fiasco, the star signing from Oxford United deciding on day two of his contract that West Ham wasn't for him. To the utter astonishment of many, apparently including Redknapp, on 10 August, aged 47 and feeling he still had much to offer as a manager, Bonds followed Beauchamp's lead: 'They were more or less saying to me, "We don't want you now. Harry will take over the running of the team but you can come and sit with us up in the directors' box." That wasn't for me. I just couldn't do it.'

Bonds resigned with a £500,000 pay-off on the three years left on his contract, while Redknapp was installed as the main man. Despite *The Sun* loudly suggesting on its back page that Bonds had been stabbed in the back, the early official line was that everyone was happy with the arrangement. Bonds was quoted as wishing Harry 'all the best' and Peter Storrie told the press, 'We wanted Bill to stay on as a director but he wanted a break. There are no hard feelings. It was difficult for Bill and Harry but their friendship is as strong as ever.' Bonds later insisted that the words used to announce his departure were not those he had approved. 'I had agreed with the chairman what was going to be put out but I know Harry changed it because it did not look good for him,' said Bonds. 'The revised statement said I was disillusioned with the game, which hardly helped my chances of getting a new job.'

As the weeks passed and Bonds had time to brood over the finer and, in his estimation, not so fine details of his departure (the 'loads of little things' that to Billy suggested his former number two had long coveted the number one role), the phrase 'no hard feelings' began to sound like a sick joke. So sick that the pair haven't spoken since, other than a bizarre phone call from Redknapp soon after he became boss asking if Bonds would pose for a PR picture with him. Billy later blasted, 'The thought of it sickened me.'

Publicly, Bonds kept his counsel for four years, but on publication of Redknapp's autobiography in 1998, he felt provoked into a reaction, in particular to a declaration from Redknapp that, in spite of the rancour, he would give Bonds a job back at West Ham without a moment's hesitation. 'Harry offer me a job at West Ham?' Bonds growled in the *Sunday Mirror*. 'He is taking the mickey. I find that totally embarrassing. I don't want to meet Harry or work with him again. He keeps calling me a friend but I don't see him as one.'

Redknapp insists that he did nothing to be ashamed of and that going to Bournemouth or staying as Billy's number two were the only things on his mind when he went to see the chairman in Scotland. 'The fact that Bill decided to resign was his decision,' he said. 'I spent three hours begging him not to do it . . . I don't suppose I ever will talk to Billy again but I know I've got a clear conscience.'

The awkward stand-off continues to prevail. Given the many controversies which have dogged Harry's subsequent managerial career at West Ham, Portsmouth, Southampton, Portsmouth again and Spurs, few Hammers fans would not have some sympathy with Bonds' take on the saga. Although he surmises that he may have got it all wrong and that perhaps there was indeed nothing underhand about the events leading up to 10 August 1994, Bonds says he is simply not prepared to give Redknapp the benefit of the doubt.

At the same time, equally few Hammers fans would disagree that the board's decision to appoint Redknapp wasn't, ultimately, the right one. Redknapp is indisputably an excellent manager; Bonds' subsequent career as a gaffer petered out with a whimper at Millwall.

This unfortunate episode may not have reached 'closure', but at least the remarkable playing career of Billy Bonds left nothing to question. Everyone, Redknapp included, agrees on that.

········

Thrilling Joke

'I ended up with too many floaters' – Harry Redknapp, May 1997

EVER HEARD the one about the 'genius', the 'horrible bloke', the 'glamour boy' and the 'big tart?' It's not a joke as such, but former West Ham boss Harry Redknapp has been known to trot out the tales of four players he signed in 1996 when looking to raise a laugh or two. The match-day walkouts, missed training sessions, badly scheduled shopping expeditions and gripes with government officials might have seen Harry grimacing rather than grinning at the time, but they have helped the likes of Paulo Futre, Florin Raducioiu, Ilie Dumitrescu and Daniel da Cruz Carvalho (otherwise known as 'Dani') retain a place in Hammers history that is distinctly disproportionate to their limited playing contributions. Their failure to live up to expectations as a result of poor fitness, attitude, temperament or lifestyle, reflects a period when West Ham's forays into the foreign market were hugely speculative. As Redknapp later admitted, he was buying 'second-hand motors with no MOTs'.

Futre certainly had plenty of miles on the clock having played for Sporting Lisbon, Porto, Atlético Madrid, Benfica, Marseille, Reggiana and AC Milan before rolling up onto the Upton Park forecourt in July 1996 on a free transfer. 'I don't think people realise how big a signing this is for West Ham,' whispered agent Jerome Anderson as the Portugal playmaker was introduced to the media, while Futre declared his 'love' for London. 'The city is so beautiful,' he said, clearly not having seen the East End. The thirty year old's accumulated transfer fees might have exceeded £20 million but the fact was that the forty-one-cap international had played just once in a year owing to a serious knee injury, while his record over the previous four seasons amounted to ten goals in thirty-three games for four different clubs. 'A genius doesn't have to run all over the field,' insisted Redknapp when it was questioned how much gas was left in the tank. 'We've just got to get the ball to him and he'll make something happen.'

It didn't take long for Futre's name to hit the headlines – for the wrong reasons – with it being reported that the Portu-geezer had stormed away prematurely from the opening-day game at Arsenal after learning he hadn't been allocated his favourite No. 10 shirt. 'What a load of cobblers,' said Harry, who claimed the player was injured and that his name had appeared on the initial teamsheet by mistake. 'I pick up the papers and have to spend the rest of my time answering to a silly story that somebody's made up,' he grumbled. 'Paulo can't speak English and I can't speak Portuguese so how are we supposed to have had a row?'

The reports were spot on, of course, but, in fairness to Redknapp, he had little choice but to stick to the same explanation he'd given referee Paul Durkin as to why his teamsheet needed amending. The manager set the record straight when appearing on stage at Jongleurs comedy club in Bow a couple of years later. 'We give Paulo the No. 16 shirt at Highbury and all I get is: "Me Futre, me No. 10!" The next thing we know is that he's hailed a cab and gone home!'

Futre would display his special talents in a memorable 2–1 home win against Southampton on 24 August, as he linked up with substitutes Raducioiu and Dumitrescu to inspire a second-half comeback that had the critics purring. The triumvirate was light years ahead of everybody else in terms of speed of thought and movement – not least striker Iain Dowie who might have had a Masters degree in engineering but was left looking like the village idiot as he struggled to join in.

Unfortunately, a pulled hamstring ended a run of four successive starts for Futre, while his ongoing knee problems restricted him to just four more outings as a substitute before the Hammers decided to activate the injury-related clause that allowed them to terminate his contract. 'I was in too much pain with my knee,' he conceded, while club physio John Green was scornful of the signing. 'I wouldn't have even let him train with the first team, let alone play for them,' he said.

Raducioiu, a £2.4 million signing from Espanyol, was also in pain after being introduced to the more brutal aspects of English football, via the elbow of Torquay defender Jon Gittens, when making his debut in a not-so-friendly pre-season game. The Romanian striker received rather more sympathy from Torquay chairman Mike Bateson, who fined his player two weeks' wages, than he did from his new manager, who accused him of 'jumping out of the way of every tackle'. Raducioiu had impressive credentials, having scored 21 goals in 35 games for his country – for which he starred at the 1994 World Cup finals in the USA – and whose recent clubs included AC Milan. The 26 year old had insisted he was ready for the Premiership, saying, 'I'm not worried about the physical side of things. I have faced some of the hardest defenders in Italy and Spain – it is all part of the game.'

Yet Redknapp immediately took a dim view of the player in a West Ham shirt. 'He had a terrible start and during pre-season it was obvious he didn't like the physical side of our game,' he said. 'He was always getting knocks and complaining.' Indeed, the manager would later use his autobiography to describe the striker as 'a fairy', adding, 'The players didn't take to him – they all thought he was a big tart. Futre poked him in the chest and said, "You are like a big girl, try being a man.'"

First-team starts were hard to come by and Raducioiu quickly became concerned about his international prospects. 'I can't stay on the bench,' he complained. 'I've been patient but I must play.' While Redknapp was proving hard to convince, the fans remained supportive of the striker they believed would prove his worth if only he was given an extended run. 'We want Radi on the pitch!' they chanted and felt duly vindicated when he made late appearances and scored wonderful solo goals against Manchester United and Sunderland in December.

Redknapp dismissed the second effort as 'not all that good', but by that time he'd already decided to get rid of Raducioiu after the striker famously failed to show up for the Coca-Cola Cup fourth-round replay at Stockport. After scoring in the first game against the Second Division outfit, the Romanian had apparently mentioned to journalists that he might be doubtful for the replay as his wife Astrid was due to give birth to their son. Yet the West Ham management was oblivious to his whereabouts as they tried in vain to make contact with him on their way to Edgeley Park. Redknapp would later – having admitted there were 'other reasons why I haven't played him and they will come out when I'm ready' – claim that a friend had 'spotted Raducioiu shopping with his wife in Harvey Nichols' on the night in question.

The story has since entered Hammers folklore to the extent that the Romanian's name – for West Ham fans at least – will always be synonymous with the famous department store. 'I had problems with the manager,' moaned Raducioiu after being sold back to Espanyol for £1.5m in January 1997. 'He wanted me to do what Dowie did, but I'm not Dowie.' Maybe that was just as well considering that the Northern Ireland international scored even fewer goals for the Hammers than Raducioiu did that season.

Florin's departure from West Ham came just a week after that of compatriot Dumitrescu following an ill-fated spell, not that Dowie was too upset to see the latter go. 'He was a horrible bloke,' said the striker during an off-the-record chat. The midfielder's failure to make his mark at Upton Park – owing to a lack of fitness, form and favour – was all the more amusing to outside observers given the huge effort required on West Ham's part to secure his services in the early part of 1996. Never mind that he had 52 Romanian caps, the fact he had failed to play in 75 per cent of Tottenham's games, following his arrival from Steaua Bucharest two years earlier, was enough for the Department of Employment to reject the renewal of his work permit and block his £1.5 million move.

As West Ham appealed, Redknapp spoke of the 27 year old 'crying his eyes out' in his office – a scenario that was somewhat difficult to picture – while there was little help provided by the Professional Footballers' Association. Indeed, PFA chief executive Gordon Taylor, fearful of the influence of the new Bosman ruling in terms of English football being flooded with foreign imports, went so far as to complain about 'managers not thinking about the best long-term interests of the game', which was harsh on Redknapp given he had already shaken up the club's youth academy system. 'I am a member of the union and they should support me,' moaned Dumitrescu, who added, 'All this is bad for my image.' And this from a man who, just a year earlier, had been pictured in bed with two girls in *The Sun*.

Dumitrescu was finally granted his permit, thanks to the intervention of local MP Tony Banks and West Ham's decision to apply for a brand new permit rather than a renewal of his old one. After making just three appearances for the Hammers in March 1996, a hamstring injury ended his season and it was perhaps appropriate that the last of his ten outings the following term came in the humiliating Cola-Cola Cup defeat at Stockport. He was summarily offloaded to Mexican outfit Futbal Club de America for just under £1 million. 'I ended up with too many floaters,' said Redknapp when explaining why he no longer needed Dumitrescu, who bizarrely blamed his poor form on the inability to follow his Christian faith. 'The reason I didn't perform very well at Tottenham and West Ham is probably because there aren't too many orthodox churches in England,' he said, clutching his bible in one hand and some straws in the other.

Hammers fans have rather better memories of Dani, who arrived on a three-month loan deal from Sporting Lisbon in February 1996 amid a blizzard of hype and hope. Stories of the 19 year old having made records, appeared in films and strolled along the classiest catwalks of Europe might have been largely fictitious, but he would never lose his playboy image. 'He's so good looking,' said Redknapp, 'that my players in training don't know whether to mark him or f**k him.'

Dani had already won over the fans by heading a fifth-minute winner on his debut at Tottenham – described by *The Sun* as 'West Ham's greatest performance in years'. But while Redknapp recognised the forward as a 'terrific young player', he was fighting a losing battle to keep the 'glamour boy with film-star looks' under strict control. Dani's gratitude at being fined £1,000 for missing a training session during a break in Tenerife had assistant boss Frank Lampard quipping, 'He must have had a good night if it was worth a grand!' The end of his time was signalled when he failed to show up for training before the penultimate game of the season at QPR. 'I can't run a football club like that,' said Harry. 'How can I tell Ian Bishop or Danny Williamson, who turn up for training every day, that they're not playing and Dani is? The next thing is that everybody will be on the golf course every morning!'

Redknapp is philosophical about a period in time when, by his own admission, he was venturing into 'a market I knew nothing about'. 'When you look at some of the names I brought to West Ham, it almost makes the mouth water,' he added in his autobiography. 'Unfortunately, some of those players didn't live up to their fancy reputations.'

....

Ballyhoo Under Blue Lou

'What I want is a fighting team on the pitch'
– Lou Macari, August 1989

LOU MACARI took a bit of a kicking during his ill-fated time as the manager of West Ham – in more senses than one. Whether it was from unhappy fans following poor results, unsettled players who resisted his methods and ideas, the national press who disliked his direct style of play, the high-street bookmakers he frequently visited, the frowning FA following allegations of illegal betting or a hot-headed Julian Dicks in the gym, the Scot collected enough bumps and bruises during his period at Upton Park that it was little surprise when he limped away licking his wounds after just seven months. He was known as 'Blue Lou' by some associates because of his colourful language; maybe 'Black and Blue Lou' would have been a more appropriate moniker.

In succeeding the sacked John Lyall in the summer of 1989, there's no denying the 40 year old had an extremely tough act to follow, even though the Hammers had been in decline for three years and had just suffered relegation. Player unrest was high, discipline levels and morale at the club were low and with Macari lacking any previous association with West Ham – having played for Celtic and Manchester United and managed Swindon Town – the popular perception was that his face just didn't fit at the Boleyn Ground.

While he will never be remembered with much fondness by supporters, it's worth mentioning that Macari did some good work – bringing popular players such as Ludek Miklosko, Martin Allen, Ian Bishop and Trevor Morley to Upton Park and making 21-year-old Dicks the club's second youngest captain (after Bobby Moore), as well as his penalty-taker. Anyone who tells calamity keeper Allen McKnight that he'll never play for West Ham again can't be so bad.

Former skipper Billy Bonds, then in charge of the youth team, admitted that it was 'always going to be difficult for Lou to win the players over' and referred to a 'culture shock' as the new boss tried to implement philosophies that were very different to old-school life under Lyall. One of these related to what the players were allowed to eat and drink (with alcohol being frowned upon) and Macari immediately clashed with Dicks who had established a routine of guzzling two cans of coke before games. 'Had Julian played in the days of Billy Bonds and Trevor Brooking then maybe he wouldn't have been so misguided,' said Macari. 'But if you are in an environment where everyone is a little bit sloppy, you've got a job on your hands to change their attitudes.'

Indeed he did. Chips were among the other fattening foods struck off the menu – a decision that would have drawn a wry smile from all those Manchester United fans who had sampled the menu at the Lou Macari Fish & Chip Shop right outside Old Trafford over the years – and Dicks remembered one particular overnight stay before an away fixture. 'It was the Friday evening and we were having our food when Mark Ward asked, "What's for dessert?" Lou turned round and said, "You're not having any." Wardy thought "bollocks" and went over to the dessert table, grabbed a great big piece of gateau and sat down eating it.'

It's even been rumoured that once the approved meals were finished, the players ordered takeaway pizzas to be delivered to their hotel rooms behind Macari's back. Striker Jimmy Quinn, a £340,000 signing from Bradford, admitted, 'A lot of the players didn't really get on with Lou. The training ground used to do food such as sausage sandwiches but Lou cut all that out and put salads in and that upset a lot of people. Having played for Lou at Swindon I knew what to expect, so it didn't bother me too much. But it was a big thing for West Ham to change at the time because it had been going on for ages.'

Far more disturbingly, Macari also tried to change the way the Hammers played – and many felt his ideas were simply not compatible with either the personnel or the history of the club. His direct style of play might have worked in the lower divisions when guiding Swindon to two successive promotions, but it went totally against the grain of West Ham's proud traditions. 'Lou's teams were predictable,' said Dicks. 'It would be: get the ball and whack it up front. And you can't do that if the players are geared to play football. When you've got people like Liam Brady in the side, you can't just lump it.'

'That's not entertainment, Lou,' moaned one newspaper after another dour game, but Macari hit back at criticism by insisting a change in approach was needed if the Hammers were going to be successful and win back their place in the top flight. 'West Ham's style of play did not do them much good last season,' he said, 'otherwise I wouldn't be sitting here today. Maybe the skill emphasis tended to overshadow the need for a fighting spirit. What I want is a fighting team on the pitch.'

The Littlewoods Cup fourth-round game against Wimbledon fulfilled his wishes, a two-footed tackle by Dennis Wise on Dicks sparking a 17-man brawl – 'there were punches everywhere and even the Chicken Run got involved,' remembered Julian – with the Hammers full-back receiving his marching orders after seeking retribution.

'Many people may regret that even [West Ham] are falling into line with professional football's more unsavoury aspects,' said Harry Harris in the *Daily Mirror*, after both clubs were fined £20,000, while Bobby Moore wrote in future Hammers co-owner David Sullivan's *Sunday Sport*, 'West Ham have certainly changed their style since I led the Hammers. But the get-tough policy looks like paying dividends.'

Despite being undermined by the furore surrounding midfielder Paul Ince's decision to pose in a Manchester United shirt long before he moved to Old Trafford, as well as losing striker Frank McAvennie to a broken leg after a clash with Chris Kamara at Stoke, Macari enjoyed a decent start, with his side losing just one of their opening eight league games. West Ham were also on a journey that would take them to the Littlewoods Cup semi-finals, but a run of ten matches that produced just one victory saw them slip to a mid-table position by the end of the year.

Bemused players were told in the dressing-room before losing at Wolves that the starting line-up would be 'as per the programme', while the empty team bus was deployed by the manager to pay a trip to the bookies before the 5–4 defeat at Blackburn. If signing striker Justin Fashanu (on loan from Manchester City) was the answer then it must have been a really silly question, while Phil Parkes vowed 'never to play for West Ham again' if Macari was in charge after being dumped from the side for Perry Suckling.

The undercurrent of dissent behind the scenes continued, with disillusioned players being penalised for breaches of discipline, while some – including the slightly built Kevin Keen – were ordered to a health farm on the basis of being overweight. Dispirited assistant boss Mick McGiven brought his 16-year association with the club as player and coach to an end by resigning and complaining, 'It's no longer the club I'd served for so long.'

Sadly for Macari, the writing wasn't just on the wall but also all over the newspapers, with it emerging on the eve of West Ham's FA Cup third-round tie at Torquay that the FA had charged him in relation to a winning bet made against his former club Swindon during his time as manager at the County Ground. 'That was when Lou went missing,' remembered Dicks. 'We were in the hotel on the Friday and he wouldn't answer his door because the press had arrived. We went up there the next morning and he wasn't there. God knows where he went.'

To heap further embarrassment on Macari, the Hammers slumped to a 1–0 defeat to a side sitting 87th in the league which did little to encourage him to face the media. Although West Ham forced their way through to the last four of the Littlewoods Cup following three tough battles with Derby, the cloud hanging over the manager's head was as black as the ones that drenched his players as they splashed and crashed their way to a 6–0 defeat at Oldham to end any hopes of reaching Wembley.

That very week it was confirmed that Macari had been fined £1,000 by the FA for his part in the betting scandal that saw his former chairman Brian Hillier banned from football for six months. The Scot complained that he'd been punished heavily for 'making a single phone call', while a West Ham statement pledged support for their·manager and insisted the size of the fine suggested his involvement had been 'minimal'. By sheer coincidence, the fixture list next took the Hammers to Swindon, but when the team bus arrived at the County Ground the manager wasn't on it. 'I don't think we saw him again,' said Dicks, with it being announced just two days later that Macari had resigned to bring the curtain down on a turbulent and traumatic era. 'Most people were pleased to see him go,' added Dicks.

Club photographer Steve Bacon had been one of Macari's confidants during his brief spell at the club and he said, 'Lou did admit that he felt like a real outsider. He conceded that he should never have resigned when he did and should have brought his own backroom team in. But he didn't want to be the one who sacked the likes of Ronnie Boyce, Mick McGiven and Tony Carr.'

Indeed, Macari has since described his decision to walk out on West Ham as 'a moment of madness', adding, 'I felt embarrassed for the club and made a stupid reaction. I was crazy to resign.' Lou's reign would be the briefest of any manager in the club's history – although his record of 14 victories from 39 games puts his win ratio of 35 per cent alongside that of the legendary Ron Greenwood, which, as far as the majority of Hammers fans would believe, just goes to show how misleading statistics can be.

···················

Agony Over Ecstasy

'If I kept trying to play football, I might never walk again'
– Dean Ashton, December 2009

SURELY SOME mistake? Where was the snag, the catch? Dean Ashton's arrival at West Ham in January 2006, for a club record £7.25 million, was a hen's tooth example of the Hammers beating the big guns to a young British player with proven ability and massive potential.

Supporters were so used to new signings arriving at Upton Park with some kind of 'baggage' – be it a questionable temperament, a patchy CV, inexperience at the highest level, too many nerves in front of goal, a dodgy injury record, too many wrinkles, living too far from Oxford – that for many the striker's arrival from Norwich appeared too good to be true.

As it turned out, it was – but through no fault of Ashton's. Or that of Alan Pardew, the manager whose powers of persuasion saw the West Ham board part with a fee even he admitted was a little over the odds, stating at the time, 'I'm quite content with that because I feel that in the scheme of things it will prove to be good value. Dean will bring another dimension to our pool of strikers.'

Instead, the fault could be traced to the training field on which the England squad prepared ahead of a friendly against Greece in August 2006. The boot of Chelsea's Shaun Wright-Phillips and the ankle of Ashton were both involved, but above all it was the hand dealt him by Lady Luck that did for the striker's football career. That Ashton was on the field, taking part in a practice game tailored specifically for him, was precisely because the 'dimension' Pardew said he would bring to the Hammers had worked such a treat in the nine months since his arrival.

Labelled an old-fashioned centre-forward, but evidently far more than a mere battering ram, 6 ft 2 in. Ashton hit five goals in his first seven West Ham appearances, including two in the FA Cup quarter-final win against Manchester City that demonstrated his finely tuned understanding of space and how to exploit it. Schooled at the renowned Crewe Alexandra Academy, Ashton's goals always seemed to entail something special from him in the build-up, be it an angled turn or dynamic positioning when heading the ball, a fact not lost on England manager Steve McClaren.

If McClaren was uncertain about what Ashton might add to his selection of top class strikers, then the FA Cup final surely made up his mind. The bundled second goal scored by West Ham's No. 9 in the 3–3 classic may have been one of the less artful moments of the game, but his all-round play, his eye for a defence-splitting assist and imposing presence amid a nervy Liverpool last third had the unmistakable mark of quality.

The former England Under-21 player was widely tipped to make the step up for his full debut against Greece, but the broken ankle he sustained at Manchester United's Carrington training facility rudely interrupted Dean's dream scenario. Give or take the odd teasing reminder that here was a player who could make an impact for club and country, the next three and a half years would see that dream descend into the most harrowing of nightmares.

Sidelined for the entire 2006–07 campaign, Ashton's loss compounded a season in which so many things went wrong at Upton Park. 'It was a massive blow,' said Pardew. 'We had built a lot around him in the pre-season. Teddy Sheringham had come and played that withdrawn role for us and then I had gone and got a player to replace him who, potentially, could be as good as Teddy in his prime.'

With Sheringham, Marlon Harewood, Bobby Zamora and Carlton Cole misfiring and shock new signing Carlos Tevez – with whom Ashton never played – unable to find his feet until the last frantic quarter of the season, Pardew's assistant Peter Grant was also acutely aware of how sorely Ashton was missed before the corner was turned. 'We just couldn't score. Dean was a natural and I'm sure he would have got goals in that period to turn things around.'

As the striker had been injured while on England duty it was understood that the FA paid an initial £300,000 towards his salary costs. However, a further £950,000 in compensation would reportedly be outstanding by the end of the season, allegedly causing West Ham some frustration as they waited for the underwriters to make a decision on their claim.

Such financial frustrations would seem like chicken feed a bit further down the line. The 2007–08 campaign afforded Ashton a fresh start, a mood reflected in the sunny bleach blondness of his thinning thatch. That's not to say there weren't occasions when he had the supporters, who had been so looking forward to seeing him back in a Hammers shirt, sprouting a few grey hairs of their own. More than a touch lardy – his girth exacerbated by West Ham's shirt sponsor, XL Holidays – Ashton's goals tended to come in short bursts rather than with any great consistency.

One thing that hadn't changed was his ill luck where England was concerned, a knee injury once again forcing his withdrawal ahead of Euro 2008 qualifiers in October 2007. Nevertheless, in thirty-six domestic appearances he managed an encouraging haul of eleven goals, three of which came in the last four games of the season and included an eye-catching bicycle kick at Old Trafford.

Fabio Capello, McClaren's successor as national boss, although reportedly displeased with Ashton's penchant for pizza, was impressed enough with his rejuvenation to award Dean his first full cap in a friendly against Trinidad & Tobago. Equally smitten were the West

Ham board, which despite being aware that Ashton's ankle break had taken far longer to heal than expected, threw caution to the wind and offered him a new megabucks contract to run for five years.

Five games rather than five years later, it was effectively all over for Dean Ashton, footballer. Season 2008–09 actually started in the best possible fashion, Ashton scoring both goals in a home 2–1 win over Wigan Athletic. With Capello watching the game and World Cup qualifiers on the horizon the newspapers once again started to speculate about whether the time had finally come for Ashton to properly fulfil his international promise.

It wasn't to be. In Gianfranco Zola's first training session after replacing Alan Curbishley as Hammers manager, Ashton twisted his ankle. It was predicted it would take him one month to get over the latest setback. The forward's wracked bones and ligaments thought otherwise.

Zola would later lament, 'I had him training only for one day and that is sad for me. If he'd not had the injury it is probable he would have been going to the 2010 World Cup. Everybody knows how skilful he is.'

Heartbreakingly, after more operations, more grinding hours of tentative step training in the gym and month after month of physio, Ashton was forced to draw a line under his career after 19 goals in 43 games for West Ham and a superb 111 goals in 279 games in all for Crewe, Norwich and the Irons. In December 2009, three weeks after his twenty-sixth birthday and fourteen months after he last kicked a ball, Ashton announced his retirement from the game.

'My health is obviously more important than football. I was told if I kept trying to play football, I might never walk again,' he told the press ahead of a fifth operation on his ankle.

Tony Cottee, a goal scoring forebear for West Ham and England, was one of hundreds to express their sympathy in media interviews and on Internet message boards. 'When you get these major injuries you often seem to get secondary injuries and eventually it all seems to have caught up with Dean. Psychologically, it is very difficult giving up your career. He is 26. I found it hard at the age of 36 but I had 20 years as a player. I really, really feel for Dean and wish him well.'

In March 2010, West Ham, now under new joint owners David Sullivan and David Gold, announced the financial accounts. Although they revealed how, under the previous Icelandic regime, lavish contracts had been drawn up with players who had contributed much less than Ashton, the folly of awarding him a lengthy new deal despite lingering concerns over his ankle became evident when it transpired that West Ham were liable for a handsome lump-sum figure upon his enforced retirement.

Ashton himself even appeared to hint to Radio Five live that the scenario was a tough one for the club to swallow. 'In hindsight I'm sure they [the new owners] are ripping their hair out. At the time, five years seemed a lot . . . it wasn't up to me but I felt like I'd earned my place back in the team.'

In the same interview, a philosophical Ashton revealed he had not received an insurance payout following his retirement because he had returned to action after his first ankle injury and, thereafter, his insurance did not cover him for future problems with his ankle. For their part, West Ham were reported to be pursuing a £10 million compensation claim with the FA insurers at the time of his original ankle injury, while rumours persisted that Ashton was considering suing Chelsea and Wright-Phillips, something he appeared to pour cold water on.

As of July 2010, some of the major financial repercussions of Ashton's retirement remain unresolved. What is certain is that West Ham supporters were, relatively speaking, afforded just a tantalising glimpse of a player capable of lighting up Upton Park and Wembley, for years to come.

■■■■■■■■■■■■■■■■■■■

Cream of the Milk Cup

'West Ham tore poor Bury to shreds' – Tony Cottee,
October 1995

THE DATE: Tuesday, 25 October 1983. The time: 10.30 p.m. The place: a bus stop in Elm Park, Hornchurch. The scene: two college mates share a snatched conversation as one, West Ham scarf around neck, alights off the bus and the other gets on. The dialogue:

'All right, mate. How did West Ham do tonight?'

'Won 10–0.'

'Shut up, you muppet. Seriously, how did they do?'

'Won 10–0.'

'Ah forget it then, you piss-taker. See ya tomorrow.'

Next morning the sceptic wakes up to a sports page headline screaming: 'West Ham hotshots Bury 'em alive!' – and the unbelievable truth suddenly hits home. The Hammers really did hit ten goals in one game.

The scoreline was jaw-dropping enough, especially given the fact it came between two goalless league games against Norwich and Watford. What was even more bewildering, however, was that manager John Lyall promptly splashed out £100,000 on one of the defenders who had just helped Bury suffer the worst defeat in the history of the League Cup.

Centre-half Paul Hilton and his Lancastrian cohorts showed little lambs-to-the-slaughter inclination in the first leg of the second-round Milk Cup tie at Gigg Lane. The Third Division side suffered a narrow 2–1 defeat to keep alive slim hopes of a giant-killing down in London.

The prospect of a midweek tie between an out-of-sorts West Ham and unglamorous minnows from the north didn't exactly set Cockney hearts aflutter. If anything, a first chance for many to see the mysterious words 'Avco Trust' displayed across the front of the West Ham jerseys was the bigger talking point ahead of the game.

A paltry 10,896 turned up with the expectation of seeing Lyall's team routinely finish the job and progress to the third round of a competition they had come so close to winning two years previously. However, it soon became apparent that this display was going to be anything but routine. As star of the show Tony Cottee later put it, 'West Ham absolutely tore poor Bury to shreds.'

With typically ruthless efficiency, little marksman Cottee netted a first-half hat-trick, his first for the club, as Hammers had the Shakers wobbling all over their back line. At the break the score stood at 5–0 and most in the ground, including the players, expected perhaps a couple more goals at most before the hosts took their foot off the gas and spared Bury any more humiliation.

TC had other ideas. He was compassionate enough to wait until the 63rd minute before firing his fourth, the signal for others to rejoin the party. Alan Devonshire pitched in with a rare brace and right-back Ray Stewart added another, but perhaps Trevor Brooking, who netted his second goal in the 83rd minute, provided the most poignant statistic. Almost exactly 15 years earlier, Brooking had scored in West Ham's joint record league victory, an 8–0 stuffing of Sunderland. That he and Billy Bonds played in two of the three highest scoring games in the club's history is a testament to their remarkable impact and durability.

Another link to the 1960s and Sunderland came via the eighteen minutes it took Hammers to net five of their ten goals against Bury. That ratio lies second only to the five scored in thirteen minutes in a 5–1 thrashing of the north-east whipping boys in 1967.

Alvin Martin, the other scorer on the night, was probably as surprised as anyone that within weeks of a game that finished 12–1 on aggregate, Hilton would join him in West Ham's pool of defenders. Lyall's oddest piece of transfer business certainly left Cottee perplexed. 'Nothing against Paul Hilton, but the thought we could sign anyone from a team we had just stuffed by ten goals simply didn't make any sense to me.'

Curly-haired 'Hilts', a former England schoolboy, was added to a squad lacking defensive cover, although he also found himself utilised in midfield and even up front during six years (sixty-five games, seven goals) as a useful squad player at Upton Park. Two days after joining the club he twisted his knee and lost a tooth in training, but he eventually played eight times and even added two goals in 1983–84, one of them coming against Arsenal in a 3–3 classic at Highbury. Unfortunately, by the time of his arrival it was too late for the future Hammers youth coach to slay his League Cup demons; West Ham were knocked out of the competition by Everton in round four.

Hilton's strange story would become synonymous with the most prolific 90 minutes ever seen at Upton Park. The 10–0 score has since been equalled by Liverpool's rout of Fulham in 1986, but never bettered in this competition.

For Cottee the match will always have special significance, but lesser lights such as Neil Orr, Steve Walford and Dave Swindlehurst also get an annual reminder that they achieved something unique in claret and blue. When that statto bible, the *Rothman's Football Yearbook*, receives its annual update, there they are listed in the Hammers' line-up beside the 'highest ever score' entry on the pages dedicated to West Ham.

No one can take away from Swindlehurst the fact that he is a Hammers record-breaker – even if, as a centre-forward, he achieved the impossible by NOT scoring against Bury!

·······················

The Omoyinmi Incident

'He said he didn't think' – Harry Redknapp, December 1999

'THERE'S NO Manny in this house!' Such was the regular response from the most senior member of the Omoyinmi family in the late 1990s, whenever callers innocently failed to refer to his son by his full name of Emmanuel. Following the crazy events of 15 December 1999, supporters chose to call him far worse things – most with four letters, not five – with the young winger eventually being ejected from Upton Park as a matter of necessity. Indeed, during one of the loan spells which pre-empted his departure, the popular joke among the more grammatically aware Hammers faithful was that 'there are now two of them in Scunthorpe'.

It had all seemed so insignificant when the 21 year old of Nigerian descent appeared as a West Ham substitute in the Worthington Cup quarter-final against Aston Villa, with just seven minutes of extra-time remaining. The academy product, with just a dozen first-team outings to his name, exerted little influence on the game as both sides failed to add to the 2–2 scoreline, and he was restricted to the role of cheerleader as the Hammers won the resulting penalty shoot-out by five goals to four to reach their first cup semi-final in eight years.

Yet Omoyinmi's meagre contribution – in his one Hammers appearance of the season – would prove critical, with those seven minutes costing the player his Upton Park future, two club officials their jobs and, ultimately, West Ham their place in the semi-finals of the competition. And all because the forward had neglected to mention he had already played in the Worthington Cup earlier in the campaign while on loan at Gillingham and was, therefore, cup-tied when he returned to the Boleyn Ground. Omoyinmi had started both of the second-round games against Bolton and racked up some 110 minutes of action as the Gills crashed out 6–1 on aggregate, yet – for reasons best known to himself – elected to keep this information to himself.

That is, of course, until it came to Aston Villa's attention. Naturally aggrieved that they had lost to a team featuring an ineligible player, Villa complained to the Football League. Given that the Hammers could potentially have been disqualified from the competition, it was with some relief that it was eventually decided the quarter-final tie should be replayed – not that company secretary Graham Mackrell and manager Harry Redknapp were jumping for joy. 'The club acted in good faith and we're very disappointed to have this decision imposed on us,' complained Mackrell, while Redknapp asked, 'Why should 26,000 people who love this football club have to suffer for a slight oversight by somebody? It's very harsh.'

Not surprisingly, fingers were pointed in all directions as West Ham tried to comprehend how such a situation could have been allowed to develop. Redknapp dismissed it as 'an administrative error' and claimed that Hammers football secretary Alison O'Dowd had 'checked it out with Gillingham and got a message that Manny hadn't played'. Some fans blamed the manager after he'd granted Omoyinmi the freedom to play in the competition while on loan, although, as Harry said, 'There's a difference between giving permission and actually knowing he has played.'

Meanwhile, the vast majority questioned why Manny himself hadn't declared himself unavailable when mistakenly called into the squad. Publicly, Redknapp tried to shield the player from criticism, saying, 'I'm not going to blame the kid. I asked him why he didn't say anything and he said he didn't think.' But privately it was a different story, with a 'gutted' Omoyinmi later claiming that Redknapp had refused to speak to him from that moment on before hastily deciding to loan him out to Scunthorpe United and Barnet, and then handing him a free transfer to Oxford United at the end of the season. 'It's a decision based purely on football,' said Harry. Few could be blamed for not believing him.

Mackrell and O'Dowd both accepted ultimate responsibility for the fiasco by tendering their resignations – just six months after joining the club. By the time a reprieved Villa returned to Upton Park in January, it's fair to say they strongly fancied their chances. As if being given a second bite of the cherry wasn't enough to put a renewed spring in their step, the Midlands outfit went into the game on the back of three wins and a draw during a period in which the Hammers had failed to win any of their four games since the controversy arose. 'That's negative thinking,' said Harry when one journalist suggested that Villa had the psychological advantage ahead of the re-match. 'You would say we haven't won in the last four, while I would say we haven't lost in the last three.'

West Ham duly lost the replay, having led through Frank Lampard with less than ten minutes to go and seen Paolo Di Canio squander a chance to make it 2–2 with an extra-time penalty before Villa sealed a 3–1 success. 'Tonight will haunt me for ever,' complained Redknapp as he surveyed the wreckage of his Worthington Cup dreams.

Needless to say, the traumatic experience didn't exactly do wonders for the confidence of Omoyinmi, who made just thirty-two league starts in his four years at Oxford before seeing out his career in the non-league wilderness at Margate and Ebbsfleet.

As far as West Ham's Hall of Fame goes, a case of 'no Manny in this house' indeed.

Some Refs Can't Hackett

'It's like having a criminal record' – Tony Gale, April 1991

WEST HAM are losing 4–0 and a pair of West Ham fans in their late twenties are blubbing like babies. Ordinarily one might have been tempted to tell them to grow up, that they should be used to such humiliations by now, but more than a degree of sympathy and empathy was justified on 14 April 1991, as the Hammers were crushed by Nottingham Forest in an FA Cup semi-final meeting at Villa Park. If the scoreline was difficult enough to accept, the controversial first-half dismissal of defender Tony Gale was so demoralising that it was impossible for these two sensitive souls to hold back the tears. That said, the six pints of cider and four double vodkas (each) didn't do much for their emotional fortitude as events unfolded that afternoon.

As a Second Division team, albeit one heading for promotion, West Ham always had the odds stacked against them as they took on a Brian Clough side that was destined to finish eighth in the top flight that season. After needing two matches to see off both Aldershot and Luton, before making hard work of squeezing past Crewe, the Hammers had produced a heroic performance to beat Everton 2–1 in an epic sixth-round clash at Upton Park. So fingers were crossed that Billy Bonds' men could rise to the occasion once again to secure their first FA Cup final appearance since 1980.

What they didn't need in their path was one of football's most disputed decisions to go against them with only 25 minutes of the game played. Gale was entitled to chase a through-ball intended for Gary Crosby and when the two men tumbled to the ground, referee Keith Hackett produced a red card that stunned the entire 40,041 crowd and saw him become one of the most reviled figures in Hammers history.

West Ham fought like tigers, even hitting the post through George Parris shortly after Gale's dismissal, but Forest eventually made the breakthrough just after half-time when Crosby fired home past Ludek Miklosko. Stuart Slater also hit the woodwork for the luckless Hammers before goals by teenage midfielder Roy Keane and future West Ham full-backs Stuart Pearce and Gary Charles confirmed Forest's second-half superiority.

Inevitably, it was Gale's sending off that proved the game's major talking point and the 31-year-old defender, who had never been red-carded before, pleaded his innocence after the event. Gale said, 'As I see it, Gary knocked the ball over me and he chased after it quicker than I expected him to. I waited for the bounce because it was a very dodgy pitch and then he got in front of me and virtually stopped. A collision was inevitable; it was like being cut up on the motorway. To get sent off is ridiculous. It's like having a criminal record.'

The national media also disagreed with the decision, with *The Independent* describing Gale's challenge as 'clumsy, not cynical' while the *Daily Telegraph* believed it was 'certainly a foul but didn't warrant a red card'. With angry West Ham fans wanting Hackett's head on a stick, it's perhaps no surprise that the Sheffield official took charge of just one more game involving the club – at Blackburn in September 1993 – before sticking his whistle where it belonged. The ultimate irony, given some people's view of him, was that Hackett would eventually be appointed as the general manager of the Professional Game Match Officials Board and become responsible for improving the standards of top-level referees in England.

Hackett's name would always be synonymous with that infamous red card at Villa Park and, as he admitted many years down the line, he would never forget it himself. He was sympathetic towards West

Ham but insisted his decision to send off Gale had been the right one. 'A few days before the game we got a fresh instruction from the FA telling us to change the way we interpreted the laws about the professional foul,' he said. 'Suddenly the law was different, but only the referees were told. I don't think anybody was more surprised than Tony Gale or more disappointed than me when I had to bring out a red card for something that, a week before, wouldn't even have been a yellow. It dramatically affected the game, it ruined a lot of people's day out and it has stayed with me ever since.'

A new instruction regarding Law XII had indeed been circulated to referees in the form of a letter from the FA's chief executive, Graham Kelly. However, it was distributed in February – two months before the FA Cup semi-final – and appeared to be intended for the consumption of everybody in football rather than just match officials. It read:

> The Football Association having received a circular from FIFA draws the attention of all concerned (referees, players, managers, coaches and spectators) to the interpretation issued.
>
> Referees are required to apply the mandatory instruction issued by the International FA board more consistently so that it achieves its primary objective, that is, to protect attacking players and combat destructive play.
>
> Referees and players should understand that the offence punished with expulsion is serious in terms of the game and not necessarily in terms of the opponent who is the victim of the offence, intentionally sabotaging an obvious opportunity of scoring is punished, rather than merely the act of unfairly physically impeding an opponent.
>
> The implication of this is that it is of little significance whether the physical offence is considered minor (e.g. seizing hold of the shirt) or major (e.g. wildly tripping an opponent from behind); what is important is that it is considered a serious case of unsporting conduct.
>
> If the unfair physical impeding of the attacking

player results in the sabotage of an obvious goalscoring opportunity, the offending player shall be <u>sent off</u> and the game restarted appropriately.

Readers of West Ham's monthly publication, *Hammers News*, became aware of this letter after a copy was submitted by Mark Lufton, a supporter from Surrey. He said, 'Like all West Ham fans, my initial reaction to Tony Gale's sending off was to voice my instant disapproval. However, from the moment the referee blew for a foul, I knew that the red card was going to be shown. As a minor league referee, I had recently received a letter from the FA clarifying the rules concerning the dreaded professional foul. As you can see, it does not matter how serious the offence is, it is the fact that a goal-scoring attempt has been prevented. Therefore, once the referee had decided that Gale had committed a foul, he had no alternative but to send him off.'

Hammers News editor Tony McDonald admitted that Hackett might have applied 'the letter of the law' but argued that there were 'two big areas of doubt', questioning if a foul had actually been committed and if a goal-scoring opportunity had genuinely existed given the direction Crosby was heading.

There was no doubt that there needed to be strong punishment for players guilty of a cynical act to prevent a goal being scored. West Ham had seen Liverpool midfielder Terry McDermott deliberately punch the ball over the bar in the final minute of the 1981 League Cup final and yet remain on the pitch. Yet what Hackett had seemingly overlooked in his interpretation of the new rule was the word 'intentionally'. Even if Gale had fouled Crosby and denied him a goal-scoring opportunity, there's no way it could ever have been considered deliberate. Also, how could it be right that a referee was aware of the new rules but the players weren't, as Hackett has since claimed?

Gale still looks back on that red card as his 'worst moment as a player' and thinks of Hackett as a 'busy referee who wanted to make a name for himself'. He added, 'My career was over 700 games and I played with [George] Best, [Rodney] Marsh and

[Alan] Shearer, yet the only thing most people remember me by is that bloody sending-off.'

Gale also rues the fact that the decision denied West Ham their chance of getting to Wembley, something his team-mates are equally angry about. Kevin Keen remembers the red card as 'a diabolical decision', while fellow midfielder Martin Allen claims he has 'still not got over it'. While managing Brentford he attended a meeting with Hackett who, as the chief of referees, was discussing yet more rule changes. 'Five minutes in, I hadn't heard a single word he said,' admitted Allen. 'My mind flashed back to 1991, my hand started shaking and suddenly the red hot cup of Rosie was spilling onto my lap.'

Yet that day at Villa Park will also be remembered for one of the most extraordinary displays of crowd support the game has ever seen, with the West Ham fans out-singing their Forest counterparts with chants of 'Billy Bonds' claret and blue army' that continued for most of the second half. Steve Ward-Humphrey of Crawley wrote to *Hammers News* and said, 'The pride I felt from our fans singing and dancing when we were 4–0 down is impossible to describe.'

Future Hammer Paul Konchesky was also in the crowd that day and recalled, 'After Gale was sent off the memories were just of the fans from that minute on. They gave their all.' Thankfully, there were cheers as well as tears on that memorable afternoon.

■■■■■■■■■■■■■■■■■■■

The Terminator

'I would have loved to have chinned him a few times'
– Billy Bonds, May 1996

IT'S A few years after Julian Dicks has retired from football and the former West Ham defender is hard at work. 'And would you like peas or salad with that, madam?' he politely asks of the little old lady ordering her Saturday evening meal in the country pub and restaurant he owns.

This surreal image is in stark contrast to the memory that most fans will have of the shaven-headed left-back known as 'The Terminator', who terrorised the opposition and took few prisoners during his two spells at Upton Park in which he became a Hammers hero and cult icon. An unforgettable photograph perfectly captures Julian's confrontational nature; manager Billy Bonds is racing down the touchline, with his jacket flapping in the wind, in a desperate bid to prevent Julian from lunging at Wolves midfielder Paul Birch having already taken out his team-mate Steve Bull. 'F**k off, you twat!' was the typically blunt response from Dicks as he walked away from the referee's red card – the second of three he received in one particularly crazy five-month period.

The controversies – of which there were many – inevitably created the headlines but Julian's career and character were full of contrasts. His full-blooded tackles might have been heavier than a stack of his favourite Metallica albums, but his commitment to the cause was matched by his class on the ball and cultured left foot. As John Lyall, the manager who paid £300,000 to Birmingham for the Bristol-born defender's services in 1988 (on the advice of former Hammer Steve Whitton), was keen to emphasise, 'I wouldn't have bought just a physical player. There was a great touch there as well.'

Dicks had little affection for Lyall's successor Lou Macari, who called him 'a fat bastard' on his first day in charge and suffered the consequences when participating in five-a-side games. 'I used to kick shit out of him,' boasted Julian. Even Bonds, who remembers Dicks as 'a terrific player', said of their clash of personalities, 'I would have loved to have chinned him a few times.'

As, perhaps, would David Mellor, the Conservative MP-turned-broadcaster and columnist, who branded Dicks an 'animal' following an incident in 1995, which left Chelsea striker John Spencer with blood dripping down his face after the West Ham man trod on his head. 'I wanted to sue Mellor's bollocks off,' insisted Julian, who protested his innocence. Yet even boss Harry Redknapp had his doubts, calling his player 'a f**king liar' during the behind-the-scenes inquest.

To make matters worse, Dicks was sent off just a few days later against Arsenal to cement his reputation as Public Enemy No. 1. Headlines appeared on the front pages of the tabloids to claim that one of Julian's twin daughters had been the victim of a 'revenge attack' at school – 'the stories were a load of crap,' he insisted – and the FA eventually imposed a three-game ban after finding him guilty of bringing the game into disrepute.

None of which did anything to promote Julian's chances of being called up by England boss Terry Venables for Euro '96, which his performances for West Ham certainly merited. Indeed, he won the third of his four Hammer-of-the-Year awards in 1996, but after England scout Ted Buxton allegedly told West Ham defender Slaven Bilić that his team-mate should 'grow his hair', Dicks responded by insisting he'd rather 'spend the summer building dog kennels' than represent his country under Venables. Julian failed to add to his two international B caps and was described by Graeme Souness – the manager who took the player to Liverpool in September 1993 for an ill-fated 13-month period – as 'one of the greatest left-backs never to play for the full England team'.

Life was frequently just as turbulent off the pitch, with Julian's then-wife Kay revealing how being idolised in his early days at Upton Park affected their relationship. 'It's very difficult when your husband is going out four nights a week and people are phoning you up with stories,' she said. Dicks blamed his hedonistic behaviour in the early 1990s – 'I'd go and get pissed out of my head,' he admitted – on his disciplinary problems, candidly revealing all for his warts 'n' all *Terminator* biography. The irony was that another big story was set to explode at the very time Kay was being interviewed, with the *News of the World* making front-page allegations about Julian's exploits while on holiday in Spain with some West Ham team-mates; claims that he would dispute and later win an apology for. 'There are wars going on and kids dying but they put me on the front page,' he complained. 'It just doesn't make sense.'

What also didn't make sense for some observers was that Dicks was still able to play football at all, the defender having suffered a career-threatening knee injury in 1990 that, in the words of manager Bonds, 'would have finished the majority of players'. Julian's relationship with West Ham suffered due to a lack of support, with even physio John Green admitting, 'He had gone from club captain to being treated like a leper.'

Dicksy returned to action the following year but when he later required surgery on the same knee – and was forced to miss the entire 1997–98 season – his career appeared to be over. Yet just like Arnold Schwarzenegger in his *Terminator* role, he emerged from the ashes to fight again, with Redknapp describing his comeback against Northampton as 'one of the greatest performances I've ever seen'. However, following a torrid outing against Charlton in which Julian felt he was unfairly asked to play in an unfamiliar wing-back role, Redknapp clearly lost faith in the player who could no longer train properly. 'He can't f**king run,' he confided on one occasion. Dicks was restricted to just a dozen games – 'not bad for somebody repeatedly told he'd never kick a ball again,' said Julian – before West Ham announced his retirement in the spring of 1999.

According to his agent in private, the club had been eager to publicise the news to avoid making another transfer payment to Liverpool. 'West Ham wanted to get rid of me,' complained Dicks after saying goodbye at the age of 30 to the club for whom he made 315 appearances and scored 61 goals – most of which were fiercely smashed penalties.

Fittingly, his benefit match featured a huge melee between West Ham and Athletic Bilbao's players (with Dicks later complaining about being charged costs for a game that formed part of the club's pre-season preparations), but not everything with Julian is as predictable. He loves Guns N' Roses but has been caught listening to R&B star Mark Morrison in his car. He betrayed his Hammers hardman image by employing a female agent, and after hanging up his boots, he planned to swap the passion of the Premier League for the calm of the golf course by relocating to Spain, although his damaged knee put paid to any professional aspirations.

Dicks admits that he 'hated the world' when being forced out of football but has since rediscovered his appetite for the game and, in September 2009, he took on the almost impossible task of trying to keep Grays Athletic in the Conference. 'I'd love to manage West Ham,' he says today, and while that seems some way off, many of the Upton Park faithful will always be happy to welcome him back with open arms.

·····················

Car Trouble

'It was probably the worst three days of my life'
– Rio Ferdinand, September 1997

THE BIG-NAME football journalist thought he was onto a winner when he rang the offices of West Ham's monthly magazine with his cunning plan. 'Look, I hear you're running an interview with Rio Ferdinand in your next issue,' he said. 'Let my paper run it several days in advance and we'll give your front cover a plug.'

The editor wasn't buying it, believing he'd sell more copies if he retained his exclusive piece while being eager to preserve the magazine's relationship with Ferdinand, whose trust would be destroyed if he saw his comments pop up in a tabloid newspaper instead of the place intended. 'Well, put it this way,' said the aggrieved hack, 'play ball or we'll just lift the interview when it comes out – and then you'll get no publicity whatsoever.'

Needless to say, the journalist was told to sling his hook. His efforts might have come to nothing but his devious approach spoke volumes about the desperation of the tabloids to gain access to Ferdinand in September 1997. This was understandable given that the highly rated Hammers defender had just been convicted of drink-driving . . . on the day he was set to join up with Glenn Hoddle's England squad for the very first time.

'I obviously had to speak to Glenn and when he told me he was omitting me from the squad I was gob-smacked,' admitted Rio, who had been handed a year's ban from driving and a £500 fine. 'It was literally the biggest punch in the mouth anyone has ever given me. It was probably the worst three days of my life. I have never been so depressed.'

Ferdinand has had his dark days since, of course, not least when he was banned for eight months for missing a drugs test at Manchester United's training ground in 2003, but at the time, the 18 year old was enjoying a meteoric rise and looking forward to becoming the youngest person to play for England since Duncan Edwards in 1955 – not to mention the first Hammer since Tony Cottee nine years earlier – if he figured in the forthcoming World Cup qualifier against Moldova.

Those hopes were dashed as soon as the Football Association learned of Rio's indiscretion, which just happened to take place on the same weekend as the tragic death, in a car accident, of Diana, Princess of Wales. With Diana's chauffeur suspected of having been under the influence of alcohol when he lost control of his vehicle, it was inevitable that the FA would need to be seen, contrary to previous instances of leniency, to be taking decisive action against a player caught drinking and driving. It was even suggested that former England skipper Tony Adams, who had previously been jailed for crashing his car when drunk but escaped FA penalties, should take the youngster under his wing and offer advice.

'A lot of people have portrayed me as having an alcohol problem and that I need to be taught a lesson,' said Ferdinand, who was found to be over the limit the day after a night on the town. 'That is what upsets me about the whole thing. I am not normally a drinker. This was a one-off thing and it turned out to be the biggest mistake I've ever made.'

Not one that he was alone in making, if Hammers team-mate John Hartson was to be believed, with the Welsh striker admitting, 'I'm not telling tales out of school if I say that Rio's bad luck was to be caught. If we are honest, we must admit we have all done it. There but for the grace of God . . .' Hartson would quickly apologise for his ill-judged comments that sparked outrage, but it didn't stop boss

Harry Redknapp from banning the sale of alcohol in the players' bar at Upton Park.

Down the years, several other West Ham players have been pursued by the boys in blue for drink and motor-related offences, although the headlines generated were nothing like Ferdinand's. Making just three starts for the club in fifteen months following a £1 million move from Benfica, full-back Gary Charles was often accused of going missing. In January 2001, he really did, when it was revealed that police were searching for Charles after his Mercedes CL5 Coupe was found abandoned in Hornchurch following a collision with another vehicle. A half-full bottle of whisky was left on a front seat and it was reported that the man fleeing the scene had told the other driver to take his car instead of his insurance details as he was 'a bank robber and on the run'. Two days after the bizarre incident, Charles handed himself into police, but escaped punishment on that particular occasion. However, two years after leaving Upton Park he was jailed for dangerous driving – not the last time he would find himself behind bars – and later admitted to alcohol problems.

Popular winger Matthew Etherington was reportedly found to be just 2mg over the 80mg alcohol limit when stopped by police in Harlow while behind the wheel of his Land Rover, but that didn't stop him from being slapped with a 12-month driving ban in 2007 and a fine of £2,000.

And veteran Spanish striker Diego Tristan was disqualified for 32 months and fined £3,500 after he admitted to being three times over the limit when crashing his Porsche into a minicab in January 2009. West Ham fans would have cared little if he'd been banned from playing football, too, given his dismal displays during a short period at Upton Park that saw him released after seventeen appearances and just three goals.

Tristan's arrest came just four months after fellow Hammers centre-forward Carlton Cole was arrested on suspicion of drink-driving after his Audi Q7 was stopped on Victoria Embankment at 4.25 a.m. on a midweek morning. The 24 year old was subsequently fined £8,000 by West Ham for his late-night excursion and admitted, 'I've learned my lesson and I won't make a mistake like this again.' Yet it wasn't the first time that Cole had made the news in relation to motoring matters. In February 2007, he was embarrassed when Transport for London chiefs sent bailiffs to West Ham's Chadwell Heath training ground in a bid to recover £800 of unpaid congestion-charge fees that the player had disputed. Senior coach Keith Peacock reportedly told them where to go with some colourful language, and a few months later it was reported that Cole had seen four vehicles, worth a total of £265,000, repossessed after he allegedly failed to keep up with payments. Something suggests he'd be better off using some of Transport for London's bus or Tube routes in future.

At least Cole avoided becoming embroiled in a scheme that resulted in West Ham strikers Teddy Sheringham and Bobby Zamora being arrested by police and eventually cautioned for handing over speeding tickets to team-mate Shaun Newton, in a bid to avert penalty points and potential bans. It was reported that Newton took £550 from the two players and passed the tickets over to a friend who would subsequently invent fictitious drivers to take the rap.

Newton denied nine charges of attempting to pervert the course of justice, but evidence supplied by Sheringham and Zamora helped convince Croydon Crown Court, in July 2008, that the midfielder, who had joined Leicester City the previous year, was indeed guilty on all counts. The 32 year old escaped an immediate jail term but was duly handed a 28-week suspended prison sentence, 180 hours of unpaid community service and a 12-month driving ban. Not that Fleet Street's finest were banging down any doors to speak to him as they had with Ferdinand 11 years earlier. This particular version of Newton's Theory was simply not weighty enough for the media, the player's fortunes falling to earth as quickly as Ferdinand's were rising.

Reykjavik Reckoning

'West Ham is one of Mr Guðmundsson's most important investments' – Asgeir Fridgeirsson, November 2008

GEORG ANDERSEN is both charming and cheerful as he speaks from his office in Reykjavik about West Ham's future and the club's possible change of ownership. 'It's easy finding people who are interested in buying West Ham but much more difficult finding those with the proper funds,' he says. 'We may have to wait three years until someone is willing to pay what the club is worth. So our position hasn't changed and we will retain control of West Ham until such time as the economic climate allows us to achieve the correct market price.'

Andersen, the head of corporate communications at Straumur-Burdaras Investment Bank Ltd, was speaking in October 2009, as speculation regarding another Hammers takeover continued to build. This was hardly surprising given that West Ham were haemorrhaging money – the club's most recent, suspiciously delayed set of accounts for the year ending May 2008 had revealed losses of £37.4 million ('a disaster,' admitted chief executive Scott Duxbury) – and yet they were in the hands of an Icelandic banking institution that was 'in moratorium' (had ceased to actively trade), fighting off its creditors and seemingly in no position to prop up an ailing football club. How on earth had West Ham's situation come to this?

Everything had looked so promising three years earlier when Björgólfur Guðmundsson took control of the Hammers in an £85 million deal that saw Eggert Magnusson installed as the club's new chairman. Magnusson spoke of substantial squad investment, a challenge for Champions League places and moving West Ham into the new Olympic Stadium in 2012. 'What I am trying to do here is genuine,' he insisted shortly after his arrival.

However, not everything was exactly as it first appeared. Magnusson had got his feet under the table but it was what he discovered under the carpet that perturbed him. 'I cannot go into details but some things have surprised me,' he confided. 'Certain things are not as I thought regarding the club and the team.' The Icelander was also concerned about possible leaks at the club after confidential documents were reproduced in the *News of the World*. 'We have been having serious discussions about where this has been coming from,' he admitted.

Guðmundsson's past wasn't as unblemished as many assumed, with it going virtually unnoticed that *The Guardian* had run a profile piece on 'the real power behind West Ham' in which they revealed how the businessman had made much of his money in Russia – along with son Björgólfur Thor Björgólfsson (try saying that after six pints) – after having been convicted in 1991 of minor accounting offences in his Icelandic homeland, following the collapse of shipping line Hafskip. 'The conviction was a long time ago,' said a spokesperson for the man listed as the 799th richest person in the world. 'Mr Guðmundsson has come a long way since then.'

Indeed he had, with his position as chairman of Landsbanki, the national bank of Iceland, ensuring a high profile in business circles. Back at Upton Park, the furniture was being rearranged, with managing director Paul Aldridge, who had succeeded Peter Storrie in 1999, leaving the club by mutual consent and Duxbury being promoted to the position of chief executive. Alan Curbishley replaced Alan Pardew as manager as the new owners tried to address the problems they felt were responsible for the team's struggles, and an inquiry for £21 million Chelsea winger Shaun Wright-Phillips was a clear statement of intent. Sadly, fans had to be satisfied with Fulham's Luis Boa Morte instead, while Lucas Neill, Matthew Upson, Calum Davenport and Nigel Quashie were also signed during the January 2007 transfer window, as West Ham spent around £17 million in a bid to lift themselves away from relegation trouble.

Reports claimed that defender Neill, who snubbed interest from Liverpool to join the Hammers in a £1.5 million deal, had been lured from Blackburn by a weekly wage of £80,000. 'I wish!' was the response from the Australian skipper – with dollar signs popping up in his eyes – when such figures were put to him. Whatever his motives, at least Neill was one of the few new recruits who played a significant role in West Ham winning their survival battle and he was subsequently rewarded with the team captaincy.

Despite being hit with a £5.5 million fine over the Carlos Tevez affair, the new Hammers hierarchy was true to its word in terms of bolstering the squad for the 2007–08 campaign and five big-name signings were made in the shape of Scott Parker and Kieron Dyer from Newcastle, Craig Bellamy from Liverpool, Freddie Ljungberg from Arsenal and Julien Faubert from Bordeaux. Much was made of the near £30 million outlay on transfer fees – and it could have been more if Charlton's Darren Bent had not snubbed a £17 million move – but it got overlooked that the club had recouped £22.5 million through the sales of Nigel Reo-Coker, Marlon Harewood, Yossi Benayoun, Paul Konchesky, Tyrone Mears and Tevez.

Of course, it was the hugely increased wage bill that carried the true financial burden, although Magnusson, when asked about the club's policy on salaries in one meeting at Upton Park, claimed that no player earned in excess of a basic £55,000 a week – still nice work if you can get it. However, it was later revealed that the club's total annual salary commitments had increased by 50 per cent to £63.3 million – a sign of the club's ambition as long as the costs could be funded.

The first indication that the club's strategy for global domination had perhaps veered off-course came when it was announced, in the autumn of 2007, that Magnusson was stepping down from his role with his 5 per cent stake being purchased by Guðmundsson, who would replace him as chairman. Magnusson spoke of needing to concentrate on his 'interests overseas' but the suspicion was that he was leaving reluctantly. Indeed, he would later try to sue Guðmundsson for £1.1 million over the terms of his departure.

The signings of Dyer, Bellamy and Ljungberg, in particular, were considered to be risky in terms of their injury records, and the fact they managed just 41 appearances between them in the 2007–08 season justified the fears. Dyer suffered a broken leg in only his fourth game, while Ljungberg's four-year contract – reportedly worth £85,000 a week – was terminated after just twelve months, with the Hammers agreeing a £6 million pay-off for the injury-plagued midfielder.

Magnusson later defended the expenditure during his reign and refuted suggestions that he was singled-handedly responsible for the financial problems the club would incur. 'There was much criticism about wages when we signed Ljungberg, Upson, Neill, Bellamy and Parker,' he said. 'But does anyone honestly think I did that without the knowledge and support of the owner, chief executive and the manager? I was told there was a lot of money to do things and everybody was aware of the deals we were doing.'

West Ham could at least boast a top-ten finish in 2008, but the club was forced to suffer a barrage of blows in the autumn that would leave them bloodied and bruised for a considerable period. First, the club's main sponsor, XL, went bust but the fact that the Hammers were initially forced to play with an embarrassing patch on their shirts before securing new endorsement was the least of their problems. It just so transpired that the Guðmundsson business empire had previously provided the loans to fund a buyout of the XL group and it was estimated they could lose up to £200 million as a result of the company's demise.

Manager Curbishley walked out on the club complaining of 'constructive dismissal', while Sheffield United won their claim for compensation in relation to the Tevez affair, meaning a figure of £20 million would eventually have to be paid to the Championship club. Yet these events would be considered small beer compared to the collapse of Guðmundsson's Landsbanki organisation – along with most of the Icelandic banking industry – in October 2008, as a result of the global economic downturn. In financial terms it was like an enormous pile of Icelandic krona being tossed into a volcano and the fear was that the Hammers would burn with it. Asgeir Fridgeirsson, who had been appointed West Ham's vice chairman, insisted there would be no need for Guðmundsson to sell the club. 'West Ham is one of Mr Guðmundsson's most important investments,' he said. However, it seemed the owner might have little choice if he could no longer bankroll the club's losses.

In December, it was revealed that Hansa, Guðmundsson's holding company, had gone into administration while the 67 year old was in talks with the Icelandic Government regarding the restructuring of his assets. There were reports that the Hammers could be seized as part of a debt and, as the 2008–09 season moved to a close, speculation grew that Straumur, one of Hansa's chief creditors, could assume control of the club. That possibility became a reality on 8 June, when it was confirmed that the ownership of West Ham had been transferred to a new company under the name of CB Holding, the majority shareholders of which were Straumur. The club's website tried to paint a positive picture, claiming the 'agreement will secure West Ham's long-term future and allow it to remain a force in the top flight of English football'. Indeed, new chairman Andrew Bernhardt promised that he would 'sanction investment in new players' but 'within the parameters of sensible budgeting based on revenues generated by West Ham'.

In effect this meant the club could only spend money it earned, but the problem was that it was running at a loss, and Straumur were in dire straits themselves, as evidenced by the announcement that the Icelandic Financial Supervisory Authority had appointed a resolution committee to take charge of its affairs. West Ham were in limbo and although Straumur, which effectively became an asset management company, considered the club a potentially valuable commodity worth holding on to, it was hard to see how it could prosper in such circumstances. Something, quite clearly, would have to give.

Young King Cole

'It's all off the cuff' – Joe Cole, October 2003

ATTACKING FOOTBALL played in a positive spirit as a form of entertainment. If that has more or less been the West Ham Academy playing ethos down the years, then Joe Cole more or less embodies those qualities better than any Academician.

Cole's Hammers career was always going to be a relatively short one: salivating big club suitors, the Hammers' financial constraints and the player's own ambitions made sure of that. Yet, while he went on to achieve great things with Chelsea before joining Liverpool in July 2010, there is a school of thought that suggests it was east London, not west, where Cole came closest to fulfilling the extraordinary levels of hype foisted on his shoulders.

Most of the early headlines centred on the amazing things he could do with a ball at his feet, and during Cole's four years as a first-teamer at Upton Park he was plucky enough, naive enough and audaciously talented enough to want to dip into his bag of tricks as often as possible. For the large part, his adoring East End public, who voted him Hammer of the Year in 2003, were treated to Cole the free spirit, unfettered by militaristically defined responsibilities, unconstrained by a requirement to ceaselessly put graft ahead of craft. Like his team-mate Paolo Di Canio and his hero Zinedine Zidane, Cole was a team man by virtue of being able to turn a game, but most of all he was loved for his unquenchable thirst for attempting the impossible and very often pulling it off.

Cole explains his approach to the game thus: 'I like players who make me go "wow" when I am watching. People say I am all tricks and showboating but I am not. It's instinctive. If players are in certain positions, I will do my pirouette on the ball and then come out with it but I don't prepare that. It's all off the cuff.'

Raised in Camden, Cole had been setting tongues wagging in junior football since the age of 11. His charms won over Harry Redknapp in a trial match for West Ham, as youth director Tony Carr recalled. 'The match was only five minutes old when Harry said, "Someone find a copper who can handcuff that kid to the gates. Don't let him out of here."

'When he first came to West Ham as a 12 year old, he was just audacious in the way he played the game. He was tricky, he was cheeky, he was so unorthodox in what he did and so skilful. We worked very, very hard to convince Joe that West Ham was his club. We always felt he was destined to be a great player.'

For Cole to stand any chance of fulfilling his potential, he had to be protected. With the God-given talent and tawdry demise of Paul Gascoigne standing as both inspiration and warning, Cole's family, the West Ham coaching staff and manager Redknapp made sure their prize youth asset was handled properly. Redknapp and Carr deserve enormous credit for convincing Cole to sign professional forms with West Ham in November 1998 – sealing a reported £6,000 per week contract – despite Alex Ferguson's best efforts to get him to turn pro with Manchester United.

Who could blame United when Cole was achieving feats such as netting seven of the England youth team's eight goals in a win over Spain, or when even Redknapp himself was struggling to keep a hold on his superlatives, as evidenced by this exert from his autobiography: 'Joe Cole is still only 16 but he has incredible potential. When I first saw him I couldn't believe what I was seeing. But I don't want to put too much pressure on the lad. All I will say is that I've never seen a better prospect as a 14 year old in all my years in football.'

Others cut out the caution and went straight for sensation, the hype being piled on to such an extent that one began to wonder which would come first: Cole's West Ham or full England debut? Men's lifestyle magazine *Maxim* declared 'West Ham have acquired the future of English football – and its name is Joe Cole', while the *Daily Mail* described him as 'the best prospect since the Great Gold Rush'. A lucrative boot deal with Adidas and having his name registered as a trademark with the PFA all added to the whirl of anticipation.

Cole's youth-team colleagues, with whom he annihilated Coventry City 9–0 in the 1999 FA Youth Cup final, were better placed than most to say whether the fuss surrounding their matc 'Joey' was based on fact or fiction. 'I'd been playing with Joe since the age of eight,' said Sam Taylor, left wing-back in the Class of '99, 'and the things I've seen him do over the years . . . If he did those tricks today he'd probably get his head taken off. You couldn't get close to the boy; you just knew that the next stage for him after the youths was the Premier League.'

Former youth-team striker Bertie Brayley concurred, 'Joey took everyone's breath away. Ian Wright used to call him "the conjurer". He'd be in a tight situation with three or four around him and he'd do something unreal to get out of it. He's an exceptional talent.'

By the time of the Youth Cup final Cole had already played nine times for the West Ham first team. On his debut, aged 17 years and 55 days, in the FA Cup third round against Swansea City in January 1999, Cole became the second youngest outfield player after Paul Allen to appear for the club. West Ham were dreadful that day, scraping a 1–1 draw against the bottom-division minnows, but the gurns turned to grins when Young King Cole/Joe Cool/The New Gazza replaced Eyal Berkovic. As *Hammers News* magazine's Steve Blowers put it, 'The red and white bulbs on the fourth official's electronic board shone like beacons in the Upton Park haze to signal Joe's first taste of the big time.' In the same article, Cole showed there was a level head behind the slight frame, squeaky voice and melodramatic reporting: 'It would have been nice if I'd been able to come on and make my debut as an unknown just like most other young players do. In the end, though, I didn't find it too much of a problem because I know that I'm going to have to deal with all sorts of things during my career.'

His Premier League bow came eight days later as a substitute in the televised game at Old Trafford. Again, the Hammers were abject against the Red Devils, who cruised to a 4–1 win, the only positive note being a piece of sublime touchline trickery from Cole, the first sign to a mass audience that there really was some substance to all those Fleet Street gushings about magic in his boots.

By the end of the month he was already getting Man-of-the-Match ratings, his desire to make an impression being fully encouraged by boss Redknapp, who raved after a 0–0 with Wimbledon, 'I told him to play like Zola and thought he was tremendous.' *The Sunday People* was similarly impressed: 'Joe Cole came low down on the billing on a day when many more famous players were on parade. But in the end his was the name everyone was talking about.'

Shimmies, dummies and nutmegs were all great, but what about goals? Playing in midfield in a free role behind the strikers, Cole was undoubtedly less prolific than had been expected. The fans had to wait until his 24th appearance, a 3–2 win at Birmingham City, for the papers to be able to legitimately alliterate 'Cole' with 'goal' in a headline. The relief was tangible as he ran towards his jubilant Cockney flock in the away end, but it was the maturity of Cole's overall performance that had Brum boss Trevor Francis, himself a one-time wonder-kid, opining, 'This young man will play for England within the next year.'

Cole's first goal at Upton Park came in the farcical 5–4 win over Bradford City just over a year after his debut, his old pal from the youth team Stephen Bywater almost stealing the headlines with a calamitous debut between the sticks. Three months later, Cole's fortunes also took a dive when he broke his leg, swiftly putting paid to the row brewing as to whether the mercurial youngster was ready to be included in England's squad for the European Championship finals in the summer of 2000.

Francis's prediction was eventually about seven months out. Under Sven-Göran Eriksson, Cole won his first England cap in May 2001 in a 4–0 rout of Mexico. His great friend and fellow Hammers product Michael Carrick also appeared from the bench in that game. After Rio Ferdinand and Frank Lampard, Cole is the most-capped of Hammers' 'golden generation' (Glen Johnson, Jermain Defoe and Carrick being the others), with 56 appearances to his name by the end of the 2010 World Cup.

His ten international goals, including a blinder against Sweden during the 2006 World Cup finals in Germany, represent a decent haul for a midfielder, but the fact that Cole has largely underperformed on the global stage can be partly attributed to the doubts that persist over where best to deploy his talents. This was a thorn in his side during much of his Chelsea career and one which first became an issue at West Ham under Redknapp, where despite the buzz he created as an attacking force, his defensive limitations too often saw him start games on the bench or even excluded altogether.

Under Redknapp's replacement Glenn Roeder, Cole was utilised on the left wing and later on as an orthodox central midfielder, with an instruction to tackle back more than he had been used to in the past. Many saw both roles as an impingement on Cole's free spirit but Alan Devonshire, similarly adored for his creativity and speed of thought, saw things differently. 'I really think Joe Cole would be lethal out there on the left,' Devonshire commented in *Boys of '86*. 'He knows that the main point of his game is running at players with the ball and beating them with pace and skill, so the next job is to find him a position where he can express that to the maximum.' Frustratingly, that search has never really stopped.

It was during the last throes of Roeder's tenure as manager at Upton Park that Cole was given the captain's armband. Some saw it as a boon to the 21 year old's development, others as an unnecessary burden for such a mercurial talent. Cole remained an inventive force and upped his strike-rate to five goals that season, but his tally of yellow cards was twice that as the frustrations of a doomed relegation fight, including an ugly spat after the final whistle against Bolton, took their toll on the jewel in a team that was supposedly too good to go down.

With depressing inevitability, Cole became the 14th player to exit Upton Park before the Championship campaign began, heading to Chelsea for a criminally undervalued £6.6 million. The huge financial repercussions of relegation demanded a fire sale, although Sir Trevor Brooking, stand-in manager for the ailing Roeder, revealed that Cole's departure after 150 games and 13 goals wasn't a result of book-balancing alone. 'It's a huge shame to see Joe go but the fact is that we made him a really good offer last summer and he refused. Even if we had remained in the Premiership, Joe was going to leave next season and no club wants to lose a player like that for next to nothing.'

Five years later in May 2008, the ultimate sign of just how far Cole and three other Academy graduates had progressed came when he and Lampard of Chelsea lost out to Manchester United's Carrick and Ferdinand in the Champions League final. Two years after that, the same foursome, plus fellow West Ham products Glen Johnson and Jermain Defoe, made it into the England squad for the World Cup finals in South Africa, with Cole suppressing doubts about his club form with a reassuringly effervescent performance in the final friendly before Fabio Capello named his 23-man squad.

Sadly for Joe, the 'Curse of the Luxury Player' struck him in the tournament, with two cameo appearances from the bench hardly doing his talents justice or England any favours as they crashed out in ignominious circumstances.

Cole once said: 'I would be happy to be the most boring player in the world and have stacks and stacks of medals. But that's not what I have been given in terms of talent.'

There was never a hope in hell of stacks and stacks of medals at West Ham, but as a stage for him to launch his talents on the footballing world, the Academy fitted Joe Cole like a glove.

The St Valentine's Day Massacre

'I can't ever recall feeling so much for the fans'
– Alvin Martin, February 1990

WEST HAM have suffered more than their fair share of cup disasters over the years. Yet despite the various egg-on-face embarrassments at the hands of lower league minnows, the 6–0 thrashing by Oldham Athletic in the first leg of the Littlewoods Cup semi-finals in 1990 is considered one of the most humiliating in Hammers history. Taking place on 14 February, it will forever be remembered as West Ham's very own St Valentine's Day massacre.

Forget that the Latics finished just one place behind the Londoners in the Division Two table that year; getting hit for six at Oldham represented West Ham's biggest ever cup defeat and was all the more painful for the fact that Wembley's famous Twin Towers were so tantalisingly in sight. They had come so far – having played eight full-blooded games to reach the semis – only to implode in the most spectacular fashion and render the second leg at Upton Park virtually redundant. To make matters worse, particularly for the 6,000 West Ham supporters standing on the exposed terraces at Boundary Park that evening, it was raining.

Not that the miserable weather conditions turned the pitch into a muddy quagmire that thwarted the Hammers' traditional passing game. Oldham's infamous all-weather plastic pitch scratched out that excuse at the same time as providing one of its own, together with a sense of déjà vu. West Ham had slipped up on a synthetic surface in the previous year's semi-finals at Luton, although given they had already collapsed 3–0 in the first leg at Upton Park, they had few excuses for their exit.

Going into the game the omens certainly seemed to be with Oldham. Joe Royle's plastic perfectionists had gone 13 months and 31 matches since allowing the opposition to walk away victorious. West Ham, meanwhile, were not in the best frame of mind despite having beaten three Division One sides in Aston Villa, Wimbledon and Derby on the way to the last four of the cup. Many players were unhappy with the methods of boss Lou Macari, who had succeeded John Lyall following the previous summer's relegation, while the manager's credibility had been further damaged before the Oldham game when he was found guilty of breaching FA rules in relation to betting while at his former club Swindon.

Macari was evidently in defensive mood – in more senses than one – as his starting line-up included three centre-halves in the shape of Alvin Martin, Tony Gale and Gary Strodder, with David Kelly plying his trade alone up front. The negative formation allowed Oldham to seize the initiative and the hosts never looked back once Neil Adams opened the scoring in the 11th minute, with a long-range strike that went in off a post.

Maybe the outcome could have been different had Stuart Slater's effort for the visitors a few minutes later not hit the woodwork, but further goals by Andy Ritchie and Earl Barrett put Oldham firmly in command well before the break. Macari's half-time pep talk clearly made little impact, as the second period had barely started when Rick Holden put the hosts 4–0 ahead. Although Alan Devonshire was immediately brought on as a replacement for the hapless Strodder, the midfielder could do little to prevent Roger Palmer and Ritchie from pouring further salt into West Ham's gaping wounds. 'Has Macari had a bet?' sang the delirious Oldham fans as they celebrated their side's annihilation of the southern Fancy Dans.

Macari admitted his men had been 'outpaced, outworked and outclassed', while first-team coach Ronnie Boyce, a veteran of several cup shockers in the 1960s, described the experience as 'traumatic'. Skipper Julian Dicks was reluctant to make excuses but believed that the home side had enjoyed a clear advantage in terms of being familiar with the surface. 'For visiting teams to play on their AstroTurf is always going to be hard, especially when Oldham's players train on it every day. Mind you, 6–0 is a bit extreme.'

Fellow defender Martin, meanwhile, reflected on the game by describing it as 'possibly the worst moment' he had suffered as a West Ham player. 'It's very difficult to translate our feelings into words,' he admitted. 'Once the fourth goal went in we knew it had the makings of a disaster. In hindsight, we could have done with Devonshire being on the pitch earlier, but it's easy after the event to say what might have happened if we had played with four at the back instead of five.'

And he added, 'I can't ever recall feeling so much for the fans. They stood out in the sleet and rain only to go home thoroughly depressed and disillusioned. At 5–0 they were still trying to get us back into the game by chanting that we would get six at our place.'

West Ham fans are known for their gallows humour, but there was no laughing from Devonshire and goalkeeper Phil Parkes, who both saw their distinguished Hammers careers end in the most ignominious of fashions as they made their final outings for the club at Boundary Park. The match also signalled the end for Macari, who had resigned long before Oldham returned for the second leg at Upton Park. Needless to say, the Hammers could not get the six goals their fans had promised but the team, now under the control of Billy Bonds, did ease to a comfortable 3–0 win – through Martin, a Dicks penalty and Kelly – to make the aggregate score a little less embarrassing. Not by much, though.

■■■■■■■■■■■■■■■■■■

Psycho Killer

'A great night for the fans' – David Cross, September 1981

DAVID CROSS – or 'Psycho', as dubbed by the West Ham fans – admits he could be 'a horrible, nasty bloke on a Saturday afternoon'.

If anyone was entitled to describe the striker in such disparaging terms, it was the supporters of Tottenham Hotspur after he proved he could be just as unpleasant to the opposition on a Wednesday evening.

On 2 September 1981, Cross produced the most astonishing performance of his career to score all the goals as West Ham thrashed local rivals Spurs 4–0 and romped to their biggest ever win at White Hart Lane. 'If we'd have carried on for another half an hour I'd have probably scored a couple more,' Cross said, confirming that it was one of those nights when he could do no wrong.

Before the game, everything had pointed to a Tottenham triumph. The north London outfit, with Glenn Hoddle in his pomp, were playing their first match at home after lifting the FA Cup in May and had kicked off the new campaign with a 3–1 success at Middlesbrough a few days earlier. Newly promoted West Ham, meanwhile, had been held to an unimpressive 1–1 home draw by Brighton on their return to the top flight following a three-year absence, were without the talismanic talent of Trevor Brooking through injury and had not won at White Hart Lane for ten years. Yet John Lyall's team – and that man Cross – defied the odds to ensure that England goalkeeper Ray Clemence, recently signed from Liverpool, suffered a home debut to forget.

Clemence was forced to pick the ball out of the net with just ten minutes gone after failing to prevent a shot by Cross from creeping in at the near post. He found himself repeating the experience shortly into the second half when Cross, now into his fifth season as a Hammer, poked home from eight yards after the Spurs defence failed to clear.

If Tottenham believed the first two goals had been thoroughly avoidable, there was nothing they could have done to stop the striker from claiming his hat-trick in sensational fashion just before the hour mark. Frank Lampard, Paul Goddard and Geoff Pike zig-zagged the ball into the danger area with a series of instinctive first-time passes, and there was Cross to volley into the top right-hand corner and put the east Londoners three goals up. The ball seemed to fly off the player's right shin but that didn't stop

England boss and former West Ham supremo Ron Greenwood from describing it as an early contender for goal of the season. With just a minute remaining, the rugged Cross completed the rout with his scruffiest effort of the game when he converted from close range following a goalmouth scramble. The West Ham contingent among the 41,200 crowd was in seventh heaven; Tottenham's fans were already halfway down Seven Sisters Road as they trudged away in disbelief.

Cross had scored four times in a 5–1 win at Grimsby five months earlier, but this was something else – as he acknowledged after the final whistle. 'It was a great night for me, a great night for the club and a great night for the fans,' he beamed. 'I loved every minute of it. My third goal was special and probably the best I've ever scored.'

'Four-goal Hammer leaves Spurs in a shambles!' screamed the *Daily Express*, while it also emerged that Cross had generously handed the match ball to goalkeeper Phil Parkes after the game. 'I gave it to Phil because the last time I got a hat-trick Phil complained that he was never going to be in a position to get the ball himself,' he explained. 'So I made a promise I'd give him the next one I got.'

The emphatic win at Tottenham provided West Ham with a huge boost in confidence as they started the season with a ten-game unbeaten run that set them up for the rest of the campaign. The Hammers eventually finished a creditable ninth, with Cross scoring 19 goals as he took his overall tally to 97 in 223 games for the club before joining Manchester City in the summer of 1982.

One of the supporters' funniest memories of the striker was when he pulled his bearded face out of the Upton Park mud during a game and asked team-mate Lampard who had sent him sprawling. Moments later, the guilty party was seen flying through the air having been sent on his way by the right boot of Cross. 'I'm normally a placid bloke but when I snap all hell breaks loose,' he said. In the best possible sense, that was certainly the case on an unforgettable night in north London.

■■■■■■■■■■■■■■■■■■■■

Rio Grand

*'I owe West Ham a hell of a lot' – Rio Ferdinand,
December 2000*

RIO FERDINAND has never been shy of enjoying a goal celebration. It doesn't matter which of his team-mates has scored, Rio is usually the one who appears last on the scene – well, he is a defender – and jumps onto the throng to milk the occasion more than anybody. He's there in all the photos.

Yet there was little revelry from Ferdinand over his very first goal at Upton Park – because it was scored *against* West Ham rather than for them. Instead, just five months after making his British record £18 million move, his body language suggested embarrassment at having put Leeds United 2–0 ahead against the club that had made him the player he was.

'I didn't think it was right to get too excited,' he said, deeply appreciative of the warm reception he had received from the West Ham fans on that April 2001 day. 'That's why I didn't celebrate.' And that's why the man described as a 'Rolls-Royce of a footballer' by former boss Harry Redknapp will always be welcomed back to the Boleyn with open arms – not just because he is one of the finest players ever produced by the club but also because he has never forgotten where he came from.

This was evidenced in his determination to appear in youth academy boss Tony Carr's testimonial on 5 May 2010 – starting alongside younger brother Anton and playing for nearly half an hour – despite his club Manchester United still being in the hunt for the Premier League title. 'Tony was brilliant and laid down the foundations for the rest of my career,' said Rio, whose hopes of emulating Hammers legend Bobby Moore in leading England to World Cup glory in 2010 were sadly dashed by a knee injury in South Africa.

Ferdinand's show of support was no surprise given that Carr was the man who recognised that his special talents would best be deployed in defence rather than in midfield, where he had been playing as a child. It's anyone's guess what kind of future Ferdinand might have had if he had joined Millwall, QPR or Middlesbrough, who all showed interest in the Peckham-born youngster, instead of giving the Hammers the nod when signing YTS forms in 1993. 'Frank Lampard went round to his house and talked to his mum,' recalls Redknapp. 'I don't know if he turned on the charm, but he picked us.'

Frank Lampard Jnr, meanwhile, remembers team-mate Rio having a terrible time when he was 15 years old as a result of 'outgrowing his body' and 'going all gangly'. However, it's generally recognised that the 1995 South East Counties League Cup final was the key turning point, with Ferdinand scoring in a 4–1 second-leg win at Chelsea that saw West Ham draw 6–6 on aggregate before claiming the trophy via a penalty shoot-out. Redknapp recalled, 'My dad rang me up saying, 'What a player you've got in your midfield.' I said, "Who's that, Frank Lampard?" And he said, "No, a tall dark boy." From then on we knew we had a real player.'

As Ferdinand turned professional, it was Carr who decided he had the attributes to play a role in defence. 'I attended a course at Lilleshall where [former Scotland manager] Andy Roxburgh appeared as the UEFA technical director,' he said. 'Andy said that a European philosophy was to play with three centre-backs, using a midfield player – who was comfortable with the ball and had reasonable defensive qualities – in the middle of the back three. The idea would be to encourage that player to break out from the back with the ball. I immediately thought, "That's Rio!" To be honest, he wasn't sure if he wanted to play in that position. But all the ingredients were there – height, pace, agility, mobility and great technical ability. And that switch was the making of him.'

With Carr given permission by Redknapp to adopt a 3–5–2 formation, the youngsters won the South East Counties League in 1996 and reached the final of the FA Youth Cup (where they lost over two legs to a Liverpool team containing Michael Owen). The great progress of the youth team meant there was a considerable buzz about Ferdinand by the time he made his first-team debut as a second-half substitute in a 1–1 draw against Sheffield Wednesday, on the final day of the 1995–96 campaign.

Rio was promptly loaned to Bournemouth for a 10-game period to further his education before returning to make 11 league starts for West Ham in which he impressed enough to win the Young Hammer-of-the-Year award in 1997. The Upton Park crowd loved Ferdinand, not just because he was a product of the club's Academy but also because he was exactly what they wanted from a West Ham player. With his midfield roots he enjoyed keeping possession and his class and composure in the middle of defence was always going to win him comparisons with Moore. He impressed against cousin Les as the Hammers beat Tottenham 2–1 at the start of the 1997–98 campaign and said, 'I would say that was my best game yet. It's nice to hear the fans chanting your name but I know I've got a long way to go.' Maybe so, but there was always a feeling of inevitability that Rio was going to reach the highest pinnacle of the game – in stark contrast to how team-mate Lampard was viewed by many fans in his early days.

Ferdinand's maturity was there for all to see and, although he occasionally overplayed situations, the supporters forgave him because they recognised he was trying to do the right things. It wasn't the West Ham way to just hoof the ball upfield or find Row Z when a team-mate could be located instead. 'He made mistakes and sometimes appeared too casual,' admitted Carr. 'But we stuck with it and the rest is history.'

At the end of the 1997–98 season, Ferdinand became the youngest ever player to collect the Hammer-of-the-Year trophy. 'The supporters have been brilliant to me and my relationship with them is fantastic,' declared the 19 year old. He also won his first full England cap that term and it was an acknowledgement of his fantastic promise that he was included in Glenn Hoddle's squad for the 1998 World Cup finals, although he didn't get to play in France.

His impressive form during the following campaign, as West Ham finished fifth to qualify for Europe, even saw him linked with a £12 million move to Real Madrid, which he dismissed as 'hype'. Speculation it might have been, but it was always going to be a case of when, as opposed to if, the stylish defender moved on to more glamorous pastures. In that respect, his loss of momentum during the 1999–2000 season was perhaps a blessing in disguise; it ensured he remained at the club for a further year. Rio admitted he had 'probably become a bit complacent', but the fact he played alongside six different centre-halves – including hardmen Neil Ruddock, Stuart Pearce and Igor Stimac – during that campaign should be taken into account.

Ferdinand was left out of Kevin Keegan's Euro 2000 squad but he rediscovered his form in the early part of the following season as Leeds emerged as the favourites to lure him away from Upton Park. Several £15 million bids were rejected before Rio's excellent display in a 1–0 win at Elland Road, in November 2000, convinced the ambitious Yorkshire outfit to increase their offer to £18 million – a new world record for a defender.

Carr admitted he had mixed feelings about Ferdinand's departure. 'Part of me recognised that it was a fantastic amount of money that couldn't be turned down,' he said, 'while another part of me thought it was a shame we couldn't produce and keep our own players.'

Former England boss Terry Venables believed it was money well spent as he declared, 'There hasn't been a player like Rio in this country for years.' After impressing at the 2002 World Cup finals, Ferdinand was on the move again, with Manchester United breaking the British transfer record to hand over £30 million for his signature.

Rio would spend the peak years of his career pursuing the game's top honours for club and country, but Redknapp's favourite 'Rolls-Royce' remained forever grateful to West Ham for putting him on the right road. 'I owe the club a hell of a lot,' he said. Not that his former youth boss wants to take too much credit. 'I never made Rio the player he was,' said Carr. 'I just helped him along the way.'

■■■■■■■■■■■■■■■■■■■

The Incredible Sulks

'We need grown-up men at this club' – Eggert Magnusson,
June 2007

'IF PEOPLE want to see me as obnoxious, arrogant or bitter, that's their prerogative,' said Nigel Reo-Coker after completing his £8.5 million move from West Ham to Aston Villa in the summer of 2007. With such perceptive mind-reading abilities, surely a more cerebral profession awaits Reo-Coker, especially with his football career failing to live up to expectations. Inconsistent form, a training-ground bust-up with Villa boss Martin O'Neill and an ankle injury saw the former England Under-21 skipper restricted to just six league starts during the 2009–10 campaign. West Ham fans were not exactly sympathetic to one of their old boys, having been glad to see the back of a player (dubbed 'Nigel Mediocre') who sulked his way through a season of struggle and showed remarkable immaturity before demanding a transfer to more lucrative pastures. 'We need grown-up men at this club,' said Hammers chairman Eggert Magnusson as he pointed the 22 year old towards the door.

Reo-Coker's miserable mood was in stark contrast to the keen and confident teenager who attended a press conference after joining West Ham, in a £500,000 switch from Wimbledon, in January 2004. The south Londoner gave an articulate and intelligent interview that suggested a very promising future – if he kept his feet on the ground. Perhaps that was always going to be difficult as he became the youngest ever Hammers skipper at the age of 20, before helping the club win promotion in 2005 and reach the 2006 FA Cup final. Just a few months later, when he learned that West Ham had turned a blind eye to an enquiry for his services (believed to be from Arsenal) just hours before the mid-2006 transfer window closed, he appeared resentful and his form, not to mention his attitude, started to deteriorate.

Assistant boss Peter Grant believed it was understandable that

Reo-Coker's 'head was going to get twisted a bit' by links with top clubs, but recognised it was counterproductive for toys to be ejected from prams. 'The best way to mump and moan is to play exceptionally well and keep other clubs interested,' he said. 'But the fans got on his case, he wasn't performing as well as he can and there's only one man who suffers for that – and that's the player himself.'

The coach also attributed the midfielder's below-par displays to the side struggling as a whole at the start of the 2006–07 campaign. 'Nigel needed the team to be playing well for him to perform at his best,' he said. 'He could be a moody little boy and had that sulkiness about him anyway, but things weren't going well and he got frustrated about that.' Not that Grant believed that Reo-Coker was ready to play for the very top clubs at that time anyway. 'Nigel knew he had to improve,' he said. 'The best midfield players are judged on their final selection of pass and how many goals they score.'

By the time Reo-Coker scored his first – and only – goal of the season, manager Alan Pardew had been fired and the midfielder was guilty of a huge over-reaction when it was suggested that certain underachieving players were responsible. 'Everyone keeps saying it's all my fault that we've been doing so badly,' he complained. 'I've been really getting it in the neck and now Pardew has gone it's only going to get worse.' His goal in the shock 1–0 home win against Manchester United, in Alan Curbishley's first game as boss, provided the perfect opportunity to rebuild some bridges with the fans who had been jeering his name.

However, instead of sharing in their joy – as any player with a less twisty head would have done – a surly Reo-Coker simply cupped his hand to his ear as if to say, 'That's shut you lot up.' The relationship between the captain and the West Ham supporters never recovered and Curbishley's repeated attempts to heal the situation by telling people to get off the midfielder's back only fuelled the player's persecution complex. Hammers legend Julian Dicks, meanwhile, could speak without a personal agenda. 'Certain players don't want to be at the club,' he said, 'and Reo-Coker, who seems to have spat his dummy out, is one I'd get rid of.'

Nigel wasted little time making plans when he declared just minutes after the final-day win at Old Trafford – when West Ham completed an unlikely double over Manchester United to save their top-flight skins – that 'to play my best I need to be happy'. With few others giving him much credit for his efforts, he added modestly, 'I made a promise to West Ham that I would keep the club in the Premier League and I've done that.'

He duly submitted an official transfer request, claiming that he'd not been sufficiently 'supported', moaning, 'There's been a lot of negative press that's been very hurtful and it's heartbreaking to see I'm not wanted.' The silence from England's top clubs was deafening and given the lack of interest, his poor form and the fact his position at Upton Park was now virtually untenable, the Hammers did remarkably well to entice such a generous fee from Villa. Predictably, a self-pitying Reo-Coker said farewell by complaining of having been 'hung out to dry' and made a 'scapegoat' – not that anybody at West Ham was still listening.

The boos that greeted Reo-Coker's initial returns to the Boleyn Ground were still nothing compared to those reserved for another former Hammer whose skills of diplomacy were breathtakingly poor, even for a footballer of typical intellect. With Jermain Defoe crassly demanding a move less than 24 hours after West Ham's relegation in May 2003, it's little surprise that the pint-sized striker – who bagged 41 goals for the club in 105 appearances after being nabbed from Charlton as a 16 year old – has repeatedly been subjected to chants of: 'You're just a short Paul Ince.' He might not have prematurely posed in another team's shirt as Ince had done, but in terms of insensitivity and poor judgement his plea to go was right up there. Both players, of course, would later blame other people – their agents – but that didn't prevent a storm of criticism for their actions.

The Hammers were on their knees after their 2–2 draw at Birmingham on 11 May confirmed relegation, with manager Glenn Roeder still in hospital after collapsing with a brain tumour. So the last thing the club needed – or expected – was for a written transfer request from Defoe to land on the desk of managing director Paul Aldridge before the following morning's papers had arrived. 'As much as I love the club I feel now is the time for me to move on,' said

Defoe. 'This is very much a career decision. I am very ambitious and hungry to achieve at the highest levels of the game.'

Ambition and hunger are commendable traits for sure, but neither justified the striker's unbelievable haste to make it known he saw his future elsewhere. A direct insult to the fans who had cheered him since his first-team debut in September 2000, it basically suggested he couldn't get away fast enough. Caretaker boss Trevor Brooking, a man who had remained loyal to West Ham as a player for nearly 20 years despite relegation, was quick to condemn the decision.

'I can't tell you how angry I am for Jermain's sake because I know what a good lad he is,' he said. 'Whoever advises him has made an error of judgement. I really don't understand the timing.' Fellow legend Billy Bonds also described the timing as being 'absolutely terrible', while Dicks, another former skipper, dubbed Defoe 'a rat' and declared the demand as 'nothing short of disgraceful'. He added, 'The fans are really hurting and this is a real kick in the teeth. It is wrong for him to jump ship like this.'

Thankfully, West Ham quickly made it known, both to the public and the agency (SFX) which represented Defoe, that they had no intention of honouring his selfish demands and the request was duly filed in the rubbish bin. Brooking said, 'As far as we are concerned, Jermain is a West Ham player and he has two years left on his contract.'

While other valuable assets such as Joe Cole, Fredi Kanouté and Glen Johnson were allowed to move on as West Ham raised some much-needed funds, Defoe effectively remained in a prolonged school detention at the club, very much against his wishes but to the delight of those supporters who now viewed him as the class clown. He scored fifteen times in twenty-two outings in the first half of the 2003–04 campaign – including a Carling Cup hat-trick at Cardiff – but his general discontent was reflected in three red cards in twelve games (against Gillingham, West Brom and Walsall). Previously viewed as a well-behaved Academy pupil, he was starting to become a very naughty boy indeed. Chairman Terence Brown caused some fuss when he controversially claimed Defoe's 'head is not right' and, with automatic promotion looking beyond them, the club cashed in on the player by allowing him to make a £7 million switch to Tottenham in January 2004, with striker Bobby Zamora moving the opposite way as part of the deal.

Defoe did at least express regret at his previous actions. 'I mishandled that move and can only apologise,' he said. 'I knew it was the wrong timing and so many people were saying, "How could he do that?" But it wasn't me and it's now in the past.' As the howls of derision show every time he sneaks back onto the Upton Park turf, the past has a nasty habit of catching up with you.

A Tale of Two Franks

'At times it has been difficult' – Frank Lampard Jnr

IT'S A body language expert's dream case study. Chelsea amigos Frank Lampard Jnr, John Terry and Joe Cole are photographed together on the Upton Park touchline prior to their introductions at Tony Carr's testimonial game in May 2010. A slightly hunched Lampard is pictured chewing his nails and pulling an unusually coy expression as he stares out onto his old stamping ground. Cole has got his arms folded tightly across his chest; either he is feeling cold or bashful or both, but his boyish smile in the direction of a chuckling Terry provides a telling counterpoint to Lampard's obvious apprehension.

Five minutes later and a tangible sense of relief fills the uncertain atmosphere; relief for Lampard that his reception from 14,000 fans is a warm one given the acrimony that has festered since his departure from West Ham nine years earlier. And relief for many of the supporters that the poisonous baiting of one of Upton Park's most accomplished sons might, in future, revert to the witty banter more befitting of Cockney humour. 'It was a good reception from the crowd,' Lampard said after the game. 'I was pleasantly surprised. At times it has been difficult, the relationship with the fans . . . I think everyone has to move on.'

Before moving on it's worth studying that photograph (easy enough to find with a few Google clicks) a little harder. Look closely and in the blur of the background is Frank Lampard Snr, comfortably relaxed and smiling as he chats to club officials in the players' tunnel. Talk about a picture telling a thousand words.

Lampard Snr took charge of the Academy All-Stars team on the night. 'Manager' was one of the few roles he did not occupy during a lengthy association with the club, which saw him act as assistant boss to Harry Redknapp, as a coach, scout and, most significantly, as a talented and hugely popular left-back.

Born in East Ham and raised a West Ham supporter, Lampard Snr had played the majority of his 665 games for the club – a total bettered only by his old defensive partner Billy Bonds – by the start of the time period covered by this book. None of his appearances, however, would define him more than the 1980 FA Cup semi-final replay against Everton, when his diving header and merry corner-flag jig secured West Ham a place in the final and gave rise to a terrace song in his honour that has rung out ever since.

Within days of earning his second FA Cup winners' medal, Lampard was heading to Australia to earn his second full England cap, a full eight years after his first. More call-ups should have come his way during his 1970s heyday, but as a right-footed player he was in the shadow of natural 'lefties'. He once joked, 'People used to ask me what a good left-back needs and my answer was always, "A good right foot!"'

The obvious footballing comparison between father and son – aside from the fact that they each suffered a broken leg aged 19 – is their acute awareness of the flow of a game. Many a West Ham attack started from the perceptive boot of Frank Snr, although it is for his ferocious tackling, as well as his swerving long-range shots, that he is most fondly remembered.

With his unshaven chin and ice-cool demeanour, there was something of the Spaghetti Western icon about him, especially when marauding around the pitch with fellow bearded bandits like Keith Robson, Graham Paddon and Bonds. Alongside the latter, he was superb during the record-breaking Second Division title season of

1980–81, a campaign that underlined how Bonds, Lampard and Trevor Brooking had so effectively inherited the 'Holy Triumvirate' mantle handed down by Bobby Moore, Geoff Hurst and Martin Peters. Lampard's manager at the time, John Lyall, described him as a very special player who 'typified what West Ham is about'.

Playing his last game for the club against Liverpool on the final day of the 1984–85 season, having spent much of that campaign dispensing pearls of wisdom to the reserves, Lampard took the Fenchurch Street line to Southend for a role as player/coach under Moore, his former Hammers room-mate. When that adventure petered out, he focused on his burgeoning property business, on family life and on moulding the soccer skills of a little lad who was already showing great promise on the Lampard lawn in Romford. 'There was quite a lot of pressure,' Frank Jnr told *FourFourTwo* magazine in 2001, 'although I don't regret for a minute how much Dad pushed me. He could see I had talent and he's a hard man who tells you what he thinks. I'd cry sometimes because of the stick he gave me but I'm glad of it now.'

By the early 1990s, father, son and brother-in-law Harry Redknapp – married to Sandra, sister of Frank Snr's wife Pat – were together at West Ham. Lampard Snr was doing some part-time coaching of the juniors when Redknapp arrived as Billy Bonds' assistant manager. He then took on scouting duties and when Redknapp replaced Bonds as manager, Frank became assistant manager. Meanwhile, Lampard Jnr was about to emerge from posh Brentwood School laden with O levels and a notably high IQ, but also lofty ambitions to follow in his father's Adidas boot steps.

Despite a flirtation with Tottenham youths, Lampard Jnr fulfilled his dad's hopes by signing apprentice forms with the Hammers and set about establishing a reputation as a high-octane midfielder with an uncanny knack for scoring goals. By the time he appeared in the FA Youth Cup final defeat against Liverpool, in the spring of 1996 – inevitably scoring West Ham's goal in a 4–1 aggregate defeat – Lampard Jnr had already made his first-team bow.

That summer, ahead of Euro '96, he and team-mate Rio Ferdinand were invited to train with the full England squad. Coaching staff at club and international level could clearly spot something special in both players, but while West Ham fans were mightily impressed with Ferdinand, ambivalencc was probably the best way to describe the feeling towards young Frank.

During a difficult 1996–97 season, the chunky teenager's development continued with 16 first-team appearances, but he struggled to impose himself and sections of the crowd targeted him – and the bench – with accusations of favouritism, nepotism and pie-eating. 'Silly people were thinking it was all a family act,' spat Redknapp. 'None of them knew what they were looking at but I certainly did.' His under-fire nephew added, 'Some people say I get an easy ride. And that always seems to happen when things are going badly.'

For possibly the first time in his professional life, Frank Snr started to receive stick, too; his unassuming demeanour led some supporters to question exactly what he contributed other than being Redknapp's sidekick. Even Jimmy Greaves, a colleague from the early 1970s, chipped in with a few barbed comments in his column for *The Sun*, an act which offended Redknapp who later retorted, 'Frank had played at Upton Park for 20 years. He knew the game inside out and knew West Ham inside out. It wasn't as if I was employing my brother-in-law from the local fish and chip shop.'

Frank Jnr always had bigger fish to fry than could be found in the chippies of Green Street. 'I'd be an idiot to rule out the thought of a move at some stage in my career – the player who does that is a rare one,' he said in 1999 in his column in *Hammers News Magazine*. By then he had found his footing in midfield, become a regular fixture on the scoresheet and made his full England debut in a friendly versus Belgium. However, an impressive record of thirty-eight goals in one hundred and cighty-six Hammers appearances – all by the age of twenty-two – came to an abrupt end two years later when, following his uncle's sacking and his dad's resultant departure ('I took it as a formality that we'd leave together – not that I was asked to stay'), he found himself on the springboard to greater things. All of a sudden, family ties did seem to count for something for Frank Jnr, who at the time of his £11 million switch to Chelsea reportedly claimed that his position at West Ham had become untenable.

Despite the unsatisfactory circumstances surrounding his own departure, Lampard Snr could look back with pride on the part he played during seven of the club's most productive years in terms of league placings, entertainment and home-grown success. His son, meanwhile, could look forward to a truly glittering career at Stamford Bridge (three Premier League titles, over a hundred league goals, FIFA World Player-of-the-Year runner-up in 2005), an established career with England . . . and season after season of abuse from West Ham supporters.

There is no doubting that the more extreme vitriol regularly thrown at Lampard by the Hammers' hardcore support is based on little more than repulsion at his choice of employer, jealousy of his considerable achievements and plain old bully-boy spite. For others it's a matter of principle: sportsmen paid as much as Lampard should be thick-skinned enough to take flak – including the faintly absurd 'Fat Frank' jibes – and not then turn round and criticise the supporters who used to pay their wages. Lampard Jnr has done his bit to fan the flames of this sorry saga, on occasion talking bullishly to the press about how he derives motivation from the stick he receives at Upton Park. 'I seem to mean a lot to them but they don't mean anything to me. Not any more,' he was once quoted as saying. 'I thrive on their hatred. It's an inspiration to me more than anything else. It just makes me want to climb higher and higher up the ladder with Chelsea.'

He claims the saddest aspect of the whole saga is how much upset it caused his dad and late mother Pat, who died unexpectedly in 2008. One can only imagine how upsetting it is to hear your child publicly abused by thousands, but it is not solely Hammers fans he seems to offend. England boo-boys have scapegoated Frank after below-par performances for his country and there are even 'Fat Frank' hate campaign pages on Facebook which appear to have nothing to do with irate Irons supporters. On the flipside, there are numerous pro-Frank websites, too, which goes to show just how much the man divides opinion.

Maybe all the hot air and ill feeling will start to subside in the wake of Tony Carr's testimonial. Frank Jnr held out an olive branch after that game, at the same time dropping a reminder that blue is the colour. 'I will always remember where I came from. Even though I am a Chelsea person now, I never forget.'

His dad doesn't need to kiss a badge to demonstrate his loyalties. Not so long after being rudely pushed out of Upton Park, Frank Snr remained unequivocal about where his affections lay. 'West Ham are still my team. That's something that nobody can take away from you. You're just claret and blue and that's how it is.'

●●●●●●●●●●●●●●●●●●●●

When Harry Met Terry

'I thought it was disgusting; we balanced the books'
– Harry Redknapp, April 2002

IF THE vitriolic abuse aimed at Harry Redknapp by West Ham fans during the 2009–10 season is anything to go by, it seems they remember the manager who was charged with tax evasion and secretly filmed for the BBC's investigative *Panorama* programme, about alleged corruption in football, far more than the one who took the Hammers to three successive top-half finishes in the Premier League – including a second-best-ever fifth – and a place in Europe during seven roller-coaster years as manager. Or maybe it's simply because he was in charge of rivals Tottenham Hotspur.

Either way, nothing changes the fact that when Redknapp parted company with West Ham, on 9 May 2001, it was, in purely football terms, a dark day for the club. There would be no more Cockney wit from the man who embodied the spirit of the East End entrepreneur made good, no more exciting wheeling and dealing of players and, two years later, no more top-flight football after the team was relegated thanks to the efforts of Glenn Roeder. All because of one record-breaking transfer deal that arguably changed not only the course of West Ham's future but also that of their manager.

It's fair to suggest that had Rio Ferdinand not been allowed to make an £18 million move to Leeds United in December 2000, Redknapp would probably have remained in charge of the Hammers beyond the end of that season and potentially many more. Nevertheless, it was less a case of the team's demise in the second half of the campaign and more a dispute with chairman Terence Brown about the Ferdinand money that resulted in a new four-year deal being ripped up and Harry being handed his P45 instead.

A shock 1–0 FA Cup fourth-round win at Manchester United was the highlight of a campaign that had started in disappointing fashion – no wins in the first six games – and disintegrated after a winter peak that produced five victories in six league outings, to the point that relegation fears were only erased in the penultimate match. Ten days before the Hammers finished 15th in the table, Redknapp met Brown for a meeting in which finances and budgets were discussed. Hours later, a statement was issued claiming that West Ham and their manager had 'agreed to part company', with Brown expressing 'sincere appreciation of all Harry has done'.

Speaking at his lavish Sandbanks home on the Dorset coast, Redknapp later insisted there was nothing mutual about the agreement and that he'd been sacked. 'I was pushed,' he said. 'I went into see the chairman and he was upset that I'd told the press that we needed to spend £16 million in the transfer market if we were going to get back into the top six or seven of the table the following season. I knew we needed to improve the team and it was a realistic assessment. But he felt that I was putting him under pressure and he got the hump about it.'

If leaving Upton Park wasn't bad enough, Redknapp was further angered when he read the Chairman's Report that accompanied the club's set of accounts, issued in November 2001. Brown clearly saw it as an opportunity to justify Redknapp's departure and used the statistics that suited him to present a damning indictment of his former manager's tenure. 'The team won just one of its first ten games in the Premier League and four of its last twenty-two,' he wrote. 'Only twice in 75 years of league football have we had a worse home record than last season. The team Harry took over from Billy Bonds had just finished 13th in a 22-team Premier League with 52 points and he left us with a team which finished 15th (out of 20 teams) with 42 points.

'If we add to our transfer and wage expenditure the £4 million a year invested in our youth development programme, then 15th place in the Premier League, failure to qualify for European competitions on a regular basis and continued embarrassment at the hands of lower division teams in cup competitions, it does not make financial sense.'

Good profits had been made on the sale of players such as Eyal Berkovic, John Hartson and Slaven Bilić, with the manager seemingly having to generate his own funds in the transfer market, often selling one to buy three. Yet Brown claimed there had actually been a loss on transfer dealings over the previous seven years, insisting that £79 million had been spent in gross terms as opposed to the £56 million calculated by fans. 'There is a misconception that the club has made substantial profits in the transfer market, but the truth is very different,' he said. 'During the seven years we bought and sold a total of one hundred and thirty-four players. The net deficit from this player trading was £34 million (excluding the Ferdinand sale).'

Ignoring the many successful buys or the circumstances in which his manager was working, he then proceeded to highlight recent flops such as Christian Bassila and Gary Charles: 'One of last season's loan signings, who cost £720,000 in salary and loan fee, spent 85 minutes on the pitch. Another player, who will cost the club £4.4 million in salary and transfer fee, has so far made only three starting appearances in over two years. Such expenditure cannot be justified.'

Redknapp was furious. 'I thought it was disgusting,' he said. 'This was the same man who, just a few days before I left, was offering me a new four-year contract and saying he wanted me to stay at the club for the next ten years. He can say what he wants but at the end of the day we balanced the books. I guess you find people out in these situations. The fact is that I was forced to take gambles in the transfer market and it's a punt – some come off, some don't. When we finished fifth I felt we could have continued to improve, but we didn't have the money to push on.'

Brown has since denied that Redknapp's public plea for funds was a significant factor in his dismissal. 'I have often been amused by the comment that the board were affected by an interview that Harry gave,' he said, before adding, 'My biggest regret is the way we bought and sold so many players and allowed salaries [believed to be £30 million per annum] to escalate.'

The major bone of contention was how money was spent in the wake of Ferdinand's sale for a British record fee. Titi Camara, Rigobert Song, Ragnvald Soma, Svetoslav Todorov, Hayden Foxe and Christian Dailly were recruited for around £6.5 million, as Redknapp attempted to pad out a squad he believed was too thin, but none of them looked good signings. With an unimpressed Brown choosing to include the value of their contracts to suggest that a large chunk of the Ferdinand money had already been spent, he was never going to trust Redknapp with further funds, especially with the West Stand at Upton Park being rebuilt.

According to Tom Bower's *Broken Dreams* – a book which described itself as an 'exposé of football's financial secrets . . . lifting the lid off the greed that threatens to destroy the beautiful game' – Brown 'agreed to pay Redknapp £300,000 for not spending any of the sale money on new players'. Quite why he would need to do this given the chairman controlled the club's funds is something that begs many questions. The book claimed the bonus 'proved to be wasted', with Redknapp recruiting half a dozen players, while trying to suggest that the manager was happy for Rio to be sold. 'Redknapp loved dealing – and no deal was bigger than the sale of Ferdinand,' wrote Bower.

With Norwegian agent Rune Hauge – back in action after being banned by FIFA for the secret payment that saw Arsenal manager George Graham sacked in 1995 – and Ferdinand's representative Pini Zahavi involved in a deal that Redknapp had pushed up to £18 million, there would inevitably be large commission payments. 'Redknapp knew that the transfer fee would not only benefit West Ham but also the two agents,' said Bower.

The book also, somewhat laughably, referred to Brown 'personally earning the money for someone else to waste', but Redknapp refuted everything that Bower had tried to imply without any factual evidence. 'The claims made in *Broken Dreams* are absolute rubbish,' he said. 'It's been written by a man who knows nothing about football and got an easy interview with Terence Brown. It's as if he's saying that I did all the deals. Doesn't he understand that it's the club that signs the cheques?'

Redknapp would prove his talents as a manager by taking Portsmouth into the Premier League – as West Ham were going down in 2003 – before returning to Fratton Park, following an ill-fated spell at Southampton, to win the FA Cup and then taking charge of Spurs, who he took into the Champions League. Brown has since indicated that football had little to do with Redknapp's exit. 'Harry contributed an enormous amount to West Ham,' he said. 'His knowledge of football is second to none. He did love the club, signed some great players and gave us some very exciting seasons.'

Of that there can be no question.

■■■■■■■■■■■■■■■■■■

Simply the Best?

'It was just one bunch of lads having a laugh'
– Pat Holland, October 2005

AS EMPHATIC promotion campaigns go, West Ham's charge back to the First Division in 1980–81 takes some beating. The Hammers won an incredible 19 of their 21 home league games, went unbeaten in their final 18 outings as they claimed the championship trophy and set a post-war Second Division record of 66 points (in the final season before three points for a win was introduced). They won more away games than any other team in the division (nine), were beaten just three times on the road and banged in seventy-nine goals to finish a whopping thirteen points clear of runners-up Notts County.

Meanwhile, top scorer David Cross hit the net thirty-three times to establish a brilliant fifty-six-goal partnership with Paul Goddard, during an epic campaign that stretched to an exhausting sixty-one games thanks to the club's adventures in three cup competitions. So it's little wonder that John Lyall later described the season as 'the most satisfying' of his entire managerial career.

In fact, many fans – and players involved for that matter – look back on that team as one of the greatest West Ham have ever had, which says something considering it was playing in the Second Division. Nowadays, of course, it's difficult to imagine such talents as Trevor Brooking, Billy Bonds, Alan Devonshire and Frank Lampard remaining loyal to a club about to begin its third successive season outside the top flight, while Phil Parkes, Alvin Martin, Ray Stewart and David Cross were also far too good for the level they were playing at.

That fact was evident in West Ham winning the FA Cup the previous season. Yet the team had only finished seventh in the league and with full-back Stewart its second highest scorer – thanks to his role as penalty-taker – and veteran striker Stuart Pearson struggling with injury, Lyall knew that he had to recruit another goalscorer to bolster his attack. So, for the second time in 18 months, the Hammers signed a player from QPR for a club-record fee, with Goddard following in the footsteps of goalkeeper Parkes to complete an £800,000 move to Upton Park. 'I knew instinctively that he and Cross would form a sound attacking partnership,' said Lyall.

Goddard arrived within days of West Ham's 1–0 defeat by Liverpool in a mediocre Charity Shield encounter at Wembley and had a miserable debut the following weekend when an Achilles injury forced him off during the 2–1 home defeat by Luton. 'The Hammers took the lead but then relaxed, lost control and allowed clumsiness to cost them the game,' wrote Sydney Spicer in the *Daily Express* – and what a familiar tale that has been down the years. The FA Cup had been paraded at Upton Park before the game and Lyall was forced to call his players together when they returned to training, to remind them that their shock victory against Arsenal was 'now a thing of the past' and that they needed to focus more firmly on the future.

The manager's message did the trick. Draws at Bristol City and Preston, although failing to give West Ham the first win they were looking for, provided the launch pad for what would become a fifteen-game unbeaten run in the league between August and November – until Luton provided the opposition again and beat them for the second time in three months. By that stage, the Hammers were top of the table, having won eleven of their previous thirteen games – including four- and five-goal romps against Notts County and Bristol City respectively – and Cross and Goddard taking their tally to thirty goals between them. They slipped up again when losing 2–0 at Derby, on 26 November, to make it two defeats in three games, but a 3–1 victory against the same opposition the following month not only saw West Ham gain revenge but also establish a new club record of eleven successive home league wins.

With cup games also taken into account, that figure became 16 with Tottenham becoming a notable top-flight scalp in the League Cup thanks to another strike by Cross which took the Hammers into the semi-finals. The run of successive home league triumphs also climbed to an amazing 16 – with Preston walloped 5–0 and Chelsea spanked 4–0 – before West Ham's European adventures finally caught up with them in mid-March.

A midweek visit to Dynamo Tblisi for a Cup Winners' Cup quarter-final match was always going to be tiring for the players even if everything went smoothly. Trips behind the Iron Curtain in those days rarely did – especially for British teams in the competition – and a combination of Russian red tape and black ice when changing flights in Moscow ensured that West Ham's journey was fraught with difficulty. 'We were hit by the most incredible snags that interrupted schedules, frayed tempers and brought physical discomfort,' reflected Lyall.

The Hammers eventually arrived in Tblisi nearly a day late and, although they won thc game 1–0 (to be eliminated 4–2 on aggregate), they had nothing left in the tank by the time Oldham arrived at Upton Park three days later. Thc exhausted players ran around as if they had sacks of spuds on their back, yet it was to their great credit that they still forced a 1–1 draw to remain unbeaten in the league since Boxing Day, when they had collapsed to a shock 3–0 defeat at QPR that suggested much too much turkey – or something equally festive – had been consumed the evening before.

Lyall responded to the 'lamentable' display by keeping his players in the Loftus Road dressing-room for an hour after the game. He told his men that promotion was the absolute priority and that they were good enough to go unbeaten in their remaining league games. And so they did, overcoming the loss of midfielder Pat Holland, who damaged a knee when scoring in the 1–1 draw at Notts County – an injury that effectively ended his playing career – and the disappointment of relinquishing their grip on the FA Cup with a 1–0 defeat at Wrexham in a third-round second replay. Thankfully, Jimmy Neighbour was available to step into the side and the former Spurs winger quickly won new friends by scoring the goal in the two-legged League Cup semi-final against Coventry that booked West Ham a Wembley date with Liverpool.

Other sides might have allowed their extra-curricular activities to undermine them but the Hammers shook off their 2–1 replay defeat by the Reds – West Ham's 19th cup game including the Charity Shield – to guarantee promotion just four days later, on 4 April, with a 2–0 home win against bottom club Bristol Rovers. The Second Division championship was secured the following weekend with a 5–1 success at Grimsby in which Cross scored four goals for the first time in his career. Then Goddard smashed a hat-trick against former club QPR as West Ham turned the tables on the last side to beat them in the league by enjoying a 3–0 home win. Sadly, a goalless draw at Cardiff allowed the Welsh outfit to avoid relegation, while a Nicky Morgan goal saw the Hammers round off the stunning campaign with a 1–0 win at Sheffield Wednesday.

West Ham's success was reflected in the amount of international recognition their players received, with Brooking remaining an England international regular despite his prolonged spell out of the top flight – and scoring twice in the vital 3–1 World Cup qualifying win in Hungary that booked a place at the 1982 finals – and fellow midfielder Devonshire later adding six more caps to the two already earned. Martin made the first of his 17 England outings in the friendly against Brazil in May 1981, while a rib injury denied Bonds his chance of playing in that game following his surprise call-up by former Hammers boss Ron Greenwood. 'I fancied myself and Billy to take anyone on that season,' remembered Martin. Goddard's early season form saw him break into the England Under-21 squad, midfielder Paul Allen smashed Bobby Moore's appearance record for the England youth team, while Stewart collected the first of his ten full Scotland caps.

Incredibly, West Ham called upon just seventeen players during the entire 1980–81 campaign – the joint-lowest figure in the club's history – with nine of them (Brooking, Lampard, Holland, Martin, Allen, Morgan, Geoff Pike, Paul Brush and Bobby Barnes) being home-grown. According to their manager, in the newly launched *Hammers* magazine, they boasted 'by far the best disciplinary record in the country'. As well as the goalscoring prowess of Cross and Goddard, Lyall credited the success of the team to the 'essential balance of flair and aggression' provided by the experienced Bonds, Lampard and Brooking.

'That was an absolutely wonderful team,' said Goddard. 'As a 20 year old, I didn't realise how good we really were and I just count myself lucky to have played with so many quality players at one time. Some of the football we played was out of this world.'

Parkes even believes the 1981 promotion winners were 'a better all-round team' than the one that pushed for the First Division title five years later. 'Although we were playing in the Second Division,' he said, 'we could have held our own against any First Division side. We were going out for games expecting to win and anything less than maximum points was a real shock to the system.'

Lyall later declared that winning the Division Two championship was one of his 'most cherished memories' but typically found time to reflect on the sadness of Holland's misfortune. The bubbly midfielder prefers to reflect on the tremendous spirit that existed between the players at that time. 'The dressing-room was fantastic,' he said. 'The banter was great and there were never any little splinter groups, just one bunch of lads having a laugh.'

Upton Sparks

'Hell breaks loose in war of West Ham' – The London Paper,
August 2009

ONE SPORTS journalist described the unsavoury scenes around the Boleyn Ground, before West Ham's Carling Cup second-round clash with Millwall on 25 August 2009, as 'the worst violence I have ever seen'. Funny that, given the reporter in question was rumoured to be stuffing his face in the Upton Park press lounge at the time. There was indeed a hostile atmosphere in the surrounding streets and the fact that one Millwall fan was stabbed should not be underplayed. However, the media's distortion of the events of that night, as they deliberately blurred the distinction between what took place inside and out of the ground to suit their own sensationalistic ends, reflected the fact that the Hammers will always struggle to disassociate themselves from a reputation for hooliganism that has been hanging around their necks since the dark days of the 1970s.

Horrific headlines such as 'Battle of the Boleyn', 'War Zone' and 'Hell Breaks Loose in War of West Ham', supported by images of assorted pitch invaders, had outside observers believing that Hammers and Millwall fans had engaged in a full-scale riot inside the stadium, with the football playing second fiddle to fierce and relentless fighting. The reality, however, was that while some home supporters were indeed guilty of running on to the pitch, it was more through boisterous behaviour – neither big nor clever – rather than menacing aggression, the three occasions being sparked by two West Ham goals in the 3–1 extra-time win and the final whistle.

That said, a surge in the lower tier of the West Stand did result in an overspill at the corner with the Sir Trevor Brooking Stand, where the visiting contingent were housed and isolated. With one blood-soaked Hammers fan being dragged away by police, the media had the photograph they needed and duly exploited, although few stopped to ask themselves how he had sustained his injuries.

West Ham were always going to be held accountable for the actions of their supporters inside the stadium and were understandably eager to cooperate with the authorities, who were quick to condemn the disorder. So too were various parties who jumped aboard the bandwagon with their personal agendas. Hence, in a 'name-and-shame' damage limitation exercise, the club's website ran a series of photographs depicting everybody from boozed-up, blubber-bellied bovver boys to grinning girls waving their handbags around in a bid to identify those who had trespassed on the playing surface. One fan, pictured in the papers, even carried his four-year-old son on his shoulders, suggesting he was out for an evening stroll rather than a punch-up.

Meanwhile, the real villains were those looking for trouble and clashing with police outside the ground. It was important to distinguish those running riot in Green Street from those running randomly on to the Boleyn turf, because West Ham could not be held responsible for anything that happened outside their gates. It wasn't the club's fault that several hundred ticketless Millwall fans travelled to the East End with the aim of causing chaos and conflict. Or that police ignored the warnings provided by the pre-season friendly with Napoli and allowed fans to congregate drunkenly and develop a mob mentality at a pub (between the Tube station and ground) that common sense dictated should have been closed. Certainly, questions had to be asked as to whether the authorities had underestimated the potential for problems, given the historical animosity between the two groups of fans.

It looked as if West Ham were going to be left to carry the can for the failings of others. Some suggested the club should be thrown out of the Carling Cup or forced to play future games behind closed doors. Former Hammers boss Harry Redknapp even suggested that Millwall and West Ham should never be allowed to play each other again in cup competitions, when it seemed that the most obvious solution would be to simply ban away fans on the rare occasions the two clubs met (with the Lions two divisions below the Irons at that time). Meanwhile, as if to prove that all those months spent studying the criminal mind and watching *Cracker* at Hendon had not gone to waste, the police piped up that some of the skirmishes had been 'pre-planned'. Brilliant.

Despite West Ham denying all charges against them, the FA found the club guilty of failing to ensure that their fans refrained from 'violent, threatening, obscene and provocative behaviour' and 'entering the field of play'. A £115,000 fine was duly imposed, plus £5,000 costs. The Hammers were, however, cleared of two further charges of failing to ensure their supporters refrained from 'racist behaviour' and 'throwing missiles, harmful or dangerous objects on the pitch'.

In contrast, Millwall were found not guilty of all three charges against them, despite seats having been thrown onto the pitch from the away end, where toilets were also reportedly damaged. More than 60 people were eventually arrested by police and charged with disorder offences, the vast majority of which related to pitch encroachment and resulted in banning orders.

Media clichés about 'thugs returning to drag soccer back into the gutter' are as predictable as they are lazy, yet there is no escaping the fact that there remain some people who are lured to football purely for its tribalism and trouble-making potential. The fear was that the shock headlines generated by the latest confrontation between West Ham and Millwall hoodlums would simply increase the likelihood of further violent clashes taking place in the future. The two factions have been enemies since the clubs were formed as rival docklands outfits in the late nineteenth century – West Ham as Thames Ironworks – and the intensity of ill feeling was never more apparent than in the 1970s and 1980s, when organised gangs such as the ICF (Inter-City Firm) and Millwall's Bushwackers existed as conduits for such hatred.

Indeed, the conflict of those times has been documented in numerous books about Hammers hooliganism (not least by former ICF main-man Cass Pennant, whose autobiography was turned into a film) and provided the inspiration for movies such as *The Firm*, *ID* and *Green Street* to turn football thuggery into a mini industry. The critics might argue about whether such stories glorify football violence but when retired hooligans are being asked to pose for pictures with people's children on match days, some form of celebrity status has clearly been achieved.

West Ham would have been wise to distance themselves from *Green Street* purely on the basis that it's a dreadful film, with the lead role incongruously played by Elijah Wood, better known as Frodo Baggins in *The Lord of the Rings* trilogy, and the second lead by Charlie Hunnam, purveyor of a Cockney accent so poor it makes Barbra Streisand sound like Barbara Windsor.

Yet it was only after allowing the film's cameras in for the home game against Gillingham, on 23 October 2004, that the club discovered that the film's theme concerned gang warfare between Hammers and Millwall fans. Apparently, the West Ham hierarchy demanded that the original title of *Hooligans* be dropped; *Green Street* might have sounded a little less menacing but it did the club few favours, the name clearly pinning the violence on West Ham's mast.

With that kind of conditioning, it's perhaps little wonder that so many youngsters responded the way they did when Millwall arrived at Upton Park in 2009. Nobody, particularly if they wear a claret and blue shirt, is supposed to like them . . . remember?

Hart and Soul

'It's in my nature to be honest' – John Hartson, July 1998

FOOTBALLERS DON'T come any more honest than John Hartson. Stretched out across his bed in an Edinburgh hotel room, the striker could try to make any number of excuses as to why his form dipped so alarmingly the previous season. Instead, he tells it exactly as it is. 'I got a bit complacent,' he says. 'Around about January or February, I personally felt I'd shot my bolt. I'd scored 17 goals in the first 20 games and that was frightening. Then I scored twice in my next 14 games and obviously the expectation was that I was going to keep scoring as I had done. But I went off the boil and wasn't training so hard. I honestly felt that I'd done my bit. It's not the right way to think because there was a long way to go – we were challenging for Europe and I was pushing to be top scorer – but it happens in all aspects of life, doesn't it?'

It's a stunning admission but, as John says, 'It's in my nature to be honest. It's the way I've been brought up.'

Hartson spent just two years as a West Ham player, but rarely can the two halves of a player's career at any one club have offered such distinct contrasts as those experienced by the Welshman at Upton Park. His 13-goal partnership with fellow new signing Paul Kitson, following their arrival in February 1997, rescued the Hammers from relegation, and his electrifying form in the first part of the following campaign took his tally to 22 strikes in 31 games. The world, as they say, was his lobster. But then, just as quickly, John's form deserted him to the extent that he scored just 11 times in his next 42 outings – during which time he was involved in a highly publicised training ground bust-up with Eyal Berkovic – before making a surprise move to Wimbledon. As the Everly Brothers song suggests, it was indeed 'So Sad to Watch Good Love Go bad'.

With foreign forwards such as Paulo Futre and Florin Raducioiu lasting just months at the Boleyn Ground and Iain Dowie having a barren run before getting crocked, goals were in short supply in the middle of the 1996–97 season – hardly surprising with Mike Newell and Steve Jones in attack. The Hammers were clearly heading for the drop and with the team entrenched in the bottom three, after collecting just 22 points from 24 games, boss Harry Redknapp acknowledged that 'desperate measures' were needed if he was going to turn things around. He duly put pressure on his board to provide the funds to make a £2.3 million raid on Newcastle for Kitson and then smashed the club's transfer record with the £5 million signing of Hartson from Arsenal (based on an initial payment of £3.2 million plus add-ons). Critics accused West Ham of making 'panic buys', with both strikers having struggled for first-team action at their previous clubs. However, Redknapp believed the two players would complement each other and was confident that in 21-year-old Hartson he had a star in the making. 'John is going to be the centre-forward for this club way into the foreseeable future,' he said.

'I can't promise miracles,' said Hartson on his arrival. 'All I can do is give 100 per cent and hopefully help keep West Ham in the Premier League. I'm fully committed and like to think I chase lost causes.' He was referring to hopeful punts up field rather than his new team's predicament, but it looked to be a good summary of the situation following a 1–0 defeat at Derby that saw Hartson collect a booking that incurred a two-game ban. Thankfully, he was still eligible to make his home debut against Tottenham on 24 February, and West Ham's thrilling 4–3 victory – in which both he and Kitson opened their accounts for the club – would be a game that lived long in the memory. Kitson scored twice in a home 3–2 win against Chelsea, while Hartson also bagged a brace in a 3–1 success at Coventry.

Team-mate Julian Dicks, who scored twice in that game against Spurs, remembered, 'John was exactly what we needed and his passion got the crowd going as well. When you see someone like that arrive, it really does give everyone a lift.' Suddenly West Ham were scoring for fun, although Redknapp wasn't laughing when Hartson relinquished penalty duties to give Kitson the chance of a hat-trick against Everton, only for his colleague to miss and allow the visitors to subsequently wipe out a 2–0 deficit and secure an undeserved draw.

Kitson did indeed walk away with the match ball in the next home game against Sheffield Wednesday, with Hartson scoring the other two West Ham goals in the 5–1 win. Ultimately, the Hammers finished in 14th place, two points clear of the drop zone, with Hartson insisting, 'I would never have come to West Ham if I thought we were really going down.'

The Hart was on fire in the early part of the following season, scoring a hat-trick in a Coca-Cola Cup win against Huddersfield and bagging braces against Aston Villa (twice) and Bolton. Then, seemingly with no rhyme or reason, 'Super John' morphed into 'Big Bad John', with the goals evaporating and the striker being sent off twice in seven games as his frustration got the better of him. Redknapp was furious that his star's enforced absence for seven games had undermined his team's hopes of qualifying for Europe, warning, 'John is a good player but he has let his performances and discipline drop. If he is not careful he could end up in the same situation he found himself in at Arsenal.'

As West Ham visited Scotland for a pre-season game at Hibernian, Hartson insisted he was fully focused on rediscovering his best form again. 'My biggest target is to keep myself fit,' he admitted, just moments before team-mate Berkovic paid a brief visit to his room. 'It's basically down to how well I look after myself. I like a beer, although I wouldn't say I drink more than the average 24 year old. But I like to enjoy myself and when I go out and have half a dozen pints I can put weight on.'

He would later admit to being 'about ten pounds overweight' when returning for pre-season training, although answering Redknapp's call to play while trying to shake off an ankle injury did him few favours in terms of trying to make a good impression. 'When I'm not fit it's like sending out a Formula One car into a Grand Prix with top gear missing. It's just not going to happen,' he said. Then came the autumn incident with Berkovic, with video footage revealing how Hartson kicked the Israeli playmaker in the face as tempers flared. It's something for which the Welshman has been apologising ever since and he insisted, 'I'm deeply sorry and it really does bother me that I will be remembered for what happened at Chadwell Heath. It's so worrying that people have got the wrong impression of me.'

West Ham fined the striker £10,000, while the FA later imposed a further £20,000 penalty and three-game ban. Berkovic claimed that 'had my head been a football it would have flown into the top corner of the net', but with Hartson's profligacy resulting in just four goals in twenty appearances that season, it's more likely it would have flown over the bar. Speculation was rife that Berkovic would soon be leaving Upton Park, having complained that he was 'very upset with West Ham because they tried to cover up what happened' – as if they were supposed to broadcast news of the fracas from the rooftops. However, other factors were playing a part behind the scenes. Redknapp again admitted that Hartson's form 'hadn't been good' and that he needed to work harder. Just a few weeks later, however, the striker was sold to Wimbledon; a shock development simply because nobody realised the tiny south London outfit had £7.5 million to spend on one player.

As luck would have it, Hartson made his home debut for the Dons against his former employers, where the striker was deeply saddened to find himself booed by West Ham fans during the goalless draw. 'I thought that was a bit harsh,' he said. 'Thirty-three goals and then £7.5 million, what more could I have done for them? I felt I deserved better after scoring some of the goals that kept the club up.'

John would later restore his goalscoring reputation during a successful five-year period with Celtic, for whom he netted 109 goals in 201 games, while his inclination to 'say what I think' saw him become a successful television and newspaper pundit before being diagnosed with cancer in the summer of 2009. John had expressed fears that West Ham fans might 'remember only the bad things' about his time at Upton Park, but the show of support and affection they gave him, as he fought to win the biggest battle of his life, suggested otherwise. That honesty – not to mention those goals – had not been forgotten after all.

The Roed to Hell

'If you're going to regret something, regret doing it rather than not doing it' – Glenn Roeder, June 2001

TO THIS day, football fans – and not just those of a claret and blue persuasion – still scratch their heads when pondering how a team containing top quality players such as Paolo Di Canio, Fredi Kanouté, Joe Cole, Jermain Defoe, Michael Carrick, David James, Glen Johnson and Trevor Sinclair could find itself relegated from the Premier League. The answer, as far as some people are concerned, is relatively straightforward. There is no mystery, intrigue or surprise. Indeed, it can be summarised in two words. Glenn Roeder.

Unlike some cases of relegation, West Ham surely suffered the drop in 2003 as a direct result of short-term mismanagement – from both Roeder and the hierarchy that first appointed him and then failed to remove him from office. Other factors also undermined the club's prospects that fateful season. Yet the overwhelming feeling is that the manager, who never had the credentials to deserve one of football's most prestigious jobs, was ill-equipped to solve the problems he faced that term, while his decisions were dictated by a personal agenda that ultimately worked against the club's best interests.

The trouble stemmed from the fact that nobody fancied Roeder, who had been on the club's coaching staff for two years, to succeed sacked boss Harry Redknapp on a permanent basis in the summer of 2001. As the 45 year old admitted after surprisingly being handed the job following snubs by Alan Curbishley and Steve McClaren, 'I feel a bit like Foinavon in the 1967 Grand National – I'm the only one left standing.' He also quoted 'the words of Terry Venables', whom he played under at QPR, when saying, 'If you're going to regret something, regret doing it rather than not doing it.'

Having failed at Gillingham and Watford in the lower divisions, Roeder, who openly declared he needed to 'win over the doubters', seemed primarily motivated by a desire to prove people wrong. Sadly, he wasn't the only one in danger of regretting the outcome.

With midfielder Frank Lampard sold to Chelsea, Roeder was allowed to splash £15 million on the signings of James, Tomás Repka, Don Hutchison and Sébastien Schemmel to get his reign under way. After a dodgy inaugural period of one win in eight games, which saw a 5–0 defeat at Everton followed by a 7–1 thrashing at Blackburn, the new boss eventually got to grips with things and guided the Hammers to a very creditable seventh-place finish. Not surprisingly, his initial one-year deal, which hardly suggested the club had a great confidence in him, was replaced with a new three-year contract.

Youngsters such as Cole and Carrick had sung Roeder's praises as a coach, which is where he excelled, but he was left wanting when it came to making the big judgement calls demanded of a manager when serious difficulties arose. And that's why the 2002–03 season proved Roeder's undoing.

The campaign got off to a dreadful start with a televised 4–0 defeat at Newcastle, then in the first home game the fans were left to speculate how different things might have been had Kanouté not wasted a late penalty that would have put West Ham 3–1 up against double-winners Arsenal. Having also been 2–0 ahead in a match that ended in a 2–2 draw, the Hammers missed a golden opportunity to get their season up and running in the best of fashions. Instead, West Ham had to wait until their seventh game before picking up maximum points, but the 3–2 win at Chelsea, in which Di Canio scored twice, saw Kanouté forced off with a torn groin muscle that would rule him out for the next three months.

Two 1–0 successes at Sunderland and Fulham made it three away victories on the spin but the revival was short-lived, with the Hammers embarking on an appalling run of fourteen league games without a win that dumped them back to the bottom of the table. After a 4–1 spanking at Aston Villa, the side's fourth defeat in five games, Roeder was asked if he was getting the best out of his squad – one that had done so well the previous season – and he was forced to confess that he wasn't. 'Some players have not performed as well as last year,' he reluctantly conceded before adding, 'It's difficult to put a finger on why.'

With the manager admitting he had no idea why things were going wrong, it was hardly surprising that fans were rapidly losing confidence in him. The bewildered coach was grilled again after a 1–0 defeat by Southampton, which left the Hammers still without a home win by early December, and prompted vociferous post-match protests. Roeder insisted he had no intention of resigning, even when it was suggested that he might be doing the club a favour. 'No, no, no,' he said, claiming he was still the right man for the job despite recent evidence pointing to the contrary.

If Roeder's stubbornness and self-interest wasn't bad enough, his idea of moving Ian Pearce, his best defender, into attack when Di Canio was ruled out for two months with a knee injury, proved one of complete folly. Pearce scored in a 2–2 draw at Middlesbrough, but his absence at the back did West Ham few favours as they leaked fourteen goals in eight games. Summer signing Gary Breen, meanwhile, was proving a disaster in defence and things went from bad to worse, with a 3–1 defeat at Arsenal, a 4–2 loss at Charlton and, finally, a 6–0 thrashing at Manchester United which represented West Ham's biggest ever FA Cup exit.

The failure to win any of the first 12 home games of the season was also a club record in what was, by far, the worst start in their history, but still there was no sign of Roeder admitting his best efforts were not good enough. 'I have never been somebody who gives in,' he declared, still preoccupied by his self-image. Of course, chairman Terence Brown could have sacked him, but the strong suspicion was that the cost of paying up his new contract was proving prohibitive. So the board sat on their hands and simply hoped results would eventually turn.

Thankfully, an 89th-minute goal by Defoe, on 29 January, saw the Hammers edge out Blackburn 2–1 to finally clinch their first home win of the season. By this time, Lee Bowyer and Les Ferdinand had been recruited on short-term deals in a desperate bid to improve prospects for the run-in, while Rufus Brevett would also arrive. Nevertheless, defeats against Liverpool and Leeds left West Ham five points adrift of safety and with very little room for error in the remaining eleven games.

So, for more reasons than one, the events at West Brom, on 23 February, were to prove hugely significant. Sinclair rediscovered some of his old form by scoring the two goals that earned the Hammers a crucial 2–1 success. But not everyone was happy, with a recently returned Di Canio making it abundantly clear that he disagreed with Roeder's decision to take him off, even though he appeared to be carrying a knock. 'Glenn is still a young manager and he makes mistakes,' said Di Canio. 'Just because we won doesn't mean his decisions were all good ones.'

Injury ruled the magical maverick out of action for a brief period, but with the Hammers enduring a run of six unbeaten games, Roeder had the excuse he needed to freeze Di Canio – whose presence he believed to be unsettling – out of the picture even when fit. The striker, who had been disappointed by Roeder's appointment after insisting that West Ham needed a 'strong, expert manager', was already aggrieved that the club had refused to extend his contract which was soon to expire. He was further frustrated when it became obvious that Roeder saw the latest spat between them as an opportunity to show who was boss and refused to even name him on the bench.

Roeder's decision to ignore his best player – which had many fans believing he was allowing a personal feud to cloud his professional judgement – could have been vindicated if the Hammers were picking up maximum points. However, they could only draw with Southampton and Aston Villa before losing 1–0 at fellow strugglers Bolton – the single result that, come the final shake-up, cost them their top-flight place.

Roeder's shocking collapse with a brain tumour after the 1–0 home win against Middlesbrough resulted in director Trevor Brooking being handed the reins for the final three games. The West Ham legend, with no personal axe to grind, sensibly restored Di Canio – who missed the 1–0 victory at Manchester City through illness – to his squad for the penultimate game against Chelsea.

The Italian duly grabbed the winner on what was his farewell outing at Upton Park and signed off by scoring the final goal in the 2–2 draw at Birmingham, a result rendered meaningless with fourth-bottom Bolton's 1–0 home win against Middlesbrough sending the Hammers down. 'We can't say what might have been had I come back earlier,' reflected Di Canio many years later – and that's the problem, because nobody will ever know.

'I don't think another team will ever go down like that again,' Roeder said long after he had recovered from surgery and was sacked the following season. He was referring to the record high of 42 points for a Premier League side to be relegated – a drop that forced the sale of the club's best young players such as Cole and Johnson – but he could just as well have been talking about the wealth of talent at his disposal. 'That has to be the best squad of players ever to go down,' pitched in former boss Redknapp, while his own predecessor Billy Bonds pinpointed the aspect that has been troubling those head-scratchers ever since. 'West Ham probably had the best squad they had ever assembled.'

■■■■■■■■■■■■■■■■■■■

Having a Devil of a Time

'West Ham's effort was obscene' – Alex Ferguson, April 1992

IT'S GETTING late, the walls are dripping with sweat and the predominantly male crowd has been preparing for the evening's main event by knocking back a few beers. There's a mixture of tension and excitement in the air and the sense of anticipation is rising when a voice eventually booms over the public address system. 'And the final score from Upton Park tonight is . . . West Ham United 1, Manchester United 0.' The crowd erupts and a mass of clenched fists punch the air in unison, giving the impression that everybody is a diehard Hammers supporter. This is no West Ham social gathering, however, but London's Town & Country Club and heavy metal veterans UFO are about to take the stage.

Bass player Pete Way is an ardent Aston Villa fan, but even he can't fail to be amused by rock-bottom West Ham's surprise success, or rather Manchester United's disastrous defeat. Because the result, on the evening of 22 April 1992, would effectively cost Alex Ferguson's side the league title – which, famously, they had failed to win in 25 years – placing the trophy firmly in the hands of Leeds United. If the hairy, head-banging hordes hailing UFO are anything to go by, the neutrals appear more than happy with this state of affairs.

Ferguson clearly believed that everybody was against his team – beaten by Kenny Brown's 66th-minute goal at Upton Park – given his comical post-match claims that West Ham had produced an 'obscene' level of effort to prevent them from jumping above Leeds to go two points clear at the top with just two games to play. The Hammers were all but relegated from the top flight, having fallen nine points adrift of safety with just three games remaining and needing a mathematical miracle to survive. With just one win in their previous sixteen outings, they were expected to provide little resistance as the visitors retained control of their own destiny. Never mind the UFO playing in Kentish Town, there was more chance of a real spaceship landing in the centre circle of the Boleyn Ground than there was of a shock result.

Yet it's a traditional characteristic of West Ham that they produce great results when least likely and, as far as left-back Julian Dicks was concerned, there was no way his team-mates were going to roll over and die. 'When clubs like Manchester United come to Upton Park expecting to win,' he reflected, 'it makes the lads even more determined to get a result, especially under the evening lights which help to make a great atmosphere.'

The Hammers certainly raised their game and, although Ferguson had little right to complain about the opposition for simply trying their best, it's fair to say that home supporters were left wondering what might have been had the team displayed such spirit more frequently in the campaign. Not that Billy Bonds' side was lacking in talent, with the likes of Dicks, Ludek Miklosko, Alvin Martin, Tony Gale, Ian Bishop and Stuart Slater starting the game. Manchester United, meanwhile, included such stars as Peter Schmeichel, Steve Bruce, Ryan Giggs, Mark Hughes and Lee Sharpe. Fergie conceded that his side was 'tired' as they went into their fourth game in a week, although it should be acknowledged that West Ham were playing their third fixture in five days.

Midfielder Bishop's post-match claim that the Hammers 'played United off the park' might be a slight exaggeration, but the hosts had more than one chance to open the scoring, while Ferguson complained that the result would have been different had a first-half offside decision not been given against Sharpe. However, the all-important goal eventually came midway through the second period, when Slater delivered a low cross that defender Gary Pallister could only steer into the path of Brown, who deflected the ball home.

Ferguson would later use his autobiography to describe the strike in the 'sickening loss' as 'the luckiest goal imaginable', while Brown's team-mate Dicks also believed the Hammers had enjoyed an element of good fortune. 'The ball came in, hit Kenny on the shin and went spinning into the bottom corner,' he recalled.

Yet that's not how Brown remembered the goal. 'I want to get one thing on the record,' he said several years later. 'That goal against

Manchester United was not off my knee or my shin. I opened up for it and side-footed it in – it came plum off the inside of my foot. But I never got the credit I deserved. One press report said the ball ricocheted off my shin and bobbled into an empty net! Even now, people still say, "Do you remember that goal that came off your shin?"'

As far as West Ham fans were concerned, Brown could have nudged the ball in with his testicles as long as it found the back of the net. It had been a miserable campaign and normal service would resume just three days later when the 1–0 defeat at fellow strugglers Coventry rubber-stamped relegation, but at least the team had proved what they were capable of and thrown a spanner into Manchester United's works. After all, it might be some time before the Hammers got to play them again.

As events transpired, both clubs succeeded in putting the disappointments of the 1991–92 campaign behind them by achieving their immediate targets, with West Ham winning promotion to the Premiership the following term and Manchester United ending their lengthy wait for championship glory by finishing ten points clear of nearest challengers Aston Villa.

The two sides shared a 2–2 draw when they next met at Upton Park in February 1994, as the Hammers eventually finished ten points clear of the drop zone, but United needed nothing less than victory when they returned to the Boleyn Ground on the final day of the 1994–95 season.

West Ham had been in danger of relegation but guaranteed their Premiership place with an emphatic 3–0 win against Liverpool – with former Reds midfielder Don Hutchison scoring twice – just a few days before meeting United. That at least meant the heat was off for the Hammers, who were now managed by Harry Redknapp.

Fergie's men were chasing a third successive league title but arrived at Upton Park, on 14 May, knowing the trophy would only be theirs if they collected all three points and rivals Blackburn were held at Liverpool. With West Ham having nothing apart from pride to play for and Liverpool sitting fifth, United were considered to have by far the easiest task and were strongly fancied to come out on top. After the upset in 1992, surely lightning couldn't strike twice in the same place . . .

Just to add spice to the occasion, the visiting side included former Hammer Paul Ince, who would never be forgiven by fans for posing in a Manchester United shirt several months before his controversial move to Old Trafford in 1989. The West Ham faithful predictably booed the England midfielder, but the jeers quickly turned to cheers when Michael Hughes pounced to open the scoring on the half-hour mark. The winger, who was on-loan from Strasbourg, latched onto a cross from Mattie Holmes and side-footed the ball into the corner of the net to put the cat among the pigeons.

The goal left visiting boss Ferguson questioning his decision to leave his own Hughes – striker Mark – on the bench for the first half. 'I didn't want [West Ham's] clever midfield players to grab hold of the game,' he wrote later, as he admitted to 'possibly making a tactical error'. He also complained that 'the first half was made peculiar by West Ham's insistence on sitting tight and relying on counter-attacks', but had he really expected Redknapp's side to play an open game just because it suited him?

To make matters worse for Manchester United, Alan Shearer had put Blackburn in front at Anfield, meaning that unless Liverpool hit back the outcome at Upton Park would be irrelevant anyway. But the Red Devils, dressed in their all-black strip on this occasion, were not giving up without a fight and Brian McClair made it 1–1 when he headed home from Gary Neville's free-kick seven minutes after the break. When the news then filtered through that Liverpool had indeed pegged Rovers back through John Barnes, the green light was switched on for Manchester United to hit the gas in search of a second goal.

They hadn't figured on Hammers goalkeeper Miklosko wearing his Superman cape under his green shirt – and the bouncing Czech produced his very best form to deny substitute Hughes, Ince and, most notably, Andy Cole, in a frenzied, heart-in-mouth final 15 minutes. Ferguson insisted his side should have been awarded a 'clear-cut penalty for handball' against Tim Breacker but the West Ham full-back insisted, 'I was falling backwards, it wasn't intentional.'

The irony was that while one Redknapp was trying to prevent Manchester United from claiming the league title, another was doing his best to help them, with Harry's son Jamie firing home a last-minute, 25-yard free-kick that condemned Blackburn to a 2–1 defeat at Anfield. It made no difference, however, with United unable to find a late winner despite having seventeen goalscoring attempts to West Ham's six. The corner count of fifteen to two also said everything about the visitors' dominance in the second period. After the final whistle, a less bitter Ferguson admitted that Miklosko had been 'fantastic' and enjoyed 'a marvellous game', but later insisted his men were desperately unlucky and 'had sufficient chances to have won a dozen games'.

Miklosko was typically modest, claiming it has been 'a real team performance'. He added, 'I was perhaps feeling a little bit sorry for United because they lost the title . . . but, in another way, it was like "Yes!"'

Michael Hughes reflected on the occasion by describing it as 'the most important game I've played in, even though we didn't need the points'. As for his goal, he said, 'I didn't expect it to come to me but when Holmes crossed back into my path, I just put my foot on it and the ball did the rest.' A breathless Harry Redknapp said, 'It's amazing when you think about it. If Cole had scored in the last minute they would have won the championship – that's how close it all was. They wanted it for their lives and we were certainly hanging on.'

If the Manchester United dressing-room at Upton Park, in the words of Ferguson, had been 'like a funeral parlour' in 1992, it's safe to assume the atmosphere was no less mournful three years on. In stark contrast, the champagne corks were popping for Blackburn at Anfield and the bubbles weren't confined to the liquid being sprayed around the changing room. With Tony Gale in the Rovers ranks after being released by the Hammers the previous summer, there are no prizes for guessing who might have instigated the rousing rendition of 'I'm Forever Blowing Bubbles' that was hollered in grateful recognition of West Ham's efforts that afternoon. 'I told my old team-mates to make sure they did the business against United to help us to the title,' said Gale. 'And that's just what they did.'

Another old Iron was experiencing very different emotions, however, with Ince left to grumble, 'Obviously West Ham wanted to show us what they could do. Every team seems to raise its game against United.' A week later, the midfielder's misery was compounded when Manchester United were beaten 1–0 by Everton in the FA Cup final at Wembley, as a second trophy was snatched away. West Ham's official magazine *Hammers News* was naturally unsympathetic, running a full-page image of the boys in claret and blue celebrating their final goal of the season while an aggrieved Ince stood nearby and pointed accusatory fingers. The headline? 'Forever Blowing Doubles!'

Bitten by a Pike

'It was like swinging a sledgehammer to crack a nut'
– Tony Carr, March 2002

WEST HAM are rightly renowned for quality and consistency where the production of their own first-team players is concerned. There has been the odd blip, most notably between the end of the 1980s and the mid 1990s, when just two native sons climbed the ladder up from the youth team with, seemingly, the right ingredients to make it in the big time. Winger Matthew Rush had bags of potential but was prone to inconsistency and played just 52 times, while midfielder Danny Williamson, sold to Everton in 1997, was a genuine talent whose career was blighted by ankle problems. The story of Paul Marquis summed up the whole disappointing period: the defender saw 60 seconds of action as a 90th-minute sub in 1994, and that was it, all over – the shortest Hammers first-team career ever.

Youth overlord Tony Carr is well placed to offer an insight into why the conveyor belt started jamming. 'There was a lull in the sense that perhaps we were still old school in our approach and it took us a while to wake up to the fact that our recruitment drive had to be a lot more fierce. It all became more intense and when there's more competition other factors come into play, with different kinds of promises and incentives being offered.'

Little could Carr have predicted that another factor to compound the Academy's woes would involve one of its most successful ever products. In his playing days, midfielder Geoff Pike, a 1980 FA Cup winner who stacked up 367 appearances for the club, was expert at keeping the game ticking over with his neat passes and crisp tackles. However, as a youth coaching monitor for the Football Association in the mid 1990s, a few ticks too many on his clipboard reportedly contributed to a nightmare scenario under which West Ham were banned from signing young players for an entire year.

Explains Carr, 'We put on an 11-a-side game to look at some boys when we should only have played small-sided games. It was fairly innocent as far as we were concerned. I would describe it as a minor infringement of the regulations.'

Following an FA review into this and other irregularities, West Ham were fined an undisclosed amount and were ordered to shut their Centres of Excellence for 12 months. Additionally, the FA suspended youth development chief Jimmy Hampson for the same period. Said Carr, 'Jimmy obviously felt very aggrieved by it. It was a real blow for the club. It was like swinging a sledgehammer to crack a nut and we felt that Geoff played a big part in that.'

Labelled as a whistleblower, Pike was barred from the very training ground on which he'd honed his craft, as well as Upton Park. Several years would pass before Carr and Hampson reconciled their differences with him, and Pike admitted it was an extremely difficult period in his life – being portrayed as the villain of the piece by the club he loved.

'I knew I hadn't done anything wrong,' he said. 'I just happened to drop in at Chadwell Heath when they were doing something that wasn't within the regulations. I felt it was my duty to report it and that was all. Apart from one or two very minor incidents, that was my sole contribution.

'My part in the saga involved one side of A4 paper, which later I very willingly showed Tony and Jim. There were lots of other things that the FA allegedly took into account when they closed down the club's coaching centres. They had a file on West Ham that was four or five inches thick.'

After leaving the FA to work for the Professional Footballers' Association, much to Pike's relief a situation arose whereby he was able to clear the air with Carr and Hampson. 'It came to a head after I'd been working for the PFA for a couple of years and I was asked to do some coaching qualification assessments at Chadwell Heath,' said Pike, who would later return to work on grass roots FA projects, reporting to former midfield team-mate and FA director of football development Trevor Brooking. 'I felt it was time to bury the hatchet. To be fair to Tony and Jim they were very willing to get together. We met on neutral ground, had a cup of coffee and it was all very civilised. They said, "Well, as far as we're concerned, the matter is closed," and I agreed with that 100 per cent.'

Coincidence or not, the years immediately after the ban was lifted proved to be a golden period for youth development. The emergence of starlets such as Rio Ferdinand, Frank Lampard Jnr, Joe Cole and Michael Carrick went a long way to making up for one of the more peculiar behind-the-scenes incidents to affect the Academy.

■■■■■■■■■■■■■■■■■■■

Where Eagles Dare

'Sometimes things are written' – Alan Pardew, May 2004

THERE IS a four-letter word beginning with 'F' that is used often in football and perhaps never more so by West Ham fans than after watching their team fail dismally to win promotion back to the Premier League at the first time of asking in 2004. That word, of course, is 'fate' (what else?), something which conspired against Alan Pardew's side as they qualified for the Division One play-offs with a fourth-place finish and came up against Crystal Palace in the final.

The fact is that London rivals Palace would not have even reached the play-offs if Brian Deane had not headed a superfluous last-minute equaliser for the Hammers in their final league game at Wigan, who would have claimed a top-six place instead if they had clung on to their one-goal lead. 'Who knows how important that goal will prove to be?' asked Pardew after the 1–1 draw, although the suspicion, even at that time, was that the Hammers would be left to rue the moment they threw Palace a promotion lifeline.

Of course, it's possible that West Ham might never have even reached the final at the Millennium Stadium had they returned to Wigan in the semis – as looked to be the case before Deane struck – rather than Ipswich, who they beat 2–1 on aggregate. However, once they booked their place at Cardiff, the clash against the Eagles (who squeezed past Sunderland on spot-kicks), on 29 May, started to look like an ominous prospect.

It was ironic that Pardew and rival boss Iain Dowie both found themselves leading their sides into battle against clubs they used to play for and with whom they had strong emotional ties. Indeed, Pardew spoke of Palace being 'very close to my heart' – hardly surprising after 170 games in their colours – while Dowie admitted he still had 'a lot of affection for West Ham', for whom he made 96 outings over two spells and had supported as a boy. Hammers midfielder Hayden Mullins and Palace winger Michael Hughes were also facing outfits they had previously represented, so there were plenty of connections between the two clubs.

West Ham needed promotion far more than Palace. The Hammers had dropped out of the top flight for the first time in ten years under Glenn Roeder, who was sacked after just four games of the new season. Trevor Brooking had returned in a caretaker capacity to steady the ship, winning seven of his eleven games, before Pardew was allowed to assume control once compensation had been agreed with his former club Reading. The enforced departure of many top earners following relegation resulted in a huge turnover of players, to the extent that 36 different names appeared on West Ham's shirts (24 for the very first time) the following season. Needless to say, loanees such as Niclas Alexandersson, Robbie Stockdale and Wayne Quinn will not be remembered as Hammers legends. These were turbulent times at Upton Park and, with even a play-off place looking in question, the club had cashed in on 15-goal striker Jermain Defoe by selling him to Tottenham in a £7 million deal that included the arrival of Bobby Zamora midway through the campaign, while England goalkeeper David James also moved on.

In stark contrast, the Eagles were in their natural habitat in football's second tier and fully acclimatised, having resided there for six years. The *East London Advertiser* drew attention to the fact that a revitalised Palace had collected 45 points from 22 games to storm up the table since Dowie's appointment earlier in the season and had 'enjoyed immense good fortune' at the same time. However, the paper also stressed that 'West Ham have the superior players, produce the more attractive football and enjoy the greater support' before adding, 'None of that will count for anything if the team doesn't perform on the day.'

Sadly, too few Hammers players took note as they produced a thoroughly uninspired display that failed to do their talents – or their billing as bookies' favourites – any kind of justice. Zamora had a great chance to open the scoring when clean through in the first half only to shoot straight at goalkeeper Nico Vaesen, and West Ham paid the price when Neil Shipperley prodded home on 62 minutes, after goalkeeper Stephen Bywater could only parry Andy Johnson's shot into his path.

David Connolly and Zamora both put the ball into the Palace net before seeing their efforts wiped out by a linesman's flag, while the Hammers realised it was never going to be their day when referee Graham Poll failed to award a penalty after Michael Carrick was taken out by Mikele Leigertwood. Poll later revealed he had been 'interested' in pointing to the spot but was dissuaded when few players raised their arms. 'Not even Carrick appealed,' he said, 'so on the basis that no one at West Ham was interested, I reckoned that they did not think it was a penalty and the play just moved on.'

Almost as mystifying as Poll's judgement was Pardew's bizarre decision to replace Zamora, Connolly and Marlon Harewood – three strikers who had scored thirty-three goals between them for the Hammers that term – with Deane, plus midfielders Nigel Reo-Coker and Don Hutchison, who had just twelve strikes to their name. 'I felt the substitutions were valid at the time,' said Pardew unconvincingly when he was quizzed on his unsuccessful ploy after the 1–0 defeat.

As the West Ham fans either drowned their sorrows in Cardiff or headed back to London, they hardly needed Pardew, who partially blamed the 'sticky pitch' for his team's lack of zest, to remind them that it had been 'a dark day' for the club. The future looked equally bleak with the manager admitting that play-off final failure left him facing some tough decisions in terms of trying to improve the club's promotion prospects the following season, while having to reduce costs. 'I need to cut the wage bill while trying to make us stronger,' he said.

In the end, however, he reluctantly conceded it had indeed all come down to fate. 'People kept saying Palace's good fortune would run out, but sometimes things are written,' he said. 'I just wish it had been written for us.'

Cheating the Odds

'I am entitled to an opinion and I'm sticking to it'
– John Lyall, March 1981

JAMES MOSSOP of the *Sunday Express* summed it up perfectly. 'Through all the chronicles of sporting drama, there can be little to match the bewildering finish to a match that ended with two sensational goals and a bonfire of controversy that was still raging long afterwards,' he wrote after one of the most thrilling climaxes to a game involving West Ham – or any other team, for that matter.

The date: 14 March 1981. The venue: Wembley Stadium. The teams: West Ham United and Liverpool. The event: The 21st League Cup final.

The Hammers had achieved a minor miracle in battling their way to another major final less than a year after their incredible FA Cup triumph against Arsenal, not least because they remained a Second Division side. They had seen off Burnley, Charlton and Barnsley before fighting their way past top-flight outfits Tottenham and Coventry to book their return to the Twin Towers. To give an indication of the enormity of West Ham's task, Liverpool were the reigning league champions (who had defeated the Hammers 1–0 in the Charity Shield the previous August) and, just a couple of months later, would beat Real Madrid to win the European Cup for the third time in five seasons.

Manager John Lyall, whose match strategy had proved so difficult for the Gunners to cope with at Wembley, seemed once again to have got his tactics spot on, with Liverpool being thwarted to the extent that a relatively uneventful game went into extra-time. Even then it seemed inevitable that the final would finish goalless and a replay would be required – until the last 118 seconds provided more explosive drama than the entire previous 118 minutes.

Liverpool had already seen one early effort ruled out for offside and when the linesman's flag was raised for a second time after Alan Kennedy's shot found the net, it seemed inevitable that the goal would be disallowed. With the ball having travelled over the head of the grounded Sammy Lee, who was clearly in an offside position, it was considered a formality that referee Clive Thomas would give the Hammers a free-kick. Instead, he pointed back to the centre circle and awarded the goal – much to the utter astonishment of the West Ham players.

Defenders Billy Bonds and Ray Stewart led the Hammers' protests and implored Thomas to consult his linesman, whose flag had suddenly been lowered. However, the Welsh official, after starting to walk towards the touchline, simply waved his arm to indicate he was overruling anything his assistant might have had to say. A goal it was.

It seemed that a huge injustice had placed the League Cup firmly in the hands of Liverpool – for the first time in their history – but West Ham retained enough composure to launch one final attack with just seconds remaining. A free-kick was won when Alan Devonshire was tripped by Phil Neal just outside the penalty box but, when Stewart's fierce drive was brilliantly tipped over by Liverpool goalkeeper Ray

Clemence, it seemed that the Hammers' luck was out. The ensuing corner was sent over by Trevor Brooking and Alvin Martin planted a firm header that was bound for the top corner – until Liverpool midfielder Terry McDermott used his fist to punch the ball away. PENALTY!

Thomas had no choice but to point to the spot, but it says much about the general honesty of players in those days that the laws did not need to deter such cynical actions with a mandatory red card. How times have changed. Stewart was duly handed the responsibility of rescuing the game for West Ham. The reliable right-back later revealed, 'Billy Bonds told me it didn't matter if I missed, because no one else wanted to take it,' but the full-back rarely fluffed from 12 yards and his firm shot smacked the back of the net as the final whistle sounded.

That was when, according to Lyall, 'the fun started', with the Hammers boss becoming embroiled in a furious war of words with the referee as he was leaving the field. It subsequently emerged that Thomas planned to report Lyall to the FA for branding him a 'cheat' – 'and no one in the world calls me that,' declared the official.

Not surprisingly, the West Ham manager was eager to put the record straight, insisting, 'I didn't accuse Clive of cheating. I simply said I didn't want to talk to him because I felt we'd been cheated. I wasn't the aggressor, but I felt I was entitled to my opinion. If I said something wrong I apologise. Football is a game of emotions and if you take the emotion out of it you have no game.'

Lyall found an ally in Liverpool boss Bob Paisley, who slammed Thomas for making allegations to the press after the game. He said, 'Clive was wrong to say in public that John had called him a cheat. I have never seen John so incensed as he was at the end of the game. When a situation gets as hot as that the best thing for all concerned is to sleep on it and think carefully before passing any comment. Clive made the situation worse and I hope those involved take a sympathetic line.'

What Lyall had been so incensed about, of course, was the Liverpool goal that he believed should have been disallowed. Thomas, a FIFA official who had refereed at the 1974 and 1978 World Cup finals, insisted he had made the right call. 'Lee was lying on the ground and there is no way I can say a player is interfering with play if he is on the ground,' he said. He did, however, admit he should have handled the situation differently. 'It was bad refereeing,' he conceded. 'What I should have done was gone straightaway to my linesman, instead of going halfway and then coming back.'

Nowadays, of course, the issue of whether a player is 'active' or 'non-active' when in an offside position is the topic of much debate, given that the rules have been amended to favour the attacking team and play is allowed to continue unless the man in question touches the ball. Back in 1981, however, it was far more of a cut-and-dried issue, with it generally being recognised that any person in an offside position would be flagged, although referees could indeed favour the attacking side at their discretion – on very rare occasions – if they believed the offending player was not interfering with play.

Former Tottenham skipper Danny Blanchflower used his newspaper column to draw attention to this particular clause. 'What idiot introduced this nonsense into the laws of our game?' he asked. 'Surely every player on the field is seeking to gain an advantage all the time? The offside law is an ass.' The belief of Thomas that any grounded player could not be deemed as interfering was also ridiculed. 'What if a West Ham player had tripped over Sammy, or if Kennedy's shot had been deflected by him?' pondered Blanchflower.

Hammers goalkeeper Phil Parkes tried to simplify the argument by insisting that Lee had blocked his view of the ball so had to be playing an active part in the goal. Meanwhile, Lyall rightly pointed to his side's incredible comeback, something that had almost been forgotten amid the furore regarding Liverpool's opening strike and the rumpus with Thomas. 'I don't think many teams would have fought back to salvage the game the way we did,' he said, before insisting he had total faith in Stewart to score at the death. 'I had no worries when Ray took that last-kick penalty,' he declared. 'If I had to stake my life on somebody scoring it would be Ray.'

Lyall was in defiant mood when the game was shown on *The Big Match* the following day and he was asked about his altercation with

Thomas. 'I'm entitled to an opinion,' he said, somewhat ambiguously, 'and I'm sticking to it.'

The West Ham boss insisted he had no problem with Thomas being in charge of the replay against Liverpool at Villa Park on 1 April – the first League Cup final game to be shown live on television. He later declared that the referee 'handled the game impeccably', despite the disappointment of seeing his side beaten by goals from Kenny Dalglish and Alan Hansen (the latter credited as an own goal at the time after the ball deflected off Bonds), after Paul Goddard had headed the Hammers in front. 'We're not used to living with that kind of football,' confessed Lyall.

The manager was later charged by the FA for 'insulting and improper behaviour' during the first game at Wembley, but was eventually cleared, with committee chairman Bert Millichip admitting, 'The case was not proved – it was really a question of how the word "cheat" was used and what interpretation was intended.'

Lyall subsequently revealed that he 'had lunch with Clive and we parted the best of friends' after the hearing. In his autobiography in 1989, he posed the question: 'When is an offside player interfering with play? It's a matter of opinion and a grey area within the game.' More than two decades later, the offside rule continues to flummox intellectuals and *Match of the Day* pundits alike.

Brescia By Golly Wow

'Savio will become a very important player' – Gianfranco Zola, January 2009

WHEN WEST HAM allowed Craig Bellamy to complete his desired £14 million move to Manchester City in January 2009, the club could ill afford to get their next move wrong – for both football and financial reasons. The sacrifice of Bellamy, who had made it clear that the grass of money-bags City appeared far greener than the off-colour turf at Upton Park, left the Hammers short of striking power, especially with the injured Dean Ashton sidelined for the rest of the season. With the balance sheets looking far worse than the club was prepared to admit – particularly worrying after owner Björgólfur Guðmundsson's fortune blew up in smoke with the collapse of the Icelandic banking system – it was imperative that any money spent was invested wisely.

West Ham needed a striker capable of instantly filling Bellamy's boots and proving value for money. Instead they bought Savio, a player who is likely to be remembered as representing one of the biggest errors of judgement in the club's recent history . . . and for that, technical director Gianluca Nani must accept much of the responsibility.

Savio Magala Nsereko, a Ugandan-born Germany Under-20 international, was signed from Italian outfit Brescia amid much fanfare for an initial £5 million payment that would rise to a potential £9 million based on appearances. The 19 year old was hailed as a wonder-kid, with West Ham's chief executive Scott Duxbury describing the forward as 'an exciting prospect who manager Gianfranco Zola believes will prove a valuable asset now and in the years to come'. He also referred to the 'the fierce competition for his services across Europe', with Bayern Munich and Napoli reportedly in contention, and added, 'It is a significant investment and shows our determination to continue moving this club forward.'

The club's website highlighted the fact that Savio – handed the No. 10 shirt as well as a four-and-half-year contract at Upton Park – had scored twice in a minute against Pisa in his final game in Italy, yet that obscured the statistic that he had bagged just three goals in twenty-two outings for the Serie B outfit in total. He had, however, helped Germany win the European Under-19 Championship the previous year and been dubbed the 'player of the tournament' by UEFA's technical observer, so he clearly had ability and potential.

Zola endorsed the youngster's talents but tried to play down expectations by pleading for patience. 'He will excite West Ham fans and will certainly become a very important player,' he declared. 'But don't forget that the boy is 19 years old and has come here for the future. We need to allow him time to settle.' This wasn't what the supporters necessarily wanted to hear, being well aware that the team's forward line needed immediate reinforcement, with only David Di Michele and Diego Tristan – two European veterans whose best years were well behind them – providing support for Carlton Cole.

Savio made his debut as an 86th-minute substitute in the 2–0 home win against Hull on 28 January and so the tone was set for the following couple of months, with the player coming off the bench in the next half a dozen games before, eventually, making his first start in the goalless draw with West Brom in mid-March. He was replaced after little more than an hour against the Baggies and would make just three more substitute outings, with it having become apparent that the teenager was not the striker the team required – and nowhere near ready for the physical demands of the Premier League. In brief flashes he was able to show examples of his pace and skill, more as a midfielder or wide man than striker, but he looked disturbingly lightweight and gave the overall impression of a player who appeared to be out of his depth – a little boy lost, in fact.

In fairness, West Ham seemed to be managing just fine without him in the first months of 2009, having put their early-season struggles behind them and moved into the top half of the table to make a strong challenge for a place in Europe. Such a quest eventually proved beyond them as a number of key injuries took their toll, but the fact that Savio couldn't even win a starting place when Cole was sidelined for six weeks said it all. Not surprisingly, questions were starting to be asked, with fans wondering why their cash-strapped club had invested what little spare funds they had on yet another player 'for the future' when there were plenty of other prospects – such as Junior Stanislas, Freddie Sears and Zavon Hines, for example – emerging from their academy and who needed to be developed patiently.

Savio's struggles began to reflect poorly on the decision making of Nani, who had been the driving force behind his acquisition. The Italian had been brought to Upton Park because of his perceived network of contacts across Europe, yet in this case he had simply returned to the club he had previously worked for as sporting director when needing to make an important signing. It was Nani who had taken Savio to Brescia in the first place, signing him as a 16 year old after the youngster had begun his career at TSV 1860 Munich, so it wasn't too much of a surprise that he retained a strong interest in him. There was also no denying that Nani continued to have a tangible link with his former club, being married to Silvia, the daughter of Brescia president Luigi Corioni. The deal appeared to be a good one for Brescia.

With the season nearing its climax, Nani attended a community event at Upton Park and the opportunity arose to ask the Italian about Savio's lack of impact. Nani remained bullish about the player's prospects. 'We have to wait a little bit because he is still a young boy, but we are really confident about him,' he insisted. 'Savio will be part of our future.'

Yet his optimism was no longer shared by Zola, who had grown tired of fending off questions about the youngster at press conferences and eventually admitted, during the summer, that things were not going to plan. 'Savio is really struggling with the heavy expectations and is putting a lot of pressure on himself,' he confided. 'But we're still working on the boy.'

Just three weeks later, West Ham announced that Savio had been sold to Fiorentina for an undisclosed fee, with Portuguese defender Manuel da Costa heading to Upton Park as part of the deal. In total, Savio made only 11 outings for the Hammers – including 10 as substitute – and spent just 254 minutes on the pitch.

West Ham attempted to sing the praises of Da Costa, who had been capped 23 times at Under-21 level for his country, but the fact that he had made just three appearances during the previous season for Fiorentina and on loan at Sampdoria suggested he would not have carried the biggest of price tags. In confirming the move, Duxbury claimed that the 'emergence of Junior Stanislas limited Savio's chances' – suggesting the latter was no longer considered as a forward – while emphasising that the club retained the right to 50 per cent of Savio's future sell-on value, with the CEO insisting, 'This is a good deal for everyone concerned.'

Not that Savio found first-team football any easier to come by in Florence and, without making a single Serie A outing, he was soon being linked with a loan move to Torino, with his agent trotting out the familiar line: 'There are many good players in his role at the club and he needs time to integrate.' When the January transfer window opened, Savio agreed to join Bologna on loan until the summer of 2010.

Back at Upton Park, the decision to sign Savio was again the subject of scrutiny as the arrival of new owners David Sullivan and David Gold inevitably saw Nani being shown the door. The club swiftly agreed a severance package with the Italian, who still had three years remaining on his reported £300,000 per annum contract. Former Hammers striker Tony Cottee, now a television pundit and newspaper columnist, was quick to criticise the contribution of the technical director in his two years at the Boleyn. 'Nani's transfer dealings were very poor and, for every positive signing he made, there was always a David Di Michele or a Diego Tristan,' said Cottee. 'The Savio deal was catastrophic for the club and it was clear from very early on that the German was not good enough for the Premier League.'

Nani would no doubt defend his record at Upton Park by insisting he was generally working under tight budgetary restrictions. Yet the fact remains that the decision to sign Savio was an extremely costly embarrassment for West Ham.

■■■■■■■■■■■■■■■■■■■■

Cup of Jeer

'These giant-killings just keep happening' – Harry Redknapp, January 1999

CYRIL THE SWAN appears from nowhere and sprints down the touchline to set a new 100-metre record – for a feathered beast, at least – before arriving in front of the West Ham fans in the corner of the Vetch Field. The Hammers have just conceded the goal that will condemn them to an embarrassing FA Cup third-round knockout by lowly Swansea City, who ply their trade in what used to be known as the Fourth Division. And there is Cyril, flapping his wings in a dance of delight, as the angry visiting contingent ponders the custodial sentence one might receive for lynching a 7 ft tall *Cygnus olor*.

Manager Harry Redknapp was left scratching his head after that 1–0 defeat in January 1999, a result made even more humiliating by the fact that West Ham had originally been drawn at home to the Welsh side and needed a late goal from Julian Dicks to scrape a 1–1 draw. 'I don't know the answer,' he sighed. 'These giant-killings just seem to keep happening to West Ham. It's been going on for years.'

He wasn't kidding. The Hammers have slipped up on more banana skins than any other major club in cup competition. In fact, between 1980 – when they last won a major trophy – and 2010, West Ham were elbowed out of the FA and League Cups by lower league opposition an incredible 19 times. It didn't matter whether it was Redknapp, John Lyall, Lou Macari, Billy Bonds, Glenn Roeder or Alan Pardew at the helm, the Hammers still wilted when coming face to face with the likes of mighty Torquay, Barnsley, Crewe, Grimsby, Stockport, Wrexham, Tranmere, Oldham, Northampton and Chesterfield.

Not a single year passed by between 1992 and 2002 – an unbelievable 11 in succession – without West Ham being humbled by sides from lower divisions. Taking into account that they also lost to Walsall and Huddersfield and were held to draws by another dozen minnows, including Farnborough, Aldershot, Lincoln, Orient and Barnet before eventually making further progress, it's little wonder that struggling against the lesser lights has become as much a club trademark as the stylish, attacking football for which the Hammers are renowned. Cyril the Swan certainly had plenty to crow about.

It was perhaps typical that West Ham should lose their grip on the FA Cup they won so sensationally against Arsenal in 1980 with a defeat by Wrexham after three hard-fought games – the fact that the Welshmen were playing in the same division at the time doesn't really improve the look of the history books. The Hammers were in no position to use that excuse when they crashed to a 1–0 home defeat by the same outfit in an FA Cup third-round replay in January 1997, which culminated in protests on the pitch – mainly of the 'sack the board' variety – and Redknapp talking of quitting. 'It's my worst result as a manager,' he said after watching Kevin Russell's last-minute 20-yarder secure victory for the Division Two side. 'Now I've got to do the best for West Ham and if people don't want me here then I understand.'

Redknapp offered to resign, more for the fact he had felt partly responsible for the takeover talk engulfing the club (having links with prospective owner Michael Tabor) than the Wrexham result. However, at the time there was sustained turmoil on the pitch as well as off it, with the Hammers on a dreadful run that would produce just one win in eighteen games and include a nightmarish Coca-Cola Cup exit at Stockport, another Second Division side. Brett Angell headed the winner but the 2–1 defeat at Edgeley Park, on 18 December 1996, will always be remembered most for Iain Dowie's comical own goal. 'A tie eked from the finest traditions of English knock-out football,' claimed *The Independent* of the fourth-round replay. A tie eked from the bowels of hell, spat the Hammers fans as they trudged away into the bleak night, sheeting rain merely compounding their misery.

That sinking feeling was a familiar one, of course. The previous year Hammers experienced the true grimness of Grimsby when they were trounced 3–0 at Blundell Park – just two days after a 1–0 success at Tottenham – in an FA Cup fourth-round replay. At Crewe, in the second round of the Coca-Cola Cup in October 1992, late goals by Tony Naylor and Craig Hignett saw the bottom-division boys secure a 2–0 aggregate victory over two legs. Nor did West Ham like being beside the seaside in January 1990, when a 77th-minute goal from teenage substitute Paul Hirons proved enough for Fourth Division strugglers Torquay to claim a famous scalp in the third round of the FA Cup.

Who would have thought that a team containing such talents as Paolo Di Canio, Rio Ferdinand, Joe Cole, Frank Lampard, Trevor Sinclair and Neil Ruddock could lose 1–0 at Tranmere, as they did on 11 December 1999, when Nick Henry's first-half goal took Merseyside's poorest relations into the fourth round of the FA Cup? Di Canio claimed the Hammers were 'badly organised without anyone running or working hard' after yet another cup disaster that fans would want to forget.

West Ham were undefeated in six games prior to the visit to Prenton Park and had beaten Liverpool and drawn at Chelsea and Tottenham in that sequence. So how could they get beaten at Tranmere? Some would suggest it's that very unpredictability, of never knowing which aspect of their Jekyll and Hyde character is going to emerge on any given day, that makes the Hammers such an intriguing club to follow. Yet it begs the question as to why the club continues to struggle against inferior opposition irrespective of who the manager is, which players are wearing the shirt and what kind of mood is in the camp. 'I tell the players it's all about attitude and that they've got to approach these games in the right way,' said Redknapp after another cup cock-up. 'But for one reason or another, we always seem to have problems.'

Complacency is the obvious conclusion to draw, after seeing West Ham's players fail to make their qualities tell, although the club's track record of coming a cropper against lower teams really should serve as a warning against that. Another theory is that West Ham's style of football is not particularly conducive to getting results against teams that play a more physical and direct game. Outplaying a side is one thing; outmuscling them is something else. It's one reason why the Hammers lost six successive games to Bolton Wanderers – generally recognised as one of the most physical teams in the Premier League – between 2008 and 2010, and it's why the Hammers have found it so hard to shake off the 'southern softies' tag that's long been attached to them, perhaps with some justification. West Ham might be seen as possessing a bit of glamour when arriving at some far-flung northern outpost, but that doesn't mean they have to play as if worried that physical contact might damage their latest eyelash tint.

It's got to the stage where supporters are in a real quandry when the balls go into the velvet bag for a cup draw. Indeed, there's even a sense of relief when West Ham are paired with a bigger club – they might not make it to the next round, but at least they won't be left looking silly. At least that was the theory until they were walloped 6–0 at Manchester United in the FA Cup fourth round in 2003.

Unsurprisingly, success against non-league opposition cannot be taken for granted either. Farnborough were a part-time outfit playing in the GM Vauxhall Conference in 1992 and had seemingly sacrificed any romantic dreams of an upset against the Hammers by switching their FA Cup third-round game to Upton Park, in the interests of crowd safety and financial health. Nevertheless, they were still able to force a 1–1 draw, thanks to Dean Coney's late penalty, to earn another bite of the cherry.

The Hammers had also been held at home the previous year by Aldershot, who were heading for relegation from the Football League, before romping to a 6–1 triumph in the replay. Despite West Ham sitting at the bottom of the First Division table and consumed with negativity towards the Bond Scheme, the feeling was that Farnborough would be despatched in similar style at the second time of asking. Instead, the Hammers once again huffed and puffed with little joy until Trevor Morley saved their skins two minutes from time. It seemed that even when they won they still ended up with red faces.

West Ham faced Conference opposition again just two years later, when they travelled to Kidderminster in the fifth round of the FA Cup. Smelling blood, the TV cameras were present to make sure another Hammers humiliation could be shared by the general public, only for Lee Chapman's looping header in the 69th minute to spoil the script.

There would surely be no problems for West Ham when they entertained little Emley of the Unibond League in an FA Cup third-round tie at Upton Park in January 1998 – especially after Frank Lampard gave them a third-minute lead. Emley had a population of less than 2,000 and boasted just three pubs, less than can be found in Green Street. But their supporters had something to celebrate when Paul David hauled the village side level, only for John Hartson to break their hearts with a header eight minutes from time. 'I'd be lying if I said I didn't think a nightmare was going to happen,' admitted relieved boss Redknapp.

Now what would possibly make him fear that?

■■■■■■■■■■■■■■■■■■■■

The Carr's the Star

'We feel if the kid has ability, we can bring it out'
– Tony Carr, March 2002

IT'S A rainy Tuesday morning at the Chadwell Heath training ground. A bunch of teenagers with flushed cheeks, silly grins and too much gel in their hair are mucking about on one of the practice pitches, awaiting instructions for the morning's session. Usually they would be over at the Little Heath youth-team headquarters, so this is a rare chance to make an impression on passing first-team personnel.

Three impish little entertainers, Joe Cole, Bobby Barnes and Stuart Slater, are taking the opportunity to show off their latest ball-juggling tricks. Michael Carrick and Danny Williamson are trying to hit the proverbial sixpence from 40 yards, while Tony Cottee and Zavon Hines are attempting to chip goalie Stephen Bywater. On the far touchline, Adam Newton and Kevin Keen are having a sprinting race, while near the centre spot James Tomkins and Elliott Ward are in the middle of a circle trying to intercept rapid-fire passes being made between Junior Stanislas, Paul Allen, Glen Johnson and Jack Collison.

Other lads are enjoying boisterous one-on-one sessions: Paul Ince and Mark Noble are going at it hammer and tongs; so too Jordan Spence and George Parris, while brothers Anton and Rio Ferdinand are trying to outwit one another with fancy flicks and twists. Meanwhile, at the side of the pitch, Eamonn Dolan and Frank Lampard Jnr are sitting on a mower comparing O level hauls, Alan Dickens and Steve Potts are self-consciously staring into space and, for some reason, senior pro Alvin Martin has got Matthew Rush in a headlock. Oh, and stood on his own, not quite knowing where to put himself, is little Manny Omoyinmi. Bless!

For those who relish the sight of a home-grown player in a claret and blue first-team shirt, this teenage dreamscape emphasises both the quantity and quality of players produced by West Ham United during Tony Carr's three-decade tenure as head of the Academy. In fact, just over 50 youngsters have emerged through the ranks to play first-team football since 1981, the year Carr took charge of the youths.

Not every player who has fallen under his aegis made it in the game. Some packed football in before they were even out of their teens; some soon found that professional football was beyond them and headed straight to non-leagues; other youth players, such as Bobby Zamora and Paul Konchesky, took a circuitous route to the Hammers first-team by initially establishing themselves elsewhere.

Around ten of the boys who did graduate to the First XI after working under Carr, including future Liverpool and Eire hero Ray Houghton, managed the feat only once – a source of huge frustration or immense pride depending on which way one looks at it. On the whole, however, the grounding most of these young footballers received, not just as footballers but as human beings, was the basis for long, successful and eventful careers with West Ham, other professional clubs and, in numerous instances, for their countries.

Rio Ferdinand, Frank Lampard Jnr, Joe Cole, Jermain Defoe, Glen Johnson and Michael Carrick were all once fresh-faced unknowns whose biggest dream was to perform on the Upton Park pitch.

The first three – who have gone to amass one Champions League crown, ten Premier League titles, five FA Cup winners' medals, two hundred England caps and be placed at No. 17, No. 32 and No. 54 respectively on the *Sunday Times* Sporting Rich List, with a reported £67 million between them – were able to show their debt of gratitude to Carr by attending his much publicised testimonial game at Upton Park in May 2010, as West Ham took on an Academy All-stars side.

'Tony Carr's claret and blue army' rang out from a 14,000 crowd which fully appreciated Carr's ability to spot and nurture real talent. The premature loss of much of that talent to bigger clubs is a bitter pill to swallow, one softened just a little by the £50 million in sales which has been generated through the transfer of home-grown players in the last decade or so.

'Tony has done a brilliant job, not only for West Ham, but for the whole nation,' said then West Ham boss Gianfranco Zola before playing a starring role alongside his countryman Paolo Di Canio in the testimonial. 'So many important and influential players with the national team have started here and that tells you what he is all about.'

Carr, made an MBE in June 2010, suggests the club's location as much as anything else is the secret of his success. 'London, especially east London and Essex, is a real hotbed for talent. We feel if the kid has ability we can bring it out. The club's philosophy has always been to blood young players. A lot of our success is due to the fact that we're patient.'

He had to show plenty of patience before making his own mark in the game, his insatiable desire to bring at least one youth player per season through to the first team perhaps rooted in his own failure to make the grade as a teenage striker at the club in the mid 1960s. After resorting to non-league football with Barnet and sustaining a broken leg which forced an early retirement, in 1973 Carr was encouraged to do some part-time coaching back at West Ham by John Lyall, the man he cites as his greatest influence. 'Everything I learned about coaching and about the game in general was thanks to John Lyall.'

Seven years later, at the age of 30, Carr was appointed full time and the following year, 1981, he achieved his first landmark in youth football with victory in the FA Youth Cup final. It was a sweet moment in particular for chief scout Eddie Baily, who had worked diligently to develop a scouting network in the local area, following several years of regression. Sweeter still that the 2–1 win was against Tottenham Hotspur.

The star of the show was Paul Allen, who had played such a pivotal role in the FA Cup final win in the previous season. Winger Bobby Barnes had also experienced significant first-team action, while the player widely rated as the most naturally gifted in the side, midfielder Alan Dickens, would soon make his mark with a scoring debut for the first team.

Tony Cottee, Paul Ince and Stuart Slater were the other major youth product successes of the 1980s. By the end of the decade, Centres of Excellence were being established and competition for boys as young as 11 was intense. With considerable instability throughout the club, as a result of multiple relegations and managerial upheaval, youth development hit a fallow period.

Harry Redknapp's return to the club is credited by Carr as the time the youth system started to really motor again. 'We'd gone through three or four years when there were no players coming through. Harry made us shake up the youth system. He said we should look at our coaching, scouting, be more aggressive in recruitment.' To that end, Redknapp brought in the forceful and experienced Jimmy Hampson as head of youth development. His prime responsibility? To stop the club missing out on the likes of David Beckham, Sol Campbell and other talented east London lads who had slipped through the net.

Cue a six- or seven-year period when only Manchester United could rival the Hammers for the quality of players rising through their ranks. In 1995, West Ham narrowly lost to Liverpool in the FA Youth Cup final, but out of that team came Frank Lampard Jnr and Rio Ferdinand.

Paul Ince is the player Carr rates as his greatest product, but Lampard and Ferdinand have gone on to surpass Ince's achievements in the game, at both club and international level. It was Carr who converted Rio from a midfielder into a central defender who would become the finest of his generation. Carr's adoption of a 3–5–2 formation, with Ferdinand in the heart of defence, was later mirrored successfully by the first team under Harry Redknapp.

The youths' 3–5–2 formation was still in full effect in 1999 as a Hammers side featuring Cole, Carrick, Bywater and Richard Garcia slaughtered Coventry City 9–0 on aggregate, in Hammers' third FA Youth Cup win in seven appearances in the final. The youths won the inaugural FA Premier Academy in the same season, having run away with the last South East Counties championship in the previous campaign.

Since the financial and relegation horrors of the mid noughties, when the best of the fledglings all flew the nest within a 14-month period, the run of superstar finds has tailed off. Nevertheless, England under-21 stars Mark Noble and James Tomkins, as well as Wales international Jack Collison, are just some of the established first-teamers who were once just toothy teenagers trying to impress their elders on the practice pitches at Chadwell Heath.

With Carr in charge, the production line is guaranteed to keep rolling, with the occasional gem unearthed every few years. 'We've got good people here who have the genuine interests of the players at heart,' he says. 'We have an environment that young players seem to enjoy and flourish in.'

●●●●●●●●●●●●●●●●●●●

That's Zamora

'Luck is what happens when preparation meets opportunity'
– Alan Pardew, May 2005

ALAN PARDEW was understandably walking on air as he bounced into the media room in Cardiff's Millennium Stadium after West Ham's Championship play-off final victory against Preston in 2005. Passing a familiar newspaper columnist, he slapped him on the back and grinned as if to say, 'Hah! Didn't think I had it in me, did you?'

The manager was entitled to look just a little bit pleased with himself. After all, he had guided West Ham back into the Premier League at the end of his first full season in charge and saved not only his own bacon but also that of the club following the inevitable financial struggles during two years of turbulence since relegation. 'It got very close to the board of directors having to make a decision about me,' admitted the relieved boss, while assistant Peter Grant confided, 'We knew what the consequences of defeat would be. West Ham needed promotion and there were a multitude of reasons why.'

Thirty million of the most obvious ones were stacked in English banknotes, with the Preston play-off dubbed 'the biggest domestic game ever' because of the huge jackpot that awaited the victors. The idea of the Hammers being back among the big boys, instead of again facing depressing trips to the likes of Plymouth, Burnley and

Crewe, was justification enough for the fans to party long and hard into the night.

However, knowing that failure would surely have condemned the club to years in the wilderness, it's little wonder that the wild celebrations were also fuelled by a huge sense of relief – not least from the management. 'Alan and I probably wouldn't have been at West Ham much longer if we'd have been beaten,' admitted Grant. 'We'd have also lost our major playing assets and there would have been such a dull feeling around the place if we had missed out on promotion two seasons running.'

Having flunked out in the previous year's play-off final against Crystal Palace, the Hammers were listed as favourites for promotion next time around, but mounting a sustained challenge while reducing running costs was never going to be quite the formality the bookmakers suggested.

Midfielder Michael Carrick – the last of the classic crop of home-grown Hammers of the era still at Upton Park following the departures of Rio Ferdinand, Frank Lampard, Joe Cole, Glen Johnson and Jermain Defoe – was sold to Tottenham for a £2.75 million fee (an irritatingly meagre sum when compared to the £18.6 million Manchester United paid for his services just two years later). Meanwhile, Pardew gambled on replacing 15-goal striker David Connolly with former England international Teddy Sheringham who, at 38, was 11 years Connolly's senior. Other new recruits, of varying quality, included Sergei Rebrov, Carl Fletcher, Luke Chadwick, Malky Mackay, Chris Powell and loanee Calum Davenport.

'We've definitely got a squad that's capable of winning this league,' boasted the manager and, with the Hammers picking up sixteen points from their first eight games to sit just behind early pacesetters Stoke, it didn't appear to be such an unlikely claim. However, injury problems and a lack of midfield creativity saw the team struggle to just four wins in the next dozen games and, by Christmas, it was obvious that the play-offs were a far more realistic proposition than automatic promotion. A 2–0 win at leaders Ipswich on 1 January proved West Ham were certainly good enough on their day, but when they followed up with three defeats, three wins and then another three defeats, even a top-six finish was in doubt. Speculation about Pardew's future started to build.

Former Coventry boss Gordon Strachan and Hammers invincible Trevor Brooking, who had severed his official ties with the club to become the FA's director of football development the previous season, were both mentioned as possible replacements. Managing director Paul Aldridge hardly put the warmest of arms around his manager's shoulder when he said, 'We have never put a timescale on our backing of him; we are in the results business.'

Coach Grant believed the intense pressure to win promotion, knowing that the Premier League parachute payments were set to expire at the end of that season, also told heavily on the players. 'Most of the young guys who had come to the club had never played under that weight of expectation, where they had to win games and play in a certain style as well,' he said. 'Some of the players couldn't handle that in the Championship.'

Yet one youngster did indeed make the difference. It seemed an innocuous moment when Elliott Ward made his league debut for the Hammers as an 87th-minute substitute in the 3–1 defeat at Reading on 12 March 2005. However, the introduction of the 20 year old, as a result of injuries, saw him reunited with his former youth-team colleague Anton Ferdinand to form a solid centre-half partnership that helped West Ham enjoy a run of just one defeat in their final ten league games. It proved just enough, with a 2–1 success at Watford on the final day of the regular season seeing the Hammers seal – some would say steal – the final play-off spot, after nearest rivals Reading fell apart in their last three games.

West Ham might have been full of confidence as they again came up against Ipswich, who they had beaten in the previous year's play-off semi-finals, but the pendulum appeared to swing in the East Anglian side's favour when they forced a 2–2 draw in the first leg at Upton Park after going two goals behind. Marlon Harewood and Bobby Zamora struck early goals to put the Hammers in command but Tommy Miller's deflected free-kick – recorded as a Jimmy Walker own goal – and Shefki Kuqi's second-half equaliser had Ipswich fancying their chances at Portman Road. West Ham were not to be denied, however, and

Zamora's two second-half goals – the second a wonderful cushioned volley – booked their return to Cardiff for the final.

Psychology had always been a fundamental part of Pardew's management style – not for nothing did the slogan 'luck is what happens when preparation meets opportunity' appear alongside other messages of inspiration and hope at the club's training ground. So he knew it was important to get his approach right in the build-up to the big game with Preston, who had seen off Derby in the other semi-final. Pardew wanted his players to draw from the lessons of the previous year's experience at the Millennium Stadium, but without suffering feelings of negativity. He even insisted the club used a different hotel as their base in South Wales to avoid unnecessary reminders of the failure against Palace.

Looking forward to being 'third time lucky' when being reminded that he had lost his two previous play-off finals (one with Reading), Pardew retained the positive mentality that had become something of a personal trademark. Nevertheless, with it being suggested that the club's wage bill would need to be reduced by a whopping 50 per cent if they missed out on promotion, the pressure was undeniably all on West Ham. 'I'm very aware of the financial implications,' conceded the manager ahead of the game.

Sometimes, just sometimes, it's possible to gauge the likely outcome of a game from the mood in the air – and many Hammers fans will attest to the belief that they headed to Cardiff on 30 May in more buoyant spirit than they had the previous year (despite Preston having come out on top in both the league meetings between the two sides). North End's supporters might have had the clapperboards, supplied by their club to manufacture some noise, but it was the Hammers fans that had the most to applaud, with their team always looking the more likely winners. Defender Tomás Repka hit the outside of the post early on and winger Matthew Etherington saw a shot tipped over by goalkeeper Carlo Nash, who twice denied Harewood shortly after the break, while Zamora had an effort cleared off the line by Youl Mawene.

It was Zamora who finally broke the deadlock when he swept home Etherington's cross from the left just before the hour mark. It was the striker's 13th goal of the season and by far his most valuable. Typically, the Hammers had to endure some nerve-wracking moments, with a late injury to goalkeeper Walker, who was stretchered off with cruciate ligament damage, forcing seven minutes of added time, during which substitute Stephen Bywater saved from Paul McKenna's free-kick.

It was West Ham's day, though, with Zamora admitting, 'We realised it was our chance and we knew it wasn't going to come again.' Meanwhile Pardew took time out to reflect on what may prove to be the highlight of his managerial career. 'That was the biggest game in West Ham's history,' he declared. 'If we'd not won that game, we could have been trapped in the Championship for years. So there was huge pressure on us to succeed. Yes, there was a period when I started to have doubts about whether we were going to make it. But we got promotion within the timescale discussed and achieved an end to the cycle of misery.'

The backslapping – literally and metaphorically – could begin.

●●●●●●●●●●●●●●●●●●●

Ron and John

'I'm just totally stunned' – Billy Bonds, April 2006

ONE OF the proudest statistics associated with West Ham's family club reputation is that which shows how the Hammers have employed just 13 managers in their 115-year history. So, in 2006, for the two greatest names on the list to die within weeks of each other was a cruel, cruel blow indeed.

In February of that year, 84-year-old Ron Greenwood, 'Godfather of the West Ham Way', passed away after a long struggle with Alzheimer's disease. A little over two months later, John Lyall – 'Mr West Ham', former player, coaching protégé of Greenwood's and mentor to so many – died unexpectedly from a heart attack at the age of just 66. In a case of truly uncanny timing, five days after Lyall's death West Ham made it to the FA Cup final for the fifth time in their history. With Ron and John so associated with the competition the timing could not have been more poignant.

Prior to the 1–0 semi-final victory over Middlesbrough at Villa Park, Alan Pardew, manager number ten to Greenwood's number four and Lyall's number five, said, 'Like Ron, John did so much to build the footballing beliefs and values that this club is built on. They are the managers I admire and whose legacy here will not be forgotten.' Pardew dedicated the victory to the Greenwood and Lyall families. Alas, his assertion that it was the Hammers' destiny to win the cup for the first time in 26 years was a script ruined by Liverpool – ironically, a club Lyall had always hugely admired.

The supporters, for whom Greenwood and Lyall were veritable Upton Park demigods, ensured that their feelings of grief, respect and pride were made abundantly clear. In spite of the fact that Greenwood had managed England between 1977 and 1982, the FA, for reasons best known to itself, deemed it unnecessary to honour him with a minute's silence at games throughout the land – a decision which gave an extra tingle to the emotion-charged 60-second hush prior to West Ham's home game with Birmingham City on 13 February.

In contrast, Lyall's passing was commemorated at the Villa Park semi-final in a more spontaneous but no less appropriate manner: with a tribal chant that, during the 1980s, used to peel around Upton Park and away grounds for upwards of 15 minutes at a time.

Comedian and Irons fan Russell Brand artfully conveyed the mood when he paid tribute to these two 'gentle patriarchs' in his *Guardian* column: 'At Villa Park, aside from Marlon Harewood's goal, the most exhilarating moment came before kick-off when, during Lyall's minute's silence, a solitary and bold voice sang out "Johnny Lyall's claret and blue army" . . . For a moment, Villa Park held its breath, before, as one, the West Ham faithful decreed that this transgression was a far more fitting testimony than silence. Once more his army marched.'

Lyall received a second, more orthodox tribute when West Ham played Liverpool in the league in a dress rehearsal of the cup final: a minute's rousing applause and a pitch parade of 25 players who had made their name under his aegis. Two of them, Trevor Brooking and team-mate Billy Bonds, formed a bridge between the Greenwood and Lyall management eras and would later experience their own spells at the helm.

Brooking's West Ham career started in 1967, halfway through Greenwood's groundbreaking 13-year tenure as manager during which Hammers lifted the FA Cup in 1964, the European Cup Winners' Cup in 1965 and, by common East End consent, the World Cup in 1966. Under Lyall's 14-year reign – the most successful of any Hammers manager – Bonds twice skippered the Irons to FA Cup wins in 1975 and 1980, plus defeats in the Cup Winners' Cup final of 1976 and League Cup final of 1981. Injury and retirement, respectively, meant neither Bonds nor Brooking figured in 1985–86, the season Lyall steered the club to its highest ever top-flight finish of third.

Asked for his feelings upon Greenwood's death, Sir Trevor recalled joining as a youngster soon after Greenwood introduced a European style of play, the basic premise of which has stayed with the club ever since. 'When you think that he converted Geoff Hurst from a midfielder to two years later scoring a hat-trick in the World Cup final, it shows you Ron's knowledge and expertise,' said Brooking. 'He put the players at the centre of his coaching and made sure that we went onto the pitch to express and enjoy ourselves. I don't think it's an overestimation to say he is one of the best coaches this country has produced in the last 50 years.'

With Greenwood well into old age and diminished by ill health by the time of his death, the many respectful tributes to him were made in the acknowledgement that everyone meets their maker. In contrast, where Lyall was concerned, the emotion quivering in Bonds' voice when he was interviewed by the BBC implied total shock at the loss of a man who many saw as virtually indestructible.

'It's a very sad day . . . I'm just totally stunned by it,' said Bonds in an interview that is at times hard to listen to. 'I got the news this morning when Ray Stewart phoned me up. I just can't believe it. We lost Ron a month or so ago and I knew he wasn't well, but John . . . I spoke to him last September at a reunion of the '75 and '80 FA Cup sides. John doesn't usually attend them and the only reason I went was because he was coming along. We had a lovely chat about the grandchildren; his wife and mine were there and he looked so well.'

Bonds touched on the fact that Lyall was not one for get-togethers or for dwelling on his former glories – and the same could be said for Greenwood. Lyall enjoyed a 34-year association with West Ham and was guided into coaching by Greenwood when knee damage brought a premature end to his career as a left-back in 1964, aged just 23. Loyalty – or 'Lyallty' as one clever scribe once put it – was central to his ethos as manager and man. He felt he owed it to the club and the club certainly showed it to him until sacking him following relegation to the Second Division in 1989. The press and supporters had started to round on Lyall after an abject few seasons, but it was still a curt conclusion to his Irons association which hurt him deeply.

Following a broadly successful five-year spell as Ipswich Town manager, Lyall retired to his farm in Suffolk – coincidentally the same county in which Greenwood spent his final years – keeping his contact with West Ham to a minimum. His wife Yvonne, his family and the quiet life were his priorities, although several of his former players kept in regular phone contact.

Lyall may have distanced himself from the club and the game he loved but the game had not forgotten him. Some 400 people attended a memorial service in St Mary Le Tower Church in Ipswich on 5 May 2006. Among the guests were Manchester United supremo Sir Alex Ferguson – their friendship partly founded on Lyall's pride in his Scottish parentage – and Paul Ince, one of many former charges to have declared that Lyall was *the* major influence on their career.

In January 2008, the Heritage Foundation erected a blue plaque in Lyall's memory at the Boleyn Ground, while the main gates were named 'The John Lyall Gates' a year later. Upton Park now has areas dedicated to Bobby Moore, Brooking, Lyall and Greenwood, the man to whom the first three owe their success. Blue plaques in his honour today adorn both Upton Park and the Essex house Greenwood lived in on Brooklyn Avenue, Loughton, while in the year of his death he was, belatedly, inducted into the National Football Museum Hall of Fame, an honour already bestowed on four of his protégés – Moore,

Hurst, Peters and Brooking – as well as Jimmy Greaves, who had a spell with West Ham during the Greenwood era.

With an impressive record of 33 victories in 55 games in charge of the national side, including an unbeaten run to the second group stage at the 1982 World Cup, Greenwood, who was made a CBE in 1981, retired from football the following year at the age of 60. Apart from some work in radio and the occasional visit to Upton Park, particularly during Bonds' managerial reign, involvement with football was limited. Laying a wreath on the centre circle to mark the death of former skipper Moore, with whom his own career was inextricably linked, in March 1993 was reportedly the last time he visited Upton Park.

Ron and Lucy Greenwood initially lived in Brighton during retirement, but when Ron's health worsened due to Alzheimer's disease they returned to East Anglia. Greenwood spent the last 14 months of his life in The Beeches Residential Home near Bury St Edmunds.

Season 2005–06 was an eventful one in many ways for West Ham, the club finishing ninth, reaching the FA Cup final and qualifying to play in the UEFA Cup. Most pleasing was the attractive style of play that Pardew's young side exhibited – which brings the theme right back round to the two men whose deaths tinged these good times with such sadness. Of Greenwood, the *Daily Mail*'s Jeff Powell wrote, 'He demonstrated an unyielding devotion to a game played for its beauty, not its belligerence.' Peter Shilton commented, 'Ron was a real football man in the sense that he loved to play the right way. He appreciated quality players and skill.' And Hammers legend Ronnie Boyce summed him up most succinctly, 'His philosophy was simply to attack and please the paying public.'

On Lyall, Bonds said, 'He was a great coach. In any era he'd be up there with the best of them. He had no side to him, he was a man you could trust.' Brooking added, 'He had a lasting influence on the club's development and the way the team played. He encouraged good, open, attacking football.' Paul Allen said, 'Some of the habits he instilled in me I still carry on to this day.'

Ron Greenwood and John Lyall were renowned for their capacity to talk football. The final words must go to them . . .

'It's all about painting pictures for players . . . Ron used to say to me, "All you need is a good pair of eyes." His philosophy was always: "Simplicity is genius"' – John Lyall

'At its best, the game is a joy, a battle of wit and muscle and character . . . Let's go out there to win and to win in style' – Ron Greenwood

■■■■■■■■■■■■■■■■■■■■

Absolutely Fabio?

'I can't explain the performances' – Matthew Upson, June 2010

THREE IS the magic number where West Ham and England are concerned. It's been like that ever since Bobby Moore wiped away the Wembley grime before shaking hands with the Queen.

To have a trio of Hammers in the national squad has a uniquely romantic significance in E13, regardless of the fact that their achievements can never even come close to matching those of Moore, Hurst and Peters.

In 2002, after years of nones, ones and occasional twos from Upton Park, at the World Cup in Japan and South Korea West Ham were represented by Joe Cole, David James and Trevor Sinclair.

Eight years later, with the South Africa World Cup looming, no fewer than four Hammers players – Carlton Cole, Matthew Upson, Robert Green and Scott Parker – offered serious contention for a place in Fabio Capello's squad. If the injury fates had not conspired against striker Dean Ashton and winger Kieron Dyer, it might even have been six.

When Capello named his provisional 30-man squad in May 2010, that foursome was whittled down to three. Cole, something of a Capello favourite in the preceding season with handy appearances in two World Cup qualifiers and two friendlies, failed to make the grade owing to a nagging knee injury that made it difficult for him to produce his best form at club level.

It was an anti-climactic end to Cole's World Cup ambitions. Although he had failed to hit the net in seven England appearances, mostly from the bench, the list of alternative strike partners for Wayne Rooney left much to desire. Cole's form under his biggest fan Gianfranco Zola, especially in 2008–09, at times suggested he could develop into the real deal for England (rather than Nigeria, with whom he had previously flirted due to his parentage).

The threesome was rudely reduced to two when the 23-man final cut was made. Parker, whose immense energy and spirit had done so much to keep West Ham in the top flight in 2009–10, had fully deserved entry to the provisional squad, even if it was partly to allay fears that regular holding midfielder Gareth Barry would not recover from injury in time to make the plane to Johannesburg.

Football statisticians were licking their lips at the prospect of Parker getting a run-out in friendlies against Japan and Mexico, which had been designed to give Capello the chance to run one last rule over the fringe players. If he made an appearance, the former Charlton, Chelsea and Newcastle man would have become the first player to make his first four England appearances with four different clubs.

In the end, Parker must have felt like a kid invited to a birthday party but banned from playing pass the parcel. Somewhat cruelly – and pointlessly – he remained unused in both friendlies. Barry was passed fit and Parker's ejection from the squad was as inevitable as it was shoddy, a situation that infuriated Spurs boss Harry Redknapp, among others. 'They tell me Scott trained fantastically every day and could not have done any more. Someone said to me he felt like a ghost.'

The chance of magic number three may have gone but Green and Upson were in – and there was considerable pride to be derived from the inclusion of six players – Joe Cole, Michael Carrick, Glen Johnson, Rio Ferdinand, Frank Lampard and Jermain Defoe – who had come through the youth ranks to play for the West Ham first team.

The days when Green had 'England's No. 6' stitched into his gloves as a nod to terrace wits behind his Boleyn goal now seemed a very long way off. Through a great deal of hard work and an awful lot of patience, Green had benefited from injury to England's first-choice goalkeeper David James during the World Cup qualifiers to nudge his tally of full caps into double figures, albeit becoming the first England stopper to get sent off, during defeat against Ukraine.

In truth, Green had endured a mixed season for struggling West Ham, at times cutting a disconsolate figure as 66 Premier League goals flew past him. However, the former Hammer of the Year, who'd won his first cap way back in his Norwich City days, was many observers' first choice to fill the England gloves ahead of former Hammer James and the up-and-coming Joe Hart. No less an authority than England legend Peter Shilton opined that Green's general reliability would fit the bill in South Africa.

Regrettably, when he did get the nod for the first game against the USA, one might have assumed that he had '666' stitched into his gloves. Green's misjudgement of a tame shot by Fulham's Clint Dempsey saw the ball spin out of his hands and bounce agonisingly over the goal line with Green grabbing air in its wake. It was a colossal mistake that not only let USA claw the score back to 1–1 but also signalled Green's conversion from decent keeper to internationally derided butter-fingers. Pundits and fans argued long and hard as to whether his nerves had been thoroughly shredded by Capello's insistence on not naming his side until hours before kick-off, or whether the controversial Jabulani (beach) ball was to blame. The goalkeeper, as honest and matter-of-fact as ever, simply said, 'I'm sure there's 50-odd million people disappointed with me but I'll come back, work hard and it won't affect me.'

He never got the chance. James' immediate recall meant Green's World Cup – and very possibly his England career – was over almost before it had begun.

With nineteen caps and one goal going into South Africa 2010, Upson was a veritable veteran compared to Green, Parker or Cole. Like Green, the West Ham skipper had often looked off-colour during the 2009–10 domestic season. However, also in keeping with Green, his international fortunes had benefited from long-term injury to a former Hammer, in Upson's case no less a figure than England skipper Rio Ferdinand.

Having recovered from back and knee problems in time for the World Cup, Ferdinand was a shoe-in to partner John Terry and reduce Upson to a place on the bench. However, when Rio suffered a knee injury during Capello's very first training session in South Africa, Upson moved a notch up the order.

Tottenham's Ledley King was preferred for the opening game against the USA but limped off at half-time with a groin strain to be replaced by Jamie Carragher. The Liverpool stalwart retained his place for the next game, a dismal 0–0 draw versus Algeria, but having picked up bookings in his two appearances was ineligible for the crucial third game against Slovenia. Thanks to a Defoe goal and a terrific late block by Upson, England progressed to the last 16, where Germany lay in wait.

Once again the old foe came out victorious, brushing aside Capello's team in magnificent style to record a 4–1 slaughtering – England's worst in World Cup finals' history. Once again, a West Ham player was at the centre of post-match arguments about vulnerability and experience at the highest level. Although it was Upson who brought England back into the game with a marvellous header midway through the first half, the way he and John Terry were carved open by the German attackers was widely slated as 'schoolboy stuff' by incandescent commentators and journalists. Upson said after the game, 'I can't explain the performances. I don't think they have been as bad as people are talking about but that's just my opinion.' Yet BBC pundit Lee Dixon begged to differ, groaning, 'It was probably the worst defensive team performance I've seen. Quite frankly we were awful and we got ripped to pieces.'

Such criticism was academic; England's entire World Cup campaign had been an utter shambles as a result of heavy-handed management techniques, star man Rooney's woeful form, discord in the ranks and, most importantly, the crazy levels of hype that had fooled a nation.

Patriotic Hammers fans were left to take minor consolation from the hope that the largely dependable Green and Upson had probably played themselves out of summer transfers to bigger, wealthier Premier League rivals.

A Golden Future?

'Benni McCarthy is nearly as fat as me'
– David Sullivan, May 2010

IN YEARS to come, somebody will decide to publish a book full of quotes by David Sullivan – and it will make for one hell of an entertaining read. 'We are like a government of national unity in a crisis,' said Sullivan after he and business partner David Gold had spent £50 million to buy a controlling 50 per cent interest in West Ham – a deal he then described as making 'no financial or commercial sense'. At the takeover press conference in January 2010, he referred to former chairman Eggert Magnusson as 'Eggbert', insisted that 'we've not come here to just bang it out to some Russian in five years' time' and claimed 'we wouldn't have bought West Ham if we weren't fans – it's in a serious mess'.

A few months on, after the disastrous 3–1 home defeat by relegation rivals Wolves, the 61 year old got his frustration off his chest by emailing an open letter to fans. 'I had no sleep last night,' he revealed. 'I was as angry and upset as every supporter at the disorganised way we played, allowing Wolves to look more like Manchester United. I apologise to every fan for our pathetic showing. Our recent performance against Bolton was also appalling.'

When new £2.5 million signing Benni McCarthy quickly proved to be a heavyweight flop, Sullivan said, 'McCarthy's body-fat measurement is 24.2 per cent while mine is 25.4 per cent – meaning he's nearly as fat as me! He's the one West Ham player I want to go to the World Cup – because he might just come back fitter.'

Hammers fans quickly realised that Sullivan was not afraid to speak his mind, while Gold – who, like his partner, had made his fortune in the sex publishing industry, while also running Birmingham City for 16 years – also wasn't shy of appearing in front of the cameras, with his beloved helicopter permanently parked just over his right shoulder. 'If I see another David Gold interview on the poor East

End Jewish boy done good,' moaned former Crystal Palace chairman Simon Jordan, 'I'll impale myself on one of his dildos.'

It can, therefore, be assumed that Jordan found sitting down to be a painful experience for a while after Gold and Sullivan took control of West Ham, because a whole series of 'rags to riches' features appeared in the press in acknowledgement of Gold's return to his roots. In the Boleyn Ground car park he pointed up towards the property at 442 Green Street where he was born 73 years earlier, while using the house number to suggest his preferred team formation. Sullivan spoke for both men when he said, 'For 20 years, this was the club that we wanted. The club is back in the hands of East Enders, people who understand the community and its passion for the Hammers.'

Yet it was a reflection of the times that not all fans were automatically swayed by the fact that claret and blue blood flowed through Gold and Sullivan's veins, with some preferring the idea of a super-rich foreigner pouring millions into the team – which seemed to be the only way that Premier League clubs could remain seriously competitive in the current climate. Lotus Formula One chief Tony Fernandes, finance firm the Intermarket Group and Cagliari owner Massimo Cellino were the other interested parties, but those fans who questioned what Sullivan and Gold had really achieved at Birmingham had missed the point. They simply needed to be grateful that the pair had allowed their hearts to rule their heads because West Ham could potentially have gone out of business had they not been rescued, even though the most recent set of accounts (up to May 2009) showed a 12-month loss of £16.2 million and the wage bill pegged at £60 million.

'We bought this club as fans, not from a business point of view,' said Sullivan, who revealed that at least one key player would have been sold that month to raise the £8 million needed by co-owners Straumur to keep the club afloat had major new investment not arrived.

He also divulged that West Ham's debt was around £110 million and made no secret of the gravity of the club's financial situation as a result of 'the crazy wages the original Icelandic owners paid out that have brought the club to its knees'. He said, 'We've got £50 million owed to banks and £40 million owed to other clubs, including

Sheffield United [for the Carlos Tevez affair]. In addition, West Ham are not owed a single penny by other clubs. The club has also borrowed against next season's ticket money and then there is the Alan Curbishley settlement. We've inherited these liabilities and we are going to have to work through them.'

With former Birmingham MD Karren Brady brought on board as vice-chairman, it was inevitable that chief executive Scott Duxbury would soon find himself leaving Upton Park with not the best of references from Sullivan. 'At every level the club has been badly run,' he said. 'I'll give you one example – it is now January and we have still got 21,000 first-team shirts in stock at £21 each. Ridiculous!'

He insisted that Gianfranco Zola had the new owners' support but questioned the manager's £1.9 million salary and again put the Italian's nose out of joint when suggesting that injury-plagued midfielder Kieron Dyer should retire to remove the burden of his £60,000-a-week wages from the books. In fact, one set of leaked figures suggested Dyer was actually on £83,000 a week, although the club shot down such claims.

Sullivan also indicated that technical director Gianluca Nani had no future at Upton Park by complaining about the 'unbelievably unbalanced team' and taking control of all transfer dealings himself in the final week of the January window, relying on agents Barry Silkman and Willie McKay to sign three strikers in the form of Mido, Ilan and McCarthy – the last of whom he blamed on Zola. 'He was the one player he wanted us to sign and so I signed him,' he said.

In the same way that pasta and steak 'n' kidney pie never sit comfortably on the same plate, it was hard to imagine Zola and Sullivan's contrasting personalities finding compatibility in the workplace. 'I'm more hands-on than some chairmen because I realise managers are fallible,' said Sullivan, whose eagerness to effect change left Zola feeling as if his new boss was breathing far too heavily down his neck. 'Until I find a manager who I have 100 per cent belief in, I have to have some involvement – otherwise I'm not doing my job,' he said.

Warning players they might face an end-of-season pay-cut just a day before the crucial home game with Birmingham in February had

Zola simmering with anger – as he was again when Sullivan publicly vented his spleen after the Wolves debacle. 'It wasn't controversial,' he insisted. 'It was an awful performance and sometimes you have to tell people how you feel.'

Gold also defended Sullivan's actions. 'I don't think David set out to undermine Gianfranco. He writes as he talks and is the most spontaneous man I know.' However, Sullivan's outspoken comments about first-team affairs continued to ruffle Zola's feathers to the point it became increasingly obvious there would have to be a parting of the ways once the season was over. With the club finishing just one place above the drop zone, the axe fell on Zola just two days after the final game. 'Sometimes you have to do things that are for the good of the club rather than popularity,' said Sullivan.

On 18 May 2010, Gold and Sullivan published a ten-point pledge: 1) Appoint the right manager; 2) Sign new players; 3) More investment in the Academy; 4) Continue to clear the debt; 5) Freeze season-ticket renewal prices; 6) Build status and image of club; 7) Make it enjoyable to come and watch; 8) Get closer to the community; 9) Go for the Olympic Stadium; and 10) Listen to supporters.

The first of those pledges was concluded on 3 June, with former Chelsea and Portsmouth boss Avram Grant, fifty-five, being confirmed as West Ham's thirteenth manager on a four-year contract. 'I like him very much,' said Sullivan of the Israeli. 'I imagined a dour, boring and serious man, but he's got a very dry sense of humour with an almost encyclopaedic knowledge of football. Avram is the right man for the job.'

At the same time, Sullivan and Gold increased their stakes in the Hammers to 30 per cent each after making a further investment of £8 million, the majority of which was used to help fund new purchases in the summer of 2010 as the new management looked to add quality to the squad. Headline-making links with big names such as Thierry Henry and Joe Cole reflected the new owners' ambition but predictably came to nothing. However, Germany international Thomas Hitzlsperger, Mexico winger Pablo Barrera, Lyon striker Frederic Piquionne and defenders Tal Ben Haim and Winston Reid all signed on the dotted line at Upton Park before the 2010–11 season began.

Sullivan insisted his new manager would have the final say on all transfers . . . well, almost. 'Avram will pick 95 per cent of the transfers,' he said. 'Maybe one in twenty I might beg a favour on and say I really fancy somebody.'

Meanwhile, West Ham continued to push ahead with their efforts to secure the rights to play in the new Olympic Stadium in Stratford from 2012. The dispute and debate involved politicians, councillors, the London Mayor, the Olympic Park Legacy Company and the Olympic International Committee, among others – each with their own agenda. 'It's a perfect fit,' insisted Sullivan. 'Take us on board, make us partners in a new adventure and have a legacy that could last 100 years.' If the previous 30 were anything to go by, it should be one hell of a ride . . .

■■■■■■■■■■■■■■■■■■■■